CREATION *and* NEW CREATION

CREATION *and* NEW CREATION

Understanding God's Creation Project

Sean M. McDonough

HENDRICKSON PUBLISHERS

Creation and New Creation: Understanding God's Creation Project

Hendrickson Publishers Marketing LLC
P. O. Box 3473
Peabody, Massachusetts 01961-3473
www.hendrickson.com

ISBN 978-1-68307-026-9

Originally published in the United Kingdom [under the title: Creation and New Creation]. Published by Authentic Media Limited, PO Box 6326, Bletchley, Milton Keynes, United Kingdom, MK1 9GG.

Please note that any italics in biblical quotations are the author's.

Printed in the United States of America

First Hendrickson Publishers Printing — January 2017

Contents

Preface

> We will begin, then, with the creation of the world and with God its Maker, for the first fact that you must grasp is this: *the renewal of creation has been wrought by the Self-same Word Who made it in the beginning.* There is thus no inconsistency between creation and salvation for the One Father has employed the same Agent for both works, effecting the salvation of the world through the same Word Who made it in the beginning (Athanasius, *De Incarnatione* 1).[1]

The quotation from Athanasius above offers a fine distillation of what we are attempting to do in this book. In keeping with the scriptural witness and the theological heritage, we will examine the doctrine of creation alongside new creation. Thus, rather than restricting ourselves to what God did at creation in the beginning, we are concerned with the full sweep of God's purposes for the cosmos—what Paul Blowers has termed 'the drama of the divine economy' in his magisterial book of that title. This will certainly begin with the work of primal creation, but it will also include his work of new creation: the providential and redemptive acts of renewal in history, and the consummation of all things in the new heavens and new earth.

The connection between creation and new creation has drawn renewed attention in the last several decades, whether it be in historical studies like those of Leo Scheffczyk, Colin Gunton, and Blowers; doctrinal treatises such as Jonathan Wilson's *God's Good World*; or the various exegetical studies of G. K. Beale and others.[2] The burden of the present volume is that this emphasis on creation and new creation has been a feature of the doctrine since the beginning, whether it be in the eschatological reading of Genesis 1 that predominated at least until early modern times, or the intertwining of the narratives of creation and redemption in thinkers from Irenaeus to Barth.

While the nexus of creation and new creation is a distinctive feature of this book, the volume also serves as a general introduction to the doctrine

1. Patristic translations, unless noted, are from T&T Clark's Ante-Nicene, Nicene, and Post-Nicene Fathers series. Scriptural quotations, unless noted, are from the Revised Standard Version.

2. For a summary, see the contributions in Beale's festschrift, *From Creation to New Creation: Biblical Theology and Exegesis: Essays in Honor of G. K. Beale* (ed. Daniel M. Gurtner and Benjamin L. Gladd; Peabody, MA: Hendrickson, 2013).

of creation. It will cover the traditional elements of the doctrine (creation *ex nihilo*, 'continuous creation', the role of the divine will, questions of time and eternity, the relationship of biblical and scientific accounts of creation, and so on), with a special emphasis on how these unfold in the story of what Gunton has called God's 'creation project'.

The title of the series, 'Christian Doctrine in Historical Perspective', in which this book first appeared, provides us with our angle of approach. We are concerned first with *Christian doctrine.* While creation provides a natural point of departure for interfaith discussions,[3] we will have quite enough to be getting on with surveying the contours of *Christian* views on the matter. By employing the term *doctrine*, we are presupposing that there are things Christians ought to believe about creation and re-creation, as well as things that they might believe, and things that they certainly ought not to believe. At times the categories blur: the Bible may not speak explicitly about creation *ex nihilo*, but most theologians have felt it is a necessary deduction from Scripture, and thus it has been at the heart of the doctrine of creation since the early centuries of the church. While there has been abundant variety in articulating different aspects of creation and new creation—think for example of the myriad ways theologians have groped towards an explanation of what the resurrected body will be like—the tradition has orbited around a common set of confessions and concerns. These common concerns form the basis for this book.

The preceding paragraph presupposes that what should or could be believed is represented in what has been believed: hence the importance of *historical perspective.* The word 'perspective' is key. What follows is not a history of the doctrine of creation, such as Scheffczyk and Gunton have produced,[4] but an exploration of the doctrine drawing upon the work of various theologians through the ages. Even this more modest goal of seeing things in historical perspective naturally involves some sort of perspective on history. One might employ a Hegelian dialectic of continual conflict and resolution, or an optimistic understanding of ever-increasing clarity as knotty problems are gradually untied. With respect to creation, one enduringly popular approach has been to posit an early pristine 'Jewish' doctrine, which then experiences a Fall into Platonism from which it has never really recovered.[5] I have taken a more synthetic approach: the central confessions in Scripture of God's creative power and wise purposes have been affirmed

3. See esp. David B. Burrell's interaction with Judaism and Islam in e.g. *Freedom and Creation in Three Traditions* (Notre Dame: University of Notre Dame Press, 1993).

4. Though a glance at his table of contents will show that Gunton has arguably used the historical timeline as the means for addressing a series of fundamentally systematic issues like creation *ex nihilo*, time and eternity, and so on.

5. This is true to some extent of the accounts of Scheffczyk and Gunton, though both are so skilfully done they resist caricature. Leo Scheffczyk, *Creation and Providence*

throughout the tradition, though that tradition has regularly been reshaped as it encounters various intellectual challenges ranging from Platonism to modern scientific discovery. But rather than producing a cacophony of self-contradiction, what we find is variations on the central themes.

A practical consideration arises from this: what, and who, counts as 'history'? In terms of epochs, we will generally stop in the mid-twentieth century with the death of Karl Barth. This is not to diminish the contributions of contemporary scholars: my thought has been heavily influenced by an array of modern thinkers, most notably Jürgen Moltmann, Wolfhart Pannenberg, Colin Gunton, Robert Jenson, Thomas Torrance, and David Burrell. No doubt their works will have a lasting influence on the doctrine of creation. Nonetheless, it seemed best to stop with Barth to provide a certain critical historical distance from the thinkers. As for the 'who' question, we clearly need to be selective. Since the doctrine of creation ought to be a place where all Christians might gather together, I have attempted to choose representative thinkers from Orthodox, Catholic, and Protestant traditions.[6] Thus on the Eastern side, we will make regular use of Irenaeus, the Cappadocians, Athanasius, Maximus the Confessor, and the twentieth-century Russian Orthodox theologian Sergei Bulgakov. For the West, Augustine holds pride of place as the founder of Western thought on creation. Aquinas will serve to represent the Catholic tradition, with assistance from John Scottus Eriugena, Duns Scotus, and Hans Urs von Balthasar. Jonathan Edwards represents older Reformed thought, and Karl Barth newer Reformed thought. Maximus and Edwards will prove particularly useful, since they are immensely creative thinkers who both gather up what has gone before them (in the patristic era and the Reformation respectively) and open up fresh possibilities for the thinkers after them. Various other theologians—Tertullian, Luther, Calvin, Samuel Taylor Coleridge, C. S. Lewis, and others—will drop in as needed.

After an initial chapter detailing the connection of creation and new creation in the Bible and the theological tradition, we will work our way through the material on a topical basis, dealing in turn with questions related to God as Creator; matters of time and space; the process of creation; and concluding with reflections of beauty and creation. Since other volumes in this series—not to mention the bulk of the theological tradition—treat particular questions related to humanity, we will reserve but one chapter for considerations of humanity's role in the creation, while devoting the bulk of our attention to questions concerning the creation at large.

(trans. Richard Strachan; New York: Herder & Herder, 1970); Colin E. Gunton, *The Triune Creator: A Historical and Systematic Study* (Edinburgh: T&T Clark, 2001).

6. Note, too, that in order to keep this work accessible, virtually all primary and secondary sources are cited in English translation.

Acknowledgements

I am grateful to Professor Alan Sell for inviting me to write for the series Christian Doctrine in Historical Perspective. My thoughts on creation and new creation have been profoundly shaped by Gregory Beale, while Richard Bauckham has long modelled for me the integration of biblical exegesis and theological reflection. I owe a great debt to the Trustees of Gordon-Conwell Theological Seminary for their support of the generous sabbatical programme which made the research and writing possible; and to my colleagues on the faculty who lent support in various ways. Special mention should be made of Donald Fairbairn, Gordon Isaac, Carol Kaminski, Cathy McDowell, Patrick Smith, Adonis Vidu, and David Wells, who provided much helpful counsel; and Jack Davis and Gwenfair Walters who provided extensive commentaries on the manuscript. Daniel Brown likewise provided helpful insight along the way. My teaching assistant, Kathleen Rogers, provided invaluable support in the preparation of the text. Finally, I am most grateful for the support of my wife, Ariana, and my children, Siobhan, Patrick, Keanu, and Daniel.

Abbreviations

1QHa	Qumran, *Thanksgiving Hymns*
Amb.	Maximus the Confessor, *Ambiguum*
ANE	Ancient Near Eastern
Ant.	Josephus, *Jewish Antiquities*
Apoc. Ab.	*Apocalypse of Abraham*
Autol.	Theophilus, *To Autolycus*
BA	*Biblical Archaeologist*
C. Ar.	Athanasius, *Orations against the Arians*
C. Eun.	Gregory of Nyssa, *Contra Eunomium*
Cael.	Aristotle, *De Caelo*
Cant.	Gregory of Nyssa, *In Canticum Canticorum*
CBQ	*Catholic Biblical Quarterly*
CD	Barth, *Church Dogmatics* (4 vols; Edinburgh: T&T Clark, 1956–75)
Civ.	Augustine, *The City of God*
Comm. Eph.	Calvin, *Commentary on Ephesians*
Comm. Gal.	Calvin, *Commentary on Galatians*
Conf.	Augustine, *Confessions*
De Hom. Opif.	Gregory of Nyssa, *De Hominis Opificio*
De Nat. Hom.	Nemesius of Emesa, *On the Nature of Man*
De Res.	Methodius, *De Resurrectione*
De Res.	Tertullian, *Resurrection of the Flesh*
Descr.	Pausanias, *Description of Greece*
Div. Quaest. LXXXIII	Augustine, *Eighty-three Different Questions*
EH	Pseudo-Dionysius, *On the Ecclesiastical Hierarchy*
1 En.	*1 Enoch*
Gen. Imp.	Augustine, *The Literal Interpretation of Genesis*
Gen. Litt.	Augustine, *Literal Commentary on Genesis*
Gen. Man.	Augustine, *On Genesis against the Manichaeans*
Georg.	Virgil, *Georgica*
Gk.	Greek
Haer.	Irenaeus, *Against Heresies*

Herm.	Tertullian, *Against Hermogenes*
Hex.	Ambrose, *Six Days of Creation*
Hex.	Basil, *Hexaemeron*
Hex.	Gregory of Nyssa, *On the Hexaemeron*
Hom. 1 Cor.	Chrysostom, *Homiliae in epistulam I ad Corinthios*
HP	Ephrem the Syrian, *Hymns on Paradise*
IEJ	*Israel Exploration Journal*
Inc.	Athanasius, *De Incarnatione*
Inst.	Lactantius, *The Divine Institutes*
JTS	*Journal of Theological Studies*
Jub.	*Jubilees*
Lect. In Joh.	Augustine, *Lectures on John*
LXX	Septuagint
Mand.	Shepherd of Hermas, *Mandate(s)*
Marc.	Tertullian, *Against Marcion*
Math.	Sextus Empiricus, *Against the Mathematicians*
Met.	Aristotle, *Metaphysics*
Migr.	Philo, *On the Migration of Abraham*
Mos.	Philo, *On the Life of Moses*
Mut.	Philo, *On the Change of Names*
NA27	Nestle-Aland Greek New Testament (ed. Kurt Aland, Erwin Nestle et al.; Deutsche Bibelgesellschaft, 27th edn., 1993)
NovT	*Novum Testamentum*
Op. Imp.	Augustine, *Against Julian: Opus Imperfectum*
Or. Bas.	Gregory Nazianzen, *Oratio in laudem Basilii*
Org.	Bacon, *New Organon*
OT	Old Testament
PG	Patrologia Graeca (162 vols; ed. J.-P. Migne; Paris, 1857–86)
Pirqe R. El.	*Pirqe Rabbi Eliezer*
PP	Eriugena, *Periphyseon*
Princ.	Origen, *De Principiis*
PSCF	*Perspectives on Science and Christian Faith*
RTAM	*Recherches de théologie ancienne et médiévale*
b. Sanh.	*Sanhedrin* (Babylonian Talmud)
Sent.	Lombard, *Four Books of Sentences*
1 Sent.	Aquinas, *Commentary on Book 1 of the Sentences*
Serm.	Augustine, *Sermons*
Sib. Or.	*Sibylline Oracles*
Sir.	Sirach/Ecclesiasticus
Sobr.	Philo, *On Sobriety*

Somn.	Philo, *On Dreams*
Spir.	Ambrose, *The Holy Spirit*
ST	Aquinas, *Summa Theologica*
Tg. Ps.-Jon.	*Targum Pseudo-Jonathan*
Tim.	Plato, *Timaeus*
Trin.	Augustine, *The Trinity*
VC	*Vigiliae Christianae*
Ver. Rel.	Augustine, *De Vera Religione*
WA	*Weimarer Ausgabe* (Weimar edition of Luther's works)

1

The End Is Like the Beginning: Creation and New Creation in Scripture and Tradition

The mingling of the beginning and the end arguably goes back to the primal creation narrative in the early chapters of Genesis. God's work in the six days clearly served as the template for Israel's ongoing cycle of work and rest, which in turn became the template for eschatological fulfilment in the book of Hebrews (e.g. 4:9: 'So then, there remains a sabbath rest for the people of God'). Less remarked on is the curious fact that Adam is created *outside* Eden, and only then is brought into paradise (Gen. 2:8, 15).[1] This might seem a small detail were it not for the careful wording of 2:15: 'The LORD God took the man and put him in the garden of Eden to till it and keep it.' The word 'put' can be more literally rendered 'caused to rest' (Heb. *yannichēhu*),[2] and is thus related to the name Noah and his story of deliverance:

> When Lamech had lived a hundred and eighty-two years, he became the father of a son, and called his name Noah (*noach*), saying, 'Out of the ground which the LORD has cursed this one shall bring us relief (*ynachamēnu*) from our work and from the toil of our hands' (Gen. 5:28–29).
>
> And in the seventh month, on the seventeenth day of the month, the ark came to rest (*tanach*) upon the mountains of Ararat (Gen. 8:4).

It is hard to miss the connection between Adam and Noah, since the birth of Noah in 5:28–29 concludes the genealogy of Adam begun in 5:1. It is thus possible that Genesis is inviting us to see God's transportation of Adam to Eden as a deliberate foreshadowing of the search for ultimate rest that will dominate the rest of the Bible.

Nor is this the only echo of the creation account in the story of Noah. The flood narrative in Genesis 6–8 is saturated with images of the creation.

---

1. But cf. Jub. 3:32, which notes that when Adam and Eve left Eden, they removed to the land of Elda where they had been created.

2. Thanks to Carol Kaminski for pointing this detail out to me.

In Genesis 6:6, we read that God 'was sorry that he had made man (*ha'adam*) on the earth', with the corresponding promise that 'I will blot out man (*ha'adam*) whom I have created from the face of the ground (*ha'adamah*)' (Gen. 6:7). While the sins of humanity are the trigger for divine judgement, this judgement calls into question the whole creation project: man and beast and bird will all be taken down. As Jacques Ellul has said in a related context, we are in the presence of a chaos 'that reveals the reality of the disaster that his own creation has become for God.'[3]

The mechanics of the flood are of immense theological importance: 'on that day all the fountains of the great deep burst forth, and the windows of the heavens were opened' (Gen. 7:11). This is not simply a stretch of very bad weather: it is the collapsing back of the waters above and below which God had separated on day two. Chaos replaces cosmos.

But new creation lies tucked inside the ark, which hovers over the waters even as the Spirit did in the beginning—both Genesis 1:2 and Genesis 7:17 feature the phrase *'al pne hamayim*, 'over the face of the waters'. The potential for new life is realized when God sends a 'wind' or 'Spirit' (the Hebrew word *ruach* can mean either) across the earth to drive back the waters. The allusions to Genesis 1:2 continue with the appearance of the dove: scholars have long noted the avian overtones of the verb 'hovering' (*mrachphet*) in Genesis 1:2. If anyone had missed the fairly glaring parallels with the creation narrative, they could hardly fail to hear the echoes of the commission to Adam and Eve in God's words to Noah after the flood (Gen. 8:16–17): 'Go forth from the ark, you and your wife, and your sons and your sons' wives with you. Bring forth with you every living thing that is with you of all flesh—birds and animals and every creeping thing that creeps on the earth—that they may breed abundantly on the earth, and *be fruitful and multiply upon the earth*.' Little wonder that 2 Peter speaks of the time of the flood in cosmic terms as 'the world that then was' (*ho tote kosmos*) and regards it as a foreshadowing of the looming dissolution of the universe (2 Pet. 3:5–7).

The story of the exodus is rife with allusions to both creation and flood. The theme is introduced with subtlety in the narrative of Moses' birth. English translations inform us in Exodus 2:2 that Moses was a 'fine' (NIV, ESV) or 'goodly' child (RSV, KJV), and we need not doubt that he was. But these renderings obscure the patent allusion in the Hebrew text to God's commendation of the creation: a literal translation gives us, 'And she saw him that he was good, he'. In the same way, the translations do no favours to the theologian by rendering the *tēbah* into which Moses is placed as a 'basket'. The word *tēbah* is used in only one other portion of the Hebrew bible: the

3. *Apocalypse: The Book of Revelation* (trans. George W. Schreiner; New York: Seabury, 1977), p. 75.

flood narrative, where it designates Noah's ark. Here, then, we find the good child, the hope of deliverance for Israel, floating in his ark above the Nile's chaos waters, whence he is drawn and given the name 'Moses'. We should not miss the monumental significance of the moment for the author of Exodus: God's plan is to restore all humanity to himself through Abraham's seed, and the fate of the creation is tied to that of its human vice-regents. Thus it is not too much to say that baby Moses is carrying the hope of the cosmos in his little ark.

The climactic moment of deliverance at the Red Sea is even more evidently indebted to the creation story. The sea represents the apparent end of Israel's journey, the definitive roadblock to the onward journey of God's creation project. But God's Spirit continues to make a way for order in the midst of chaos: 'Then Moses stretched out his hand over the sea; and the LORD drove the sea back by a strong east wind (*ruach*) all night, and made the sea dry land,[4] and the waters were divided' (Exod. 14:21).

The exodus is the seminal story in Israel's history, and the strands of creation and redemption entwine in a kind of double helix which will be reproduced in subsequent generations of the nation. The parting of the river Jordan at the conquest of the land is an obvious counterpart to the exodus. Isaiah's grand vision of the return from exile has likewise long been recognized as a second exodus:

> When the poor and needy seek water, and there is none, and their tongue is parched with thirst, I the LORD will answer them, I the God of Israel will not forsake them. I will open rivers on the bare heights, and fountains in the midst of the valleys; I will make the wilderness a pool of water, and the dry land springs of water. I will put in the wilderness the cedar, the acacia, the myrtle, and the olive; I will set in the desert the cypress, the plane and the pine together; that men may see and know, may consider and understand together, that the hand of the LORD has done this, the Holy One of Israel has created it (Isa. 41:17–20).

The concluding line of the passage from Isaiah 41 demonstrates the continued intermingling of creation and exodus in Israel's theological imagination.

In the historical books, God's deliverance was often embodied in a charismatic political and/or military leader of the people. While such success was sporadic and generally short-lived, the triumphs of David held out the hope of an enduring kingdom for Israel. Psalm 89 juxtaposes God's power over the creation with the coming kingdom of David's descendant:

---

4. The word for 'dry land' here is *charabah*, which differs from the *yabbasha* of Gen. 1:9—but *yabbasha* is used in the very next verse, Exod. 14:22 (my translation), 'And the sons of Israel walked between the waters on the *dry ground*.'

Thou hast said, 'I have made a covenant with my chosen one,
I have sworn to David my servant:
'I will establish your descendants for ever,
and build your throne for all generations.'[Selah]
Let the heavens praise thy wonders, O Lord,
thy faithfulness in the assembly of the holy ones!
For who in the skies can be compared to the Lord?
Who among the heavenly beings is like the Lord,
a God feared in the council of the holy ones,
great and terrible above all that are round about him?
O Lord God of hosts,
who is mighty as thou art, O Lord,
with thy faithfulness round about thee?
Thou dost rule the raging of the sea;
when its waves rise, thou stillest them.
Thou didst crush Rahab like a carcass,
thou didst scatter thy enemies with thy mighty arm.
The heavens are thine, the earth also is thine;
the world and all that is in it, thou hast founded them.
The north and the south, thou hast created them;
Tabor and Hermon joyously praise thy name (Ps. 89:3–12).

The future king's dominion is set forth in grand terms in verse 25: 'I will set his hand on the sea and his right hand on the rivers.' Jon Levenson summarizes:

> That YHWH can make such breathtaking promises follows from his own cosmic mastery, depicted in vv. 10–15 in the familiar imagery of his defeat of the surging Sea, his dismemberment of Rahab, and his subsequent creation of the world. It is now the Davidic throne that guarantees cosmic stability, the continuation of the order established through primeval combat . . . David is YHWH's vicar on earth.[5]

One could take issue with Levenson's contention that verse 10 refers to the creation—it might just as well refer to the crushing of Pharaoh at the exodus—but this simply serves to reinforce the point that the creation and the exodus were so tightly connected in the Hebrew bible. Likewise, that the 'Davidic throne . . . guarantees cosmic stability' might be seen as a bit hyperbolic on Levenson's part—but it is the psalmist who has invited the reader to connect God's cosmic sovereignty with Davidic dominion.

Israel's cosmic calling was on dramatic display in the temple service and its predecessor, the tent in the wilderness. In some respects, the temple

---

5. Jon Douglas Levenson, *Creation and the Persistence of Evil: The Jewish Drama of Divine Omnipotence* (Princeton: Princeton University Press, 1988), pp. 22–23.

evoked Eden, with its paradisiacal adornments and its cherubim guarding the presence of God.[6] But it also evoked the creation as a whole. Levenson details the connections between the creation of the world and the establishment of the tabernacle and concludes: 'Collectively, the function of these correspondences is to underscore the depiction of the sanctuary as a world, that is, an ordered, supportive, and obedient environment, and the depiction of the world as sanctuary, that is, a place in which the reign of God is visible and unchallenged, and his holiness is palpable, unthreatened, and pervasive.'[7]

New Testament

Creation and redemption remain conjoined throughout the New Testament. The introductions to the gospels contain an especially noteworthy cluster of associations. John signals his interest in creation quite explicitly in the first words of his gospel: 'In the beginning was the Word, and the Word was with God, and the Word was God. He was in the beginning with God; all things were made through him' (John 1:1–3). Matthew (1:1), meanwhile, begins with what translations generally render as 'the book of the genealogy of Jesus Christ, the son of David, the son of Abraham.' We can readily see the connection between Jesus and two of the chief figures of Old Testament (OT) covenant history. With the arrival of the Messiah, we are reaching the climax of that history. But the first two words in the Greek text, *biblos geneseōs*, suggest something more. A beginning Greek student confronted with the phrase might spit out in panic, 'The book of Genesis'; and this is probably at least part of what Matthew wants us to hear in the phrase.[8] Its most notable occurrence in the Greek OT is Genesis 5:1: 'This is the *book of the generations* of Adam.' Jesus' appearance will not only sum up the history of Israel, it will sum up the history of the whole human race. The allusions in Mark and Luke are still subtler. Mark (1:1) simply starts off with, 'The beginning (*archē*) of the Gospel of Jesus Christ' and moves straight on to John the Baptist, while Luke (1:2) tucks the expression 'those who from the beginning (*ap' archēs*) were eyewitnesses' into his dedicatory preface. Even if one wishes to minimize the presence of 'beginning' language in Mark and Luke, there is no question that all four gospels draw heavily upon

---

6. See Gregory K. Beale, *The Temple and the Church's Mission: A Biblical Theology of the Dwelling Place of God* (Downers Grove, IL: IVP, 2004).

7. Levenson, p. 86. Both Philo and Josephus depicted the temple in cosmic terms.

8. See W. D. Davies and Dale C. Allison, *A Critical and Exegetical Commentary on the Gospel According to Saint Matthew* (3 vols; London: T&T, 2004), 1:151.

the Isaianic Second Exodus motif, and thus draw ultimately upon creation themes embedded in Isaiah's vision.[9]

The theme of recapitulation—the summing up of all things in Christ—emerges with particular clarity in Matthew's gospel. Critical scholars have sometimes chided Matthew for what looks like a cavalier deployment of Hosea 11:1, 'out of Egypt I called my son', in 2:15. Does the evangelist not know that this is in fact a reference to Israel at the exodus? Of course he does, and this is precisely the point: in Matthew's view, the child Jesus as the embodiment of Israel's destiny is recapitulating the nation's experience in this little exodus. This reading is confirmed by what follows: the exodus motif is reiterated in his passing through the waters of baptism, followed by his *forty*-day sojourn in the wilderness. Just in case the parallels were not clear enough, Jesus in the temptation goes on to quote three times from Deuteronomy 6–8—a text precisely focused on the forty-year testing of Israel in the desert: 'And you shall remember all the way which the LORD your God has led you these forty years in the wilderness, that he might humble you, testing you to know what was in your heart, whether you would keep his commandments, or not' (Deut. 8:2).

Allusions to Genesis whisper throughout the synoptic narratives. Theologians have long noted the similarities between the Spirit/dove hovering over Jesus' baptismal waters with both Genesis 1 and Genesis 7. Whatever else is going on with the baptism, it represents a new beginning for Israel and humanity at large. The subsequent temptation in the wilderness clearly echoes Israel's experience of testing after the Red Sea crossing, but Mark's gospel also suggests connections with Adam.[10] The small note that he was 'with the wild beasts' (1:13)—but unharmed by them—may hint at a restoration of the dominion over the animals lost by Adam. Whether the description of the messianic community as 'light' (e.g. Matt. 5:15–16; 6:22–23) alludes to Genesis is open to question; but there is no mistaking the reference to the creation story in Jesus' teaching on divorce:

---

9. See above all Rikki E. Watts, *Isaiah's New Exodus in Mark* (Grand Rapids: Baker, 2000).

10. See Richard J. Bauckham, 'Jesus and the Wild Animals (Mark 1:13): A Christological Image for an Ecological Age', in *Jesus of Nazareth: Lord and Christ: Essays on the Historical Jesus and New Testament Christology* (ed. Joel B. Green and Max Turner; Grand Rapids: Eerdmans, 1994), pp. 3–21; cf. John Paul Heil, 'Jesus with the Wild Animals in Mark 1:13', *CBQ* 68 (2006): pp. 63–78. The text is of course susceptible to other interpretations: for instance, it might signal the angelic protection of the Messiah in the face of hostile forces symbolized by the desert beasts (cf. Ps. 91:11–13): 'For he will give his angels charge of you to guard you in all your ways. On their hands they will bear you up, lest you dash your foot against a stone. You will tread on the lion and the adder, the young lion and the serpent you will trample under foot.'

> And Pharisees came up to him and tested him by asking, 'Is it lawful to divorce one's wife for any cause?' He answered, 'Have you not read that he who made them from the beginning made them male and female, and said, "For this reason a man shall leave his father and mother and be joined to his wife, and the two shall become one flesh"? So they are no longer two but one flesh. What therefore God has joined together, let not man put asunder' (Matt. 19:3–6).

As R. S. Barbour has noted, the advent of the kingdom entails the restoration of things to their primal created rightness.[11]

This is surely true of the mighty works of Jesus, even if they lack the Genesis commentary provided by Jesus in the case above. The 'nature miracles' provide particularly vivid testimony to Jesus' dominion over the created order. The healings underscore the same principle in the particular case of human bodies. Of special note are the controversial Sabbath miracles performed by Jesus. If he pushed the boundaries of traditional Sabbath keeping, it was with a purpose, one which is most clearly revealed in the healing of the woman in Luke 13. When the indignant synagogue ruler tells the people, 'There are six days on which work ought to be done; come on those days and be healed, and not on the sabbath day' (v. 14), Jesus rebukes him sternly: 'You hypocrites! Does not each of you on the sabbath untie his ox or his ass from the manger, and lead it away to water it? And ought not this woman, a daughter of Abraham whom Satan bound for eighteen years, be loosed from this bond on the sabbath day?' (vv. 15–16). Jesus' point is not simply that the woman *may* be healed on the Sabbath—the phrase rendered 'ought' in the RSV quotation (*ouk edei*) indicates a strong necessity, and would typically be rendered *must*. Why is her healing *on the Sabbath* such a necessity? It is because the Sabbath was instituted precisely to celebrate God's works of creation and redemption (Exod. 20:8–11; Deut. 5:12–15). This woman has been kept from fully embracing Sabbath celebration by the machinations of Satan, and so there is no better day than the Sabbath on which she might be liberated. Jesus' Sabbath healings are indeed provocations, but they are not designed to have Israel turn its back on the Torah and loosen up a little; they are instead acted parables of the new creation that is dawning on the world in Jesus.

What is hinted at in the Synoptics comes into full view in John. The opening verses of John are a deft blend of creation and new creation, a revisioning of Genesis that both affirms the surface reading of the text and probes its depths. We will explore the christological dimensions of John's

---

11. See R. S. Barbour, 'Creation, Wisdom, and Christ', in *Creation, Christ, and Culture: Studies in Honour of T. F. Torrance* (ed. Thomas F. Torrance and Richard W. A. McKinney; Edinburgh: T&T Clark, 1976), pp. 31–32.

creation theology in depth in the next chapter. For the moment we will focus on John's juxtaposition of past and present realities, and his juxtaposition of physical and spiritual realities.

When John states that 'all things came into being' through Christ, he is manifestly referring to all created reality, in keeping with the narrative of Genesis. This warrants emphasis in light of the fact that John's gospel is often regarded as a purely 'spiritual' enterprise with little concern for the material world. This is a very questionable assumption in the presence of the affirmation of creation in 1:2, and it ill suits the gospel as a whole. If Jesus were solely concerned to direct people to a higher, immaterial dimension, he chose a strange way to do it; turning water into wine, feeding the multitudes, healing the sick, and raising the dead are hardly world-negating acts. They instead affirm the created order by way of restoration.

But John also unfolds Genesis 1 in a metaphorical way which will guide numerous future theologians. Consider 1:4–5: 'In him was life, and the life was the light of men. The light shines in the darkness, and the darkness has not overcome it [or 'understood it'].' As soon as the Word is described as 'the light of men', the discourse on creation begins to move in an ethical direction. John hints at it here, and like much else in the prologue, he will develop the theme at length in the remainder of the gospel. The dual sense of the verb *katelaben*, which John is well aware can be rendered 'overcome' or 'understood', also introduces spiritual matters which will be unpacked in the ensuing narrative. God's creation of light, according to John, is not simply a matter of pushing photons here and there in the Void: it consists equally in the effusion of his holiness into every corner of creation.

If one objects that there are no moral agents around on day one to resist this incursion of light, this only shows how John is willing at times to dissolve the boundaries separating past and present. John moves seamlessly from the one to the other: the light shone in the darkness in the beginning, and it shines now in the midst of a world darkened by sin. The serene overture of Genesis 1 is laced with subtle themes of conflict which will unfold in the later history of the creation project. They will reach their crescendo in the opposition faced by Jesus in his public ministry. Jesus will 'come to his own', but 'his own people received him not' (1:11).

The theme of cosmic restoration is signalled by the first of Jesus' 'signs', the transformation of water into wine at Cana. Along with the walking on the sea and the feeding of the five thousand (John 6), this passage reaffirms the Synoptics' demonstration of Jesus' power over the created order. But the miracle at Cana presses the eschatological point even more sharply. The image of water, which calls to mind both the river flowing out of Eden and the eschatological river flowing from the temple in Ezekiel 47, runs throughout the course of John's gospel. Here it functions as a symbol of the ritual washings of the old age (2:6), which must be eschatologically enhanced into the wine of the new age. Elsewhere, water will symbolize the gift of the Spirit, who will pour forth from the innermost being of believers (7:38; cf. 4:10). The source of this water is of course Christ himself, who fills the role of Ezekiel's life-giving temple (2:21). It is likely that John's cryptic reference to the 'water and the blood' coming from Jesus' side at the crucifixion speaks to the paradox that the blessings of eternal life flow precisely from his death.

John also brings out the full theological significance of the healing ministry of Jesus. When he heals the paralysed man on the Sabbath, Jesus defends his actions with the remarkable statement, 'My Father is working still, and I am working' (John 5:17). Jewish teachers had long recognized that God must in some sense still be working to uphold the world after the creation week, and that this work must continue even on the Sabbath; witness the rebuke offered to a sectarian by one group of rabbis:

> 'Wretch! Is not a man permitted to carry on the Sabbath in his own courtyard?' He replied, 'Yes.' Whereupon they said to him, 'Both the higher and lower regions are the courtyard of God, as it says, *The whole earth is full of His glory* (Isa. VI,3), and even if a man carries a distance of his own height, does he transgress?' The others agreed. 'Then,' said they, 'it is written, *Do I not fill heaven and earth?*'[12]

Using God's ongoing work as a justification for one's own labour was an entirely different matter, of course. It is as clear a statement that Jesus shares the divine identity as is his later statement, 'Before Abraham was, I am' (John 8:58). For our purposes, the miracle reinforces the point adduced above from Luke 13: Jesus is not merely 'breaking the rules because he is God'—he is bringing the eschatological Sabbath to the world, and so it is perfectly appropriate for him to heal on the Sabbath as a sign of this transformation.

Jesus is 'still working' because the act of creation cannot be relegated to the distant past; it is an ongoing struggle to bring God's purposes to fruition.[13] This is most clearly evident in the story of the man born blind in John 9. The disciples, lighting upon the man, immediately enter into a debate as to whether the man or his parents sinned in order to lead him into such a miserable state. Jesus, in typical fashion, recasts the entire discussion. The man's predicament is not an arena for theological logic chopping, but an

---

12. Exodus Rabbah 30.9; in *Midrash Rabbah: Exodus* (trans. S. M. Lehrman; London: Soncino, 1939), pp. 355–56. See C. K. Barrett, *The Gospel According to St. John: An Introduction with Commentary and Notes on the Greek Text* (Philadelphia: Westminster, 1978), p. 256.

13. This is at least part of what Levenson is getting at throughout *Creation and the Persistence of Evil.*

opportunity for God's grace and power to be displayed. The disciples assume that the fall has the last word; the affliction is a *fait accompli* and can serve only as an object lesson in divine retribution. Jesus, by contrast, works to realize God's creative design. He spits into the dirt, forms some clay, and commands the man to wash in the pool of Siloam. When he does, he can see.

Irenaeus' insights into the passage are unrivalled:

> Wherefore also the Lord spat on the ground and made clay, and smeared it upon the eyes, pointing out the original fashioning [of man], how it was effected, and manifesting the hand of God to those who can understand by what [hand] man was formed out of the dust. For that which the artificer, the Word, had omitted to form in the womb [viz., the blind man's eyes], He then supplied in public, that the works of God might be manifested in him, in order that we might not be seeking out another hand by which man was fashioned, nor another Father; knowing that this hand of God which formed us at the beginning, and which does form us in the womb, has in the last times sought us out who were lost, winning back His own, and taking up the lost sheep upon His shoulders, and with joy restoring it to the fold of life.[14]

While modern critical commentators have shied away from detecting an allusion to creation here, Irenaeus accurately discerns John's intent. While John 9 does not employ the 'dust' of Genesis 2, the word for 'clay', *pēlos* (9:6), was regularly used for the stuff of humanity both in biblical and Greek usage. Thus Aristophanes refers to people as 'creatures of clay' in *Birds* II.685–687, while Pausanias in his travelogue describes a certain riverbank whence the gods drew clay from which to form the first humans.[15] Closer to home, the LXX employs *pēlos* in the familiar prophetic metaphor of the potter and clay, and Job laments that he is 'mere clay'.[16]

Irenaeus' understanding of God's creative act is remarkable: his declaration that the Word had 'omitted to form [the blind man's eyes] in the womb' is audacious, but very much in the spirit of the text. Far from embracing a simplistic argument from design, Irenaeus recognizes that God's purposes in creation can only be read clearly in light of their eschatological fulfilment. No less than John, the bishop of Lyons can distinguish past, present, and future

14. Irenaeus, *Haer*. 5.15.2.

15. Pausanias, *Descr*. 10.4.4.

16. Isa. 29:16; 64:8; Job 10:9; cf. Qumran, 1QHa xx.32: 'a creature of clay and spat saliva'; and the even more ancient examples adduced by Gordon Wenham: 'Aruru created Enkidu from clay. Egyptian monuments portray the god Khnum making man out of clay. The classical myths tell of Prometheus creating the first man from soil and water (Ovid, *Metamorphoses* 1.82; Juvenal 14:35). It is evident then that Genesis is here taking up a very ancient tradition of the creation of man and is giving these old ideas its own distinctive flavor.' Wenham, *Genesis 1–15* (Waco, TX: Word, 1987), p. 60.

aspects of creation, and at the same time see them as an integrated whole: 'knowing that this hand of God which formed us at the beginning, and which does form us in the womb, has in the last times sought us out who were lost'.

The raising of Lazarus forms the climax of the signs in John's gospel. It is the definitive proof of Jesus' claim to share the divine identity, and the signal demonstration of his purpose in coming to the world: to fulfil the promise of life that had been inaugurated in him in the beginning. The prelude to the story reminds the reader that this life-giving work will come in and through Jesus' death. The disciples do not need supernatural insight to realize that a trip towards Jerusalem to rescue Lazarus means certain death for Jesus. The authorities have come close to killing him twice, and it is unlikely in the extreme that they will fail of their purpose a third time. Yet because Jesus loves Lazarus, he is determined to go—he will exchange his life for the life of his friend.

The crucifixion is of programmatic significance for John's creation theme. The proliferation of words with the *erga-* root in the gospel mean that Jesus' Sabbath-eve cry, 'It is finished' (John 19:30) is no sigh of resignation, nor the bare announcement that events have run their course: it is instead a declaration that his recreative work, adumbrated in his mighty works and wise words, and culminating in the crucifixion, has come to its climax.

John is arguably the single most important biblical resource for developing a fully orbed theology of creation and new creation. John affirms the classical theological distinctions between creation in the beginning (1:1); *creatio continua* ('My Father is working still, and I am working'); and new creation that begins with the advent of Jesus and comes to full flower in the age to come (cf. John 3, and the affirmation of future resurrection in John 5). Yet he also permits these three distinct aspects of God's creative work to mingle in perichoretic fashion.

John also provides the christological soil in which so much later theology was to grow. His portrait of a fully human Christ who nonetheless shares the divine identity and participates in the work of creation laid the foundation for subsequent *logos* theology and the grand theological syntheses of theologians like Maximus the Confessor. In Christ, creation and Creator meet.

Epistles

The theme of salvation as new creation permeates the letters of Paul. He makes the theme explicit in 2 Corinthians 5:17—'If any one is in Christ, he is a new creation (*kainē ktisis*)'—but citations from and allusions to the creation narrative abound. The respective deeds of Adam and Christ dominate the central portion of Romans 1–8, and this is no coincidence. Paul's reflections on Jews, Gentiles, and the law are rooted in creation history. His argument begins with the Gentiles' failure to give God the worship that is his due as Creator (1:18–23), and concludes with the exquisite portrait of cosmic renewal in Romans 8: 'because the creation itself will be set free from its bondage to decay and obtain the glorious liberty of the children of God' (v. 21). Far from being a mere treatise on how individuals can get right with God, Romans places the restitution of humanity in its necessary context: God's plan to glorify himself through a restored created order.

First Corinthians 15 offers a similarly grand view of world history, one which was to prove especially important in the theological tradition. Paul begins with a crisis in the local church community, in this case the denial of bodily resurrection by some Corinthians. He responds by reminding them that Christ has come to reclaim the dominion over all creation that had been lost by Adam (vv. 20–28). Even in humanity's fallen state, David could celebrate the fact that creation lay 'under his feet' in accordance with God's command at creation (Ps. 8:6; 1 Cor. 15:27). But this pales beside the messianic dominion wherein God puts all enemies, including death, 'under his [= the Messiah's] feet' (Ps. 110:1; 1 Cor. 15:25), so that 'God may be all in all' (1 Cor. 15:28 NIV). Adam at his best was merely a 'living soul', 'of the earth, earthy' (1 Cor. 15:45, 47; cf. Gen. 2:7). While Paul does not spell out his reading of Genesis, it appears he believes Adam would have needed to eat from the tree of life to receive enduring life before God. This has come now through Christ, the man from heaven, who will provide the 'spiritual body' capable of receiving the fullness of God's glory in the eschaton. Precisely what this 'spiritual body' consists of, and how it relates to God being 'all in all', was to spawn considerable discussion, which we will address in due course. Suffice it for now to show Paul's insistence on reading Christ's story in close connection with the creation narrative.

The quintessence of the creation–new creation theme in the traditional Pauline corpus is distilled in the 'hymn to Christ' of Colossians 1:15–20.[17] The first section (1:15–17) extols Christ as Creator, the second (vv. 18–20) Christ as Redeemer. But the tight parallels between the two sections show that these are mutually informative categories. Christ is 'firstborn of all creation' (v. 15) and 'firstborn from the dead' (v. 18). He is 'before all things' (v. 17, *pro pantōn*) and he has 'become pre-eminent (*prōteuōn*) in all things' (v. 18). He 'created all things in heaven and on earth' (v. 16) and 'all things were reconciled to God through him . . . things on earth and in heaven' (v. 20).[18] Salvation is not a remedial measure, a second-best alternative fobbed

17. Whether it is in fact a hymn remains open to question; it certainly has a poetic flavour to it, but that is all we can say with certainty.

18. Translations from Col. 1:15–20 in this paragraph are mine.

off on the world when the initial creation project fell apart—it is the fulfilment of God's plan for the world. By the same token, creation is not a sadly materialistic prelude to the appearance of the genuine spiritual kingdom. 'All things' are created by God through Christ, and 'all things' are reconciled to him through Christ. This is what Ephesians terms 'the administration of the fullness of times, to sum up[19] all things in Christ' (Eph. 1:10).

The Pastoral Epistles have not fared well in modern theological discourse: they are regularly torn from Paul by scholars and ascribed to some officious, late first-century bureaucrat intent on stifling the Spirit-filled communities of the church's exuberant youth.[20] In fact the Pastorals, whatever their provenance, contain some of the most important material in the entire New Testament for a robust theology of creation. Here above all we find an affirmation of the created order even in the midst of the dawning realities of the kingdom. Luke Timothy Johnson affirms the Pastorals' overall concern with order in the community: 'There is no radical discontinuity between the will of God and the structures of society. The structures of the *oikos* (household) and the *ekklēsia* (church) are not only continuous with each other, but both are parts of the dispensation [administration] of God in the world.'[21] Specific references to the abiding relevance of created realities abound. The most familiar is also the most controversial: the admonition to women to 'learn in silence with all submissiveness' (1 Tim. 2:11) in light of the deception of Eve, coupled with the curious assurance that they will be 'saved through bearing children' (2:15). The latter phrase is probably better translated generically as 'through the child-bearing', with an oblique reference to the birth of Christ as prophesied in Isaiah 7:14 and 9:6. As for the former, there has been no shortage of attempts to affirm it as theologically viable as is, or to read it in a way more conformable to Paul's apparent affirmation of women's teaching in 1 Corinthians 12–14. For our purposes, we need only affirm that whatever its precise meaning, 1 Timothy 2 affirms that at least some of the dynamics of the primal creation remain relevant

---

19. The Greek term for 'sum up', *anakephalaiōsasthai*, lies behind Irenaeus' noted doctrine of recapitulation, a Latinization of Paul's verb.

20. See e.g. the dismissal of the Pastorals in Richard Hays' otherwise excellent *The Moral Vision of the New Testament: Community, Cross, New Creation; a Contemporary Introduction to New Testament Ethics* (San Francisco: HarperCollins, 1996), pp. 60–61.

21. Luke Timothy Johnson, *The First and Second Letters to Timothy: A New Translation with Introduction and Commentary* (New York: Doubleday, 2001), p. 149. Johnson also notes the similarities between the Greek words *oikonomia* and *oikos*: 'The noun *oikonomia* has as its first meaning "household management," but can be extended from that root meaning to notions of "ordering" or "dispensation" in larger spheres than the strictly domestic, without thereby losing its basic point of reference in the *oikos*.' For reference and further discussion, see Alex Kirk, '1 Timothy', *Theology of Work Bible Commentary* (Peabody, MA: Hendrickson, 2016).

for Christian behaviour. Far clearer, and of more direct relevance to our argument, is the warning against deception in 1 Timothy 4:1–5:

> Now the Spirit expressly says that in later times some will depart from the faith by giving heed to deceitful spirits and doctrines of demons, through the pretensions of liars whose consciences are seared, who forbid marriage and enjoin abstinence from foods which God created to be received with thanksgiving by those who believe and know the truth. For everything created by God is good, and nothing is to be rejected if it is received with thanksgiving; for then it is consecrated by the word of God and prayer.

Godliness may indeed focus on 'the life to come' (1 Tim. 4:8), but it is to be exercised now in the grateful reception of the good world that God made in the beginning.

The book of Hebrews, in keeping with the rest of the New Testament, lays more weight than the Pastorals on the transitory nature of the present world order. But the connection of creation and new creation is still readily apparent. We have already noted that the author of Hebrews frames eschatological fulfilment in terms of 'sabbath rest'. While he writes as one living in the 'last days' (1:2) and characterizes the present world as 'shakeable' (12:27), he is happy to affirm that God made all the ages through Christ (1:2). Both the now-world and the new-world come from the hand of the almighty Creator. Abraham may have looked forward to the enduring 'city with foundations', but even that city has God as its 'architect and builder' (11:10).

The Epistle of James, when it has not been wished out of the canon altogether, has largely been relegated to ethical service. But like the similarly snubbed Pastorals, James is rooted in a thoughtful theology of creation and new creation. Echoes of Genesis may be heard throughout the epistle: the mention of the 'Father of [heavenly] lights' in 1:17 and the taming of the animals in 3:7 are two obvious examples, but the pattern of desire, sin, and death in 1:13–15 is also arguably drawn from the story of Adam and Eve. Most pertinent for our purposes is 1:18, where James writes, 'Of his own will he brought us forth by the word of truth that we should be a kind of first fruits of his creatures.' Interpreters are hard pressed to decide whether this refers to primal creation or new creation (I favour the latter), but the very ambiguity is instructive: the two aspects of the word's work are so intermingled in early Christian thought it is hard to tell the one from the other.

James's teaching on the recreative power of the word is echoed in 1 Peter 1:23: 'You have been born anew, not of perishable seed but of imperishable, through the living and abiding word of God.' Peter also makes use of the transition from darkness to light (2:9: 'But you are a chosen race, a royal priesthood, a holy nation, God's own people, that you may declare the wonderful deeds of him who called you out of darkness into his marvelous light'), a motif he shares with 1 John 1:5–7 (cf. 2:8–11):

> This is the message we have heard from him and proclaim to you, that God is light and in him is no darkness at all. If we say we have fellowship with him while we walk in darkness, we lie and do not live according to the truth; but if we walk in the light, as he is in the light, we have fellowship with one another, and the blood of Jesus his Son cleanses us from all sin.

For the rest, we might say that 2 Peter and Revelation are as concerned with *de-creation* as they are recreation, and we will deal with them in that regard in chapter 7. But this still supposes a certain symmetry between the beginning and the end; and in any case they both evoke the splendours of the new order in imagery derived from the present one.

Creation and New Creation in the Theological Tradition

Theologians through the ages have been quick to recognize the biblical connections between creation and new creation. Irenaeus' teaching of the recapitulation of all things in Christ is a particularly thoroughgoing reworking of this scriptural theme, but the tradition is full of similar intimations.[22] Origen may have coined the phrase, 'The end is always like the beginning', but the truth behind it was widely recognized.[23] Since the rest of the book will be dedicated to exploring the interplay of creation and new creation in Christian tradition, we will content ourselves here to establish the basic point through a series of *testimonia* with minimal comment.

We will explore in chapter 7 the widespread tradition that the six days of creation anticipated the six ages of world history, so we will let Lactantius' version stand here for the whole:

> Therefore, since all the works of God were completed in six days, the world must continue in its present state through six ages, that is, six thousand years. For the great day of God is limited by a circle of a thousand years, as the prophet shows, who says '*In Your sight, O Lord, a thousand years are as one day*.' And as God laboured during those six days in creating such great works,

22. Calvin, for instance, deploys *anakephalaiōsis* for the reordering of things in Christ (*Comm. Eph.* 1.8); Peter Wyatt, *Jesus Christ and Creation in the Theology of John Calvin* (Allison Park, PA: Pickwick, 1996), p. 77. For Irenaeus, see John Behr, *Irenaeus of Lyons: Identifying Christianity* (Oxford: OUP, 2013).

23. Origen, *Princ.*, 1.6.2; see E. Brian, *The Hope of the Early Church: A Handbook of Patristic Eschatology* (Cambridge: CUP, 1991), pp. 58–59.

> so His religion and truth must labour during these six thousand years, while wickedness prevails and bears rule. And again, since God, having finished His works, rested the seventh day and blessed it, at the end of the six thousandth year all wickedness must be abolished from the earth, and righteousness reign for a thousand years; and there must be tranquillity and rest from the labours which the world now has long endured.[24]

Lactantius also follows the New Testament in comparing the church's experience to the exodus:

> It is contained in the mysteries of the sacred writings, that a prince of the Hebrews, compelled by want of grain, passed into Egypt with all his family and relatives. And when his posterity, remaining long in Egypt, had increased into a great nation, and were oppressed by the heavy and intolerable yoke of slavery, God smote Egypt with an incurable stroke, and freed His people, leading them through the midst of the sea, when, the waves being cut asunder and parted on either side, the people went over on dry ground. And the king of the Egyptians endeavouring to follow them as they fled, the sea returning to its place, he was cut off, with all his people. And this deed so illustrious and so wonderful, although for the present it displayed to men the power of God, was also a foreshadowing and figure of a greater deed, which the same God was about to perform at the last consummation of the times, for He will free His people from the oppressive bondage of the world.[25]

Gregory Nazianzen employs a raft of scriptures to make a similar point in his Oration 38, combining ideas from Genesis, Exodus, Isaiah, and Revelation: 'Again the darkness is past; again Light is made; again Egypt is punished with darkness; again Israel is enlightened by a pillar. The people that sat in the darkness of ignorance, let it see the Great Light of full knowledge. Old things are passed away, behold all things have become new.'[26]

New creation has often been seen as the logical outworking of creation in the beginning. Thus Tertullian writes: 'And surely He is most competent to re-create who created, inasmuch as it is a far greater work to have produced than to have reproduced, to have imparted a beginning, than to have maintained a continuance. On this principle, you may be quite sure that the restoration of the flesh is easier than its first formation' (*De Res.* 11.4). Methodius says in the same vein: 'For in reality God did not establish the universe in vain, or to no purpose but destruction, as those weak-minded men say,

24. Lactantius, *Inst.* 7.14.

25. Lactantius, *Inst.* 7.15.

26. Gregory Nazianzen, *Or. Bas.* 38.2; see Peter C. Bouteneff, *Beginnings: Ancient Christian Readings of the Biblical Creation Narratives* (Grand Rapids: Baker, 2008), pp. 147ff.

but to exist, and be inhabited, and continue. Wherefore the earth and the heaven must exist again after the conflagration and shaking of all things' (*De Res.* 1.8). One notes that both these quotations come from discourses on the resurrection, a topic which regularly led thinkers back to creation. Thus Chrysostom: 'Let no one therefore go on disbelieving the Resurrection: but if a man disbelieve, let him think how many things He made from nothing, and admit it as a proof also of the other',[27] and Theophilus:

> The earth thus becoming visible, was yet without form. God therefore formed and adorned it with all kinds of herbs, and seeds and plants . . . Consider, further, their variety, and diverse beauty, and multitude, and how through them resurrection is exhibited, for a pattern of the resurrection of all men which is to be. For who that considers it will not marvel that a fig-tree is produced from a fig-seed, or that very huge trees grow from the other very little seeds?[28]

The linking of primal creation and new creation continued in the medieval church and beyond. Peter Lombard remarks on the computation of days from evening to evening as follows:

> In this there is a natural order of the distinction of the Days, so that the Days be distinguished and computed from morning unto morning. But afterwards it came to be in mystery, that the days were computed from evening unto evening, and the day was adjoined to the preceding night in computation, though in accord with the natural order the preceding day ought to be adjoined to the following night, because through sin man fell from the light into the shadows of ignorance and sins, (and) then through Christ returned from darkness to the light. Wherefore the Apostle (says): We were once darkness, but now (we are) light in the Lord.[29]

Aquinas, like many before and after him, linked the beginning and the end by way of the Neoplatonic exitus–reditus scheme, in which all things proceed from God and return to him: 'Just as the procession of persons is the reason of the production of creatures by the first principle, so too this same procession is the reason for the return of creatures to their end; since, just as we have been created by the Son and the Holy Spirit, so too it is by them that we are united to our ultimate end.'[30] This is not too far distant from what Jonathan Edwards says in *Miscellany* 741, 'The Happiness of Heaven':

27. Chrysostom, *Hom. 1 Cor.* 17.3.

28. Theophilus, *Autol.* 2.13–14; see Bouteneff, *Beginnings*, p. 69.

29. Lombard, *Sent.* 2.13.5.

30. Aquinas, *1 Sent. D.14 q.2 art.2*; see Gilles Emery, 'Trinity and Creation', in *The Theology of Thomas Aquinas* (ed. Rik van Nieuwenhove and Joseph Wawrykow; Notre Dame: University of Notre Dame Press, 2005), p. 67.

> Again it shows how much God designed to communicate himself to men, that he so communicated himself to the first and chief of elect men, the elder brother and the head and representative of the rest, even so that this man should be the same person with one of the persons of the Trinity. It seems by this to have been God's design to admit man as it were to the inmost fellowship with the deity. There was [as] it were an eternal society or family in the Godhead in the Trinity of persons. It seems to be God's design to admit the church into the divine family as his son's wife, so that which Satan made use [of] as a temptation to our first parents, '*Ye shall be as gods*,' shall be fulfilled contrary to his design [*Genesis 3:5*].[31]

As often, Edwards shows significant affinities with Eastern theologians, like the early twentieth-century Russian Orthodox thinker Sergei Bulgakov:

> The Incarnation is the interior basis of creation, its final cause. God did not create the world to hold it at a distance from him, at that insurmountable metaphysical distance that separates the Creator from the creation, but in order to surmount that distance and unite himself completely with the world; not only from the outside, as Creator, nor even as providence, but from within: 'the Word became flesh'. That is why the Incarnation is already predetermined in human kind.[32]

We may conclude our brief survey with a recognition of the linking of creation and new creation in the creedal tradition. While they may not always appreciate the significance of the words, churchgoers of varied denominations are habituated to reciting 'I believe in God the Father Almighty, Maker of heaven and earth' (Apostles' Creed, Nicene Creed of 381) as the entry point into affirmations of God's work of redemption in Christ and the Spirit. The later Reformed confessions, which go into even greater detail concerning the nature of redemption, are nonetheless careful to preserve the confession of God's primal creative act as a pillar of doctrine.[33]

Both Scripture and tradition, then, affirm that the mighty works of God wrought in history are predicated upon and are analogous to his works in the beginning. There is a unified divine purpose at work in the world, and this purpose will be realized in the glory of the eschaton.

---

31. Jonathan Edwards, *Miscellany* 741, *The Works of Jonathan Edwards* (26 vols; New Haven: Yale University Press, 1997–2009), 18:368.

32. From *The Incarnate Word*, trans. Andrew Louth, 'The Place of Theosis in Orthodox Theology', in *Partakers of the Divine Nature: The History and Development of Deification in the Christian Traditions* (ed. Michael J. Christensen and Jeffery A. Wittung; Grand Rapids: Baker, 2008), p. 36.

33. One could cite e.g. the Westminster Confession of Faith, ch. 4; Heidelberg Catechism 2.26; Baptist Confession of Faith 1644, ch. 4; and the Savoy Declaration, ch. 4.

2

God the Creator

> By this arrangement, therefore, and these harmonies, and a sequence of this nature, man, a created and organized being, is rendered after the image and likeness of the uncreated God—the Father planning everything well and giving His commands, the Son carrying these into execution and performing the work of creating, and the Spirit nourishing and increasing [what is made], but man making progress day by day, and ascending towards the perfect, that is, approximating to the uncreated One (Irenaeus, *Against Heresies* 4.38.3).

In the Scripture, God is repeatedly affirmed as the Maker of Heaven and Earth.[1] This is not in the first instance a unique tenet of Israel or the church. The essence of the Old Testament message may be summed up in this way: YHWH, the tribal deity of the small and perpetually beleaguered people of Israel, turns out to be none other than Elohim, the Creator and Overlord of all things and all peoples. People are expected to know that there is some such entity as Elohim out there; the shock comes from the assertion that he has tied himself up with Israel. Likewise in the New Testament, Paul in Acts 17 speak to Greeks about 'the God who made heaven and earth' in the full hope of being understood. He can even leverage the best of Hellenistic philosophical monotheism in support: '"In him we live and move and have our being"; as even some of your poets have said' (v. 28). He follows a similar, if less positive, line of reasoning in Romans 1. People can see readily enough from the creation that there must be a God behind it; the problem is they cannot resist worshipping the creation rather than the Creator.

But some important questions lurk under this serene surface. The first is this: can we finite creatures *really* know on the basis of his creation this being who is by definition infinite in glory and power, beyond space and time, and in the strict sense incomprehensible? At least since Philo, there has been a strain of Jewish and Christian thought that gives a (qualified) 'no' to this question. We cannot know God as he is in and of himself; we know him by his powers. The apophatic tradition, particularly as it was articulated by Gregory Palamas (1296–1359), has been especially powerful in Orthodox theology. This apophatic 'no' at its best evaporates the fantasy that we can get

1. See e.g. Pss. 121:2; 134:3; 146:6.

our little human minds right round God. He cannot become another object for us to measure and critique and control. This is especially pertinent to the doctrine of creation in light of the final chapters of Job: 'Where were you when I laid the foundation of the earth? Tell me, if you have understanding' (38:4). It also forms a safeguard against the allures of pantheism: if I am encountering God in this unique snowflake on my window pane, how do I keep from concluding that God (or at least 'part' of him) *is* the snowflake?

The corresponding danger of apophaticism, however, is that one might imagine that we cannot know God in any respect; and thus theologians who embrace the apophatic view of God-in-himself are generally careful to balance this with the kataphatic revelation of God. There can nonetheless creep in the nagging suspicion that God is holding something back from us. He gives us the world, but not himself. To counter this, it is important to remember that in Scripture knowing God follows the logic of personal encounter rather than that of exhaustive scientific description. One can genuinely meet the God who speaks and listens without claiming to have a comprehensive understanding of him. Even the face-to-face encounter with God in the eschaton (1 John 3:2) can be seen as an eternal process of discovery.[2]

Do we have this encounter with God through the creation? The visionaries of Scripture already move beyond the normal confines of space and time to meet God, and we are thus tempted to think this somehow represents an encounter with God that transcends created-ness. But it is critical to remember that the encounter of God with *anything else* necessarily assumes creation. Even if we were to posit a purely 'spiritual' encounter with God in the eschaton (and the doctrine of bodily resurrection does not lend much support to such a conception), this would still occur 'through the creation' in the sense that the spirits involved will have been created by God.

We might reframe the question, then, to ask whether we can gain an understanding of God through *material* creation, or as it is more commonly put, 'through nature'. This raises the spectre of 'natural theology'. The term is subject to numerous interpretations, but in its most simple and extreme form it entails people, presumed to be in a state of independence from God, coming up with a perfectly adequate knowledge of God simply by looking at the world around them and figuring him out. One need not be a full-blown Barthian to see the problems with this way of putting things. Following up on the logic of personal encounter mentioned above, it seems pretty clear that God must choose to make himself known if we are to have any hope of entering into a genuine 'I–Thou' relationship with him. The problem becomes more acute when we factor in the obscurity that arises from humanity's primordial estrangement from God.

2. See the comments from Gregory of Nyssa in this regard in chapter 6 below.

But a rejection of this radical version of 'natural theology' hardly means that we cannot at a minimum learn things *about* God via his works. Paul's words in Romans 1:20 provide a suitable point of departure, since it is directed precisely to post-fall Gentiles: 'Ever since the creation of the world his invisible nature, namely, his eternal power and deity, has been clearly perceived in the things that have been made. So they are without excuse.' This knowledge from the creation may do them no religious good (vv. 21ff.), but it is knowledge nonetheless. As Athanasius puts it (*C. Ar.* 2.32):

> And as the creation contains abundant matter for the knowledge of the being of a God and a Providence ('for by the greatness and beauty of the creatures proportionably the Maker of them is seen (Wisdom 13:5)'), and we learn from them without asking for voices, but hearing the Scriptures we believe, and surveying the very order and the harmony of all things, we acknowledge that He is Maker and Lord and God of all, and apprehend His marvellous Providence and governance over all things.

We will explore specific characteristics of God thought to be visible in the creation below. It is worth noting here, though, that many Christian thinkers have not been shy in thinking we can read the 'book of Nature' in rather specific detail. One striking example is the *Physiologus*, a massively popular text from the early centuries of the church that purports to unveil the divine mysteries hidden within the creation. The *Physiologus* goes well beyond Solomon's advice that sluggards would do well to watch ants, and finds allegories of God's ways in an imaginatively rich if zoologically suspect vision of the natural world. Witness the depiction of the panther in the Old English *Physiologus*: the creature, 'gracious, kind, and full of love':

> Once he has rejoiced
> His heart with feasting, straight he finds a nook
> Hidden among dim caves, his resting-place.
> There three nights' space, in deepest slumber wrapped,
> The people's champion lies. Then, stout of heart,
> The third day he arises fresh from sleep,
> Endowed with glory. From the creature's mouth
> Issues a melody of sweetest strains . . .[3]

The transparent connection with Christ's resurrection is duly noted in the following stanzas.

As a field guide, the *Physiologus* leaves something to be desired, particularly if one is going to encounter any actual panthers. But it does raise

3. Translation in J. H. Pitman, *The Old English Physiologus* (New Haven: Yale University Press, 1921).

an interesting theological question: if God has put his wisdom into the creation, are we warranted in drawing spiritual lessons out of the creation? Edwards was thoroughly convinced that we can do just that. For him, all the world was 'full of images of divine things, as full as a language is of words'.[4] Thus, true to the spirit of the *Physiologus*, Edwards could see the silkworm as a type of Christ: in dying the silkworm yields us that which will make beautiful clothing, just as Christ in dying yields us clothes of righteousness and glory.[5] But Edwards provides a far more detailed rationale for his moralizing than does the *Physiologus*. Christ and the apostles employed natural items to depict spiritual realities, and Edwards takes them as examples for our own practice.[6] There is also a deeper theological reason for viewing the world in this way. Edwards' idealistic philosophy encouraged him to think of the material in terms of the spiritual; in God's well-ordered creation, lower things are as it were embedded within higher things:

> Again, it is apparent and allowed that there is a great and remarkable analogy in God's works. There is a wonderful resemblance in the effects which God produces, and consentaneity in his manner of working in one thing and another, throughout all nature. It is very observable in the visible world. Therefore 'tis allowed that God does purposely make and order one thing to be in an agreeableness and harmony with another. And if so, why should not we suppose that he makes the inferior in imitation of the superior, the material of the spiritual, on purpose to have a resemblance and shadow of them? We see that even in the material world God makes one part of it strangely to agree with another; and why is it not reasonable to suppose he makes the whole as a shadow of the spiritual world?[7]

Even the works of human beings cannot escape this principle of analogy. In one particularly striking example, Edwards compares the wheel of divine providence (derived from Ezek. 1, with some assistance perhaps from James 3:6; cf. 'Images' 154) to the wheels of human contraptions:

> 'Tis because the providence of God is like a wheel, as a machine composed of wheels, having wheels in the midst of wheels, that 'tis so ordered in the constitution of nature and in the dispositions of God's providence, that almost all the curious machines that men contrive to do any notable things or produce

---

4. Jonathan Edwards, 'Types', *The Works of Jonathan Edwards* (26 vols; New Haven: Yale University Press, 1997–2009), 11:152, cited in Kin Yip Louie, *The Beauty of the Triune God: The Theological Aesthetics of Jonathan Edwards* (Eugene, OR: Pickwick, 2013), p. 78.

5. Edwards, 'Images' 35, *Works*, 11:59, in Louie, *Beauty*, p. 78.

6. Louie, *Beauty*, p. 79. Edwards adds in 'Images' 55 (*Works*, 11:66) that God himself endorses the spiritual interpretation of natural phenomena in the case of the rainbow.

7. Edwards, 'Images' 8, *Works*, 11:53.

> any remarkable effect, are by wheels, a compage of wheels, revolving round and round, going and returning, representing the manner of the progress of things in divine providence.[8]

Edwards essentially produces a counterpoint to the common assertion that the world operates like a machine: the reality is that human machines, like the world at large, are only dim reflections of the great machine of God's providence. Edwards concedes that analogies get 'more faint and languid' the further down the chain of being you go (e.g. from people to rocks),[9] but the principle obtains throughout. The world speaks of God to those willing to listen.

The Triune Creator

We have seen arguments that one might look at the world and conclude that there is a Creator. It seems far less likely that one would look at the world and conclude that this one Creator God subsists in three persons, Father, Son, and Holy Spirit. This is not to say that one might not *in retrospect* find evidence of a kind of Trinitarian logic woven into the fabric of creation.[10] But it does suggest that the primal insight would stem from revelation rather than observation of nature. Whatever its provenance, the confession of God as the *Triune Creator* has been a visible part of the doctrine of creation since the earliest days of the church, and its prominence has only increased in recent years.[11]

While there is a long-standing tendency in the church to attribute creation to the Father, redemption to the Son and consummation to the Spirit, this neat distinction overrides some critical biblical evidence. The involvement of Christ in creation was a foundational part of early Christian doctrine (see e.g. John 1:2; Col. 1:15–19; 1 Cor. 8:6; Heb. 1:2). Likewise, the Spirit hovering over the waters in Genesis 1:2 was generally identified with the Holy Spirit, a reading strengthened by the creative role of the Spirit in Psalm 104 and elsewhere.[12] The challenge for a Trinitarian theology of

8. Edwards, 'Images' 89, *Works*, 11:86.

9. See Edwards, 'Images', *Works*, 11:85–86.

10. See e.g. Augustine, *Trin.* 15; Colin E. Gunton, *The One, the Three, and the Many* (Cambridge: CUP, 1993).

11. See esp. Colin E. Gunton, *The Triune Creator: A Historical and Systematic Study* (Edinburgh: T&T Clark, 2001), and vol. 1 of Robert W. Jenson, *Systematic Theology* (2 vols; New York: OUP, 1997–99).

12. See Paul M. Blowers, *Drama of the Divine Economy: Creator and Creation in Early Christian Theology and Piety* (Oxford: OUP, 2012), pp. 113–18.

creation is then similar to the challenge for a Trinitarian theology of anything: how do we speak both to the distinction of the persons and the unity of the substance?

Omni opera Trinitas ad extra indivisa sunt has long been a watchword for the doctrine of the Trinity: all the works of the Trinity 'towards the outside' are undivided. This surely obtains in the case of creation: we would not want to say, for instance, that the Father created part of the world and the Son another part, or that the Spirit is working on certain 'independent projects' apart from the counsel of the Father and Son.[13] The divine unity is a foundational aspect of the doctrine of creation.[14] But can one still make meaningful distinctions between the persons within this unity?

Paul's formula in 1 Corinthians 8:6 assists us in exploring the diverse activities of the Trinity in creation and new creation. A literal rendering would be: 'But for us, one God the Father, from whom are all things, and we to him; and one Lord Jesus Christ, through whom are all things, and we through him.' This requires substantial unpacking, and we might begin with an expansive translation: 'In contrast to pagan polytheists, we recognize that there is only one true God, the Father, who is the source of all things that exist, and our whole lives are ultimately oriented to him; and we recognize one Lord, Jesus Christ, through whom God made all things, and we ourselves are both created and redeemed through Jesus.' As numerous scholars have pointed out, 1 Corinthians 8:6 constitutes a stunning Christian reworking of the Shema, Israel's traditional monotheistic confession: 'Hear, O Israel: the LORD our God is one LORD' (Deut. 6:4).[15] By associating Jesus with the act of creation and the classic monotheistic confession, Paul thus

13. Cf. Augustine, *Trin.* 1.12: 'But if they will have this to be understood only of the Father, then in what way are all things by the Father, as is said here; and all things by the Son, as where it is said to the Corinthians, "And one Lord Jesus Christ, by whom are all things," and as in the Gospel of John, "All things were made by Him?" For if some things were made by the Father, and some by the Son, then all things were not made by the Father, nor all things by the Son; but if all things were made by the Father, and all things by the Son, then the same things were made by the Father and by the Son. The Son, therefore, is equal with the Father, and the working of the Father and the Son is indivisible. Because if the Father made even the Son, whom certainly the Son Himself did not make, then all things were not made by the Son; but all things were made by the Son: therefore He Himself was not made, that with the Father He might make all things that were made.'

14. For a cautionary look at recent trends in emphasizing diversity at the expense of unity, see Stephen R. Holmes, *The Quest for the Trinity: The Doctrine of God in Scripture, History, and Modernity* (Downers Grove, IL: IVP, 2012).

15. This is not of course denying the existence of other 'supernatural' beings; one might equally render the Hebrew of Deuteronomy, 'Hear, O Israel: YHWH is your God, YHWH alone', in contradistinction to the nothing-gods of the surrounding nations.

included Jesus within the divine identity.[16] But within this unity there is distinction: creation is *from the Father and through the Son*. While the Spirit is not explicitly mentioned in the formula, he is a very active presence in the epistle, and it is difficult to imagine that Paul would exclude the Spirit from the act of creation. Note that in the climactic passage on the resurrection, Christ as last Adam is described as 'a life-giving spirit' (15:45). Thus 8:6 can justly serve as an introduction to a Trinitarian theology of creation.

Father

Paul identifies God the Father as the source and goal of all things ('from him . . . to him'). The idea that God is the source of all things was a commonplace in Hellenistic thought, and Paul's terse expression 'from him' fits well in the 'prepositional theology' of the day.[17] God is likewise the goal of all things. The eschatological dénouement hinted at in 1 Corinthians 8:6 is made explicit later in the epistle, in the climactic verse of 1 Corinthians 15:20–28: 'But when he [the Father] subjects all things to him [the Son], then the Son himself will be subjected to the one who subjected all things to him, in order that God might be all in all' (v. 28, my translation). Drawing out the implications of 'all in all' has been a long-standing theological pastime, and we will examine the tradition of interpretation in detail in later chapters. Suffice it to say for now that just as all things proceed from God's creative power, their unfolding history is designed to issue in eschatological praise for the one who has created them. Here we have creation, redemption, and eschatology forming a perfect circle, flowing out from God through Christ, and returning to him for his glory.

We may find an analagous structure in chapters 4 and 5 of Revelation. In chapter 4, God is again celebrated as Creator of all things: 'You are worthy, our Lord and our God, to receive glory and honor and power, for you created all things, and through your will they were and they were created' (4:11, my translation). Christ is not explicitly included in the act of creation; instead, he becomes the focal point of the redemptive narrative in chapter 5: 'You are worthy to receive the scroll and to open its seals, because you were slain and purchased by your blood people from every tribe and tongue and people and nation' (5:9, my translation). The scene climaxes with all creation praising the 'one who sits on the throne and the Lamb'. The circle is

16. Richard Bauckham, *Jesus and the God of Israel: God Crucified and Other Studies on the New Testament's Christology of Divine Identity* (Grand Rapids: Eerdmans, 2009), pp. 102–4.

17. See Ronald Cox, *By the Same Word: Creation and Salvation in Hellenistic Judaism and Early Christianity* (Berlin: de Gruyter, 2007), pp. 43–51.

complete, and again it is a matter of things flowing out at God's command and at the end returning through Christ's sacrifice to praise to him.

This image of the circle imagines the Father as a fixed point, with a concomitant 'eschatology of return' that has drawn criticism as an undesirable import from Neoplatonism.[18] The fact that the doctrine in this form is associated with Origen does not help matters. It seems a short step (if a step at all) from here to a Neoplatonic emanationism that guts the history of creation of its meaning. For this reason, it is important to supplement the image of the circle (which does capture one aspect of 1 Cor. 15 and Rev. 4 and 5 quite well) with other images. We might, for example, wish to picture God *stretched out* over the temporal continuum in accordance with his character as the one who knows the end from the beginning (Isa. 44:6; Rev. 1:4). The revelation of God's name as 'I am who I am' at the burning bush suggests a similar view, particularly in the tradition of interpretation: the LXX emphasizes the supra-temporality of YHWH in its translation 'I Am the One Who Is', while this formula is in turn unpacked in the tradition to 'the One who was and is and is to come' (Rev. 1:4, etc.; cf. *Tg. Ps.-Jon.* Deut. 32). We might also think of God *journeying with* his people—witness the fire and cloud and the Rock in the wilderness. (Here, however, we face the question of the extent to which he makes this journey in the person of the Son or the Spirit; cf. 1 Cor. 10.)

Precisely *how* all things come from God and return to him will occupy much of the rest of the book. The doctrine of *creatio ex* nihilo arose at least in part to counter the notion that matter was a kind of substance extruded from the divine essence. One could instead take 'from whom' to indicate that the Father 'thinks up' the creation; as Irenaeus says in the quotation above, 'the Father planning everything well and giving his commands'. At this point the problematic dialogue with Platonism becomes inescapable: are the Ideas of things a part of God? Is Jesus the consummate Idea of all things? Or ought the Ideas to be seen as a particular type of created thing? Even the simple phrase 'giving his commands' can be developed in a number of ways, most notably with respect to the divine will. Does God, for instance, command a certain thing because it is good, or is it good because he commands it? This is not to mention the return to God, which poses equally puzzling questions. Is the cosmos somehow absorbed into the divine essence? Issues such as these will be addressed in due course.

For the time being, we will be content to isolate a few of the Father's perfections which are particularly evident in the act of creation. The first is his *power*. The word has accrued negative connotations in recent times, though at root this is simply an assertion that *no one else is capable of producing a*

18. See Gunton, *Triune Creator*, p. 59.

cosmos as splendid as this. Nonetheless, the tradition repeatedly emphasizes the power of God displayed in his works. This emerges in different ways for different writers. In Genesis 1, the serene establishment of the world through God's word seems almost effortless. On further reflection, this very effortlessness is the supreme revelation of God's omnipotence. Unlike other Ancient Near Eastern claimants to creation, the true and living God does not need to engage in combat with his peers and raise the creation from the carcass of his enemies. He simply commands that things be, and they are. Elsewhere, however, we see him, as it were, rolling up his sleeves and wrestling recalcitrant elements to his will, as in Psalm 74:13–17:

> Thou didst divide the sea by thy might;
> thou didst break the heads of the dragons on the waters.
> Thou didst crush the heads of Leviathan,
> thou didst give him as food for the creatures of the wilderness.
> Thou didst cleave open springs and brooks;
> thou didst dry up ever-flowing streams.
> Thine is the day, thine also the night;
> thou hast established the luminaries and the sun.
> Thou hast fixed all the bounds of the earth;
> thou hast made summer and winter.

As we have already seen with respect to Psalm 89, one may debate whether the splitting of the sea and the crushing of Leviathan depict primal creation from a certain angle,[19] or whether they depict the exodus with its recreative deliverance. But even if we opt for the latter, this can still be seen as part of the ongoing creation project.[20] In either case God's power is still very much in evidence. The latter chapters of Isaiah feature the same blend of creation and new creation in their magisterial picture of God, aptly summed up in 43:13: 'I am God, and also henceforth I am He; there is none who can deliver from my hand; I work and who can hinder it?'

As is already evident in the above passages, God's power cannot be divorced from his *wisdom*, which is evident in the care with which the world has been crafted:

> O Lord, how manifold are thy works!
> In wisdom hast thou made them all;
> the earth is full of thy creatures.
> Yonder is the sea, great and wide, which teems with things innumerable,
> living things both small and great (Ps. 104:24–25).

---

19. See Jon Douglas Levenson, *Creation and the Persistence of Evil: The Jewish Drama of Divine Omnipotence* (Princeton: Princeton University Press, 1988), pp. 105–6.

20. The psalm even invites an eschatological reading—when will Leviathan's head be crushed save at the last battle?

We may compare the musings of the arachnophile Jonathan Edwards:

> Hence the wisdom of the Creator in providing of the spider with that wonderful liquor with which their bottle tail is filled, that may so easily be drawn out so exceeding fine, and being in this exposed to the air will so immediately convert to a dry substance that shall be so very rare as to be lighter than the air, and will so excellently serve to all their purposes.[21]

Proverbs 8:22–31 offers a vivid portrait of personified Wisdom rejoicing at God's side at the time of creation:

> The LORD created me at the beginning of his work,
> the first of his acts of old.
> Ages ago I was set up,
> at the first, before the beginning of the earth.
> When there were no depths I was brought forth,
> when there were no springs abounding with water.
> Before the mountains had been shaped,
> before the hills, I was brought forth;
> before he had made the earth with its fields,
> or the first of the dust of the world.
> When he established the heavens, I was there,
> when he drew a circle on the face of the deep,
> when he made firm the skies above,
> when he established the fountains of the deep,
> when he assigned to the sea its limit,
> so that the waters might not transgress his command,
> when he marked out the foundations of the earth,
> then I was beside him, like a master workman;
> and I was daily his delight,
> rejoicing before him always,
> rejoicing in his inhabited world
> and delighting in the sons of men.

The passage has had an equally vivid history of christological interpretation, to which we will return. In its original setting in Proverbs, this seems to be no more than a vivid way of expressing the wisdom of God which is made known in the structure of the world. It is an extended portrait of the same truth expressed more tersely a few chapters earlier (Prov. 3:19–20): 'The LORD by wisdom founded the earth; by understanding he established the heavens; by his knowledge the deeps broke forth, and the clouds drop down the dew.'

---

21. Edwards, 'The "Spider" Letter', *Works*, 6:167.

God's *goodness* and *love* are likewise on display in the cosmos. In Scripture, divine beneficence is usually associated with God's redemptive activity, but his providential care over the creation is implicit in texts like Psalm 104, and occasionally it finds direct expression: 'The LORD is good to all, and his compassion is over all that he has made' (Ps. 145:9). The letter of James expresses the matter exquisitely. James first establishes God's identity as 'the giving God' (a literal rendering of *tou didontos theou* in 1:5). He then elaborates: 'Every good gift and every perfect present comes down from the father of lights, with whom there is no change or shadow of turning' (1:17, my translation).[22] James alludes to the creation of the heavenly lights as part of a subtle *a fortiori* argument: if even the glorious heavenly bodies are subject to eclipse, how much greater is the changeless God who made them.

The manifestation of God's love in the creation of the world takes on greater prominence in later theology. James's sentiments are echoed by none other than the man who sometimes wished to escort him out of the canon, Martin Luther: 'This is the three persons and one God, who has given himself to us absolutely and completely, along with all that he is and has.' Oswald Bayer comments:

> But God is categorically the one who gives. His giving nature defines the form that his actions take . . . Creation and new creation are both *categorical gift*. The first Word to the human being is a gifting Word: 'You may freely eat of every tree!' (Gen. 2:16)—renewed in the gifting Word of the Lord's Supper: 'Take and eat. This is my body, given for you!' According to Luther, God's entire Trinitarian being, within his own being as well as for us—though it is not usually emphasized in the theological tradition—is to be apprehended as giving and giving as a sacrifice.[23]

Part of the attraction of divine goodness was its apologetic value in the Graeco-Roman context. Plato's *Timaeus*, which along with Hesiod's *Theogony* was about as close as the Greeks came to a 'creation account', features an introduction which could hardly fail to draw the attention of Christians: 'Why did the Creator make the world? . . . He was good, and therefore not jealous, and being free from jealousy he desired that all things should be like himself.' There might be debate as to whether Plato intended to speak of a literal Creator (or a literal act of creation, for that matter), but the opportunity to establish a bond between the Bible and the greatest philosopher of the Greeks was irresistible. Athanasius quotes the passage from the *Timaeus*

---

22. There are numerous textual issues here; we go with the NA27.

23. The Luther quote is from the Weimar edition of Luther's works (WA) 26:505.38ff.; trans. and comments in Oswald Bayer, *Martin Luther's Theology: A Contemporary Interpretation* (Grand Rapids: Eerdmans, 2008), pp. 98–99.

directly in *Contra Gentes* 41 and *De Incarnatione* 3.[24] In both cases, he sees the goodness of the Creator expressed particularly in the activity of the Word. As he says in the *Contra Gentes* passage:

> But the God of all is good and exceeding noble by nature,—and therefore is kind. For one that is good can grudge nothing: for which reason he does not grudge even existence, but desires all to exist, as objects for His loving-kindness. Seeing then all created nature, as far as its own laws were concerned, to be fleeting and subject to dissolution, lest it should come to this and lest the Universe should be broken up again into nothingness, for this cause He made all things by His own eternal Word, and gave substantive existence to Creation, and moreover did not leave it to be tossed in a tempest in the course of its own nature, lest it should run the risk of once more dropping out of existence; but, because He is good He guides and settles the whole Creation by His own Word, Who is Himself also God, that by the governance and providence and ordering action of the Word, Creation may have light, and be enabled to abide alway securely.

The note about 'abiding securely' at the close of the quotation speaks particularly to God's *faithfulness*. While the characteristic is typically associated with God's covenant love for his people in Scripture, on occasion this broadens out to include the creation as a whole. The most notable example is the covenant with the earth signified by the rainbow:

> And God said, 'This is the sign of the covenant which I make between me and you and every living creature that is with you, for all future generations: I set my bow in the cloud, and it shall be a sign of the covenant between me and the earth. When I bring clouds over the earth and the bow is seen in the clouds, I will remember my covenant which is between me and you and every living creature of all flesh; and the waters shall never again become a flood to destroy all flesh' (Gen. 9:12–15).

Presumably God's commitment to the creation did not begin after the flood, and the covenant in Genesis 9 reaffirms a prior determination to uphold the cosmos. If this be granted, God's faithfulness to the creation carries within itself the seed of eschatological promise. He will not simply prop up the world as it slouches from one crisis to the next, but instead in faithfulness he will bring it to his desired goal. This may find confirmation in the reappearance of the rainbow in Revelation 4, where it now encircles the divine throne. Richard Bauckham argues for the relevance of the background in Genesis 9 (with an assist from Ezek. 1) and concludes: 'In this

24. See the discussion in Athanasius, *Contra Gentes: Introduction, Translation, and Commentary* (trans. E. P. Meijering; Leiden: Brill, 1984).

way Revelation portrays God as faithful to the Noahic covenant and indeed surpassing it in his faithfulness to his creation: first by destroying the destroyers of the earth, finally by taking creation beyond the threat of evil.'[25]

Luther makes a similar point as he muses upon the future of creation in light of the present:

> [We] are presently in the dawn of the age to come, for we are beginning to acquire once again the knowledge of the creatures that we lost through Adam's fall. Now we can look at the creatures much more correctly, more than at any time under the papacy . . . But we begin, by the grace of God, to recognize his majestic works and wonders even within the little blossoms, when we reflect about how almighty and good God is. Therefore we praise and glorify him and thank him. We recognize the might of his Word in his creatures, how powerful it is. For he spoke and it came to be [Ps. 33:9]—even through a peach stone. Even though its outer shell is very hard, in its own proper time it must open up because of its soft center, which is inside.[26]

The God from whom all things have come may be relied upon to bring them to their proper goal.

Son

To the extent that the work of the Son is the work of the Father, all that has been said above with respect to the Father's love and faithfulness and power may be equally predicated of the Son. We are nonetheless bound to explore the distinctives that attend Paul's 'through whom' formula. The way forward will be cleared considerably by recognizing that the Messiah is by definition the deputized agent of God's rule in the world.[27] The early Christians expanded this to include the work of primal creation, even as they expanded the Messiah's identity to full inclusion in the Godhead. But based on the evidence of 1 Corinthians 8:6, they did not feel compelled to alter the basic understanding that the Messiah was authorized and empowered by God (now known as Father) to do God's will and not his own. The church has rightly resisted the idea that the Son is somehow inferior in essence to the Father, and the modern democratic impulse has encouraged an iron resistance to anything that smacks of 'subordinationism'. But a distinction is evident in 1 Corinthians 8:6. Indeed, it would be shocking

---

25. Richard Bauckham, *The Theology of the Book of Revelation* (Cambridge: CUP, 1993), p. 53.

26. WA TR 1:574.8–19 (no. 1160), in Bayer, *Martin Luther*, p. 108.

27. Ps. 110; Ps. 2; 2 Sam. 7; Ps. 89.

only if Paul's formulation lacked the fundamental idea of messianic agency on behalf of God.

The notion that God created the world through Christ receives little commentary in the New Testament texts in which it appears, so its precise origins and significance remain somewhat elusive. But it is widely agreed that the agency of Christ in creation was extrapolated from his work in the eschatological new creation which had dawned with his incarnation, life, death, resurrection, and ascension.[28] The earliest Christians experienced Jesus as the eschatological presence of the Lord in their midst, an Immanuel who did not merely represent YHWH's gracious turning to the world, but who in his mighty works of restoration and his words of wisdom fully embodied the God of Israel. Once he was thus embraced within the divine identity at the end of times, it would be difficult to imagine a time when he would not have been embraced within that identity. Couple this with the long-standing association of cosmic order and social order, and the foundation is laid for thinking of Christ as Creator.

We have already noted how the gospels and epistles entwine the themes of creation and new creation around the works of Christ. But the New Testament itself does not limn out all the implications this assertion had for understanding Christ's person and the precise role he played in the formation of the world. It fell upon later generations to explore the theme in depth.

Creation by the Son

From the beginning, the association of Christ and the act of creation was a pillar in the confession of his inclusion in the Godhead.[29] John's theology of the Word played a critical role here: Christ is the perfect self-expression of God, the effective Word who brings to reality God's desires for the creation. In his lectures on John's gospel, Augustine extols the divinity of the Word and

28. See e.g. R. S. Barbour, 'Creation, Wisdom, and Christ', in *Creation, Christ, and Culture* (ed. W. A. McKinney; Edinburgh: T&T Clark, 1976), p. 23; Sean McDonough, *Christ as Creator: Origins of a New Testament Doctrine* (Oxford: OUP, 2011), pp. 46ff. Note Athanasius, *Inc.* 18: 'For who, seeing a body proceeding forth from a Virgin alone without man, can fail to infer that He Who appears in it is Maker and Lord of other bodies also? Or who, seeing the substance of water changed and transformed into wine, fails to perceive that He Who did this is Lord and Creator of the substance of all waters? For to this end He went upon the sea also as its Master, and walked as on dry land, to afford evidence to them that saw it of His lordship over all things. And in feeding so vast a multitude on little, and of His own self yielding abundance where none was, so that from five loaves five thousand had enough, and left so much again over, did He shew Himself to be any other than the very Lord Whose Providence is over all things?'

29. See Bauckham, *Jesus and the God of Israel*, on Jewish background, in which this puts Jesus on the divine side of a divine/everything else divide.

counters the Arian notion that the Word is one creature among many (and in the process illustrates yet again the link between creation and new creation):

> Do not then believe that that was made by which were made all things, lest thou be not new-made by the Word, which makes all things new. For already hast thou been made by the Word, but it behoves thee to be new-made by the Word. If, however, thy belief about the Word be wrong, thou wilt not be able to be new-made by the Word. And although creation by the Word has happened to thee, so that thou hast been made by Him, thou art unmade by thyself: if by thyself thou art unmade, let Him who made thee make thee new: if by thyself thou hast been made worse, let Him who created thee re-create thee. But how can He re-create thee by the Word, if thou holdest a wrong opinion about the Word? (*Lect. In Joh. 1.12*)

In a similar way, viewing Christ as God's Wisdom afforded theologians another way to affirm that Christ shared the divine identity—he is God's Wisdom—while maintaining his own personhood. The personified figure of Wisdom 'at the side of' the creating God in Proverbs 8 seemed to offer a clear demonstration of at least a 'bi-nitarian' distinction within the Godhead. To take but a few examples, Justin Martyr lists 'Wisdom' as one of the names of Christ in *Dialogue with Trypho* 126, while Gregory of Nyssa (like Athanasius) expends considerable energy in *Contra Eunomius* 2.10 countering the notion that the use of the verb 'created' in the Greek text of Proverbs 8:22 means that Christ is essentially a created being. What is interesting for our purposes is that he assumes that all parties agree the figure of Wisdom in the passage is Christ. Jonathan Edwards affirmed the same in his 'Discourse on the Trinity': 'But Christ is said to be the wisdom of God (*1 Corinthians 1:24; Luke 11:49* compared with *Matthew 23:34*); and how much doth Christ speak in Proverbs under the name of Wisdom, especially in the *Proverbs 8*.'[30]

Another exegetical route to explaining Christ's role in creation was the interpretation of 'in the beginning' in Genesis 1:1. Already in Revelation 3:14 one of Christ's titles is 'the *archē* of God's creation'; but as the English translations indicate, the word *archē* could signify either 'beginning' (RSV) or 'ruler' (NIV). The latter appears to fit the context of Revelation slightly better, but the former can hardly be excluded. In any case, what John might have intended by calling Christ the 'beginning' is difficult to say. Later commentators were much more forthcoming. Origen writes in his Commentary on John (1.17):

> One might assert, and with reason, that God Himself is the beginning of all things, and might go on to say, as is plain, that the Father is the beginning of

30. Edwards, *Works*, 21:120.

> the Son; and the demiurge the beginning of the works of the demiurge, and that God in a word is the beginning of all that exists. This view is supported by our: In the beginning was the Word. In the Word one may see the Son, and because He is in the Father He may be said to be in the beginning.[31]

Augustine is clearly familiar with this line of interpretation: 'We answer them [the Manichaeans] that God made heaven and earth in the beginning, not in the beginning of time, but in Christ. For he was the Word with the Father, through whom and in whom all things were made.'[32] Interpreting 'the beginning' in this way not only bolstered the credibility of confessing Christ as Creator. As Augustine's example shows, it also provided a way of addressing the question of what God was doing 'before' he created the world.[33] (To the extent this involved merging Christ and the Platonic Ideas, however, this meant exchanging one set of theological problems for another.)

Athanasius in particular was at pains to stress that Christ functions qua God in creating the world, and is not merely a 'half-man/half-god' serving as a kind of mathematical mean between God and the world. If the world could really not bear the 'untempered hand of God' and thus needed a created Son to mediate the creation (as some of Athanasius' opponents claimed), we would end up with an infinite regress of mediators:

> And again, if because originate nature could not endure to be God's own handywork, there arose need of a mediator, it must follow, that, the Word being originate and a creature, there is need of a medium in His framing also, since He too is of that originate nature which endures not to be made of God, but needs a medium. But if some being as a medium be found for Him, then again a fresh mediator is needed for that second, and thus tracing back and following out, we shall invent a vast crowd of accumulating mediators.[34]

---

31. See Blowers, *Drama*, p. 125.

32. Augustine, *Gen. Man.* 1.2.3, in *On Genesis: Two Books on Genesis against the Manichees and On the Literal Interpretation of Genesis: An Unfinished Book* (trans. Roland J. Treske; Washington, DC: Catholic University of America Press, 1991), p. 49. It interesting that in addition to John 1:1 and Col. 1:15, Augustine cites John 8:25 in support of Christ as 'the beginning'. The Vulgate reads literally, '"Who are you?" Jesus said to them, "Beginning, who is also speaking with you."' The Latin construction mirrors the Greek, which contains *archēn* without a preposition. While the usual English translation of 'what I told you at the beginning' is probably correct (see D. A. Carson, *The Gospel According to John* [Grand Rapids: Eerdmans, 1991], pp. 345–46), it is just possible John employs this unusual adverbial accusative as a hint that Jesus is the ultimate 'beginning' of all things. This would certainly fit with his overall theological purposes. Cf. Ambrose, *Hex.* 2.5.

33. See Blowers, *Drama*, pp. 140–45.

34. Athanasius, *C. Ar. 2.26*, New Advent translation; see discussion in Jon M. Robertson, *Christ as a Mediator: A Study of the Theologies of Eusebius of Caesarea, Marcellus*

This logical difficulty gives rise to corresponding theological difficulties. In the passage from *Contra Arianos* above, the stability of the creation hangs upon the fact that it is God himself who creates the world through his Word.[35] The loving God would not contract out the creation of the world to another created entity, since this would subject the world to dissolution. For the world to endure, he must make it himself. Furthermore, he argues, his opponents demean God by the suggestion that his power extended only to the creation of the Son: is this really the God of whom Isaiah testifies, 'The Everlasting God, the LORD, the Creator of the ends of the earth, faints not, neither is weary: there is no searching of His understanding' (Isa. 40:28, in *C. Ar.* 2.25)? As for Christ, he becomes a poor sort of 'Wisdom of God' who is in need of tutelage himself (*C. Ar.* 2.28), and a dishonoured Son who exists not for his own sake, but only for the purpose of giving existence to us (*C. Ar.* 2.30). Athanasius sums up (*C. Ar.* 2.82):

> Hence the whole earth is filled with the knowledge of Him; for the knowledge of Father through Son and of Son from Father is one and the same, and the Father delights in Him, and in the same joy the Son rejoices in the Father, saying, 'I was by Him, daily His delight, rejoicing always before Him (Prov. 8:30).' And this again proves that the Son is not foreign, but proper to the Father's Essence. For behold, not because of us has He come to be, as the irreligious men say, nor is He out of nothing (for not from without did God procure for Himself a cause of rejoicing), but the words denote what is His own and like. When then was it, when the Father rejoiced not? But if He ever rejoiced, He was ever, in whom He rejoiced. And in whom does the Father rejoice, except as seeing Himself in His own Image, which is His Word?

One way to construe Christ's agency in creation, then, is to simply see him acting *as God*. God desires to extend his blessings *ad extra*, and his Word is the means of this self-expression in the act of creation. Augustine's discussion of the Word in the *Lectures on John* and *Confessions* book 11 has this flavour, with the watchword being, 'and the Word was God' (John 1:1). But one can also speak of Christ's agency in creation—still on the divine side of the ledger—as a kind of partnership with the Father: 'the Word was *with* God'. This is very much in keeping with the pattern laid down in Christ's eschatological agency in new creation, particularly in John. As we have seen, Jesus defends his work on the Sabbath with the words, 'My Father is working still, and I am working' (John 5:17). In the same passage, he declares, 'Truly, truly, I say to you, the Son can do nothing of his own accord, but only what

of Ancyra and Athanasius of Alexandria (Oxford: OUP, 2007), pp. 172–74. Augustine makes a similar point in *Lect. In Joh.* 1.11.

35. See above all Robertson, *Christ as a Mediator*.

he sees the Father doing; for whatever he does, that the Son does likewise (5:19).' This is by no means *independent* work by Jesus, or a work that is *different from* the Father's; but there remains a dynamic sense of the Father's call and the Son's response that distinguishes the persons.

It might be countered that Christ's agency in creation, while inspired by his agency in redemption, could nonetheless differ from it in certain key respects: perhaps the incarnation adds a dimension of responsive action which does not obtain in the primal formation of all things. But Athanasius' appropriation of Proverbs 8 certainly embraces the idea of mutuality: 'and the Father delights in Him, and in the same joy the Son rejoices in the Father, saying, "I was by Him, daily His delight, rejoicing always before Him".' Such a reading meshes well with the overall thrust of John's gospel, where the emphasis lies on the unity of Christ's work in creation and new creation. To take but one example, the statement in John 5:26, 'For as the Father has life in himself, so he has granted the Son also to have life in himself', presages the resurrecting work of Jesus in the world. But can we imagine that this gift of life was given only at the incarnation—particularly when the corresponding statement in John 1:4, 'in him was life', follows directly after 'all things were made through him, and without him was not anything made that was made'? Thus while we affirm the unity of the triune divine action in the act of creation, we may equally affirm the genuine involvement of the Son as Son in the formation of the world.

The Son as the idea of creation

But the Word–Wisdom Christology can be developed in another way. The *logos* could be viewed as a kind of paradigm for the creation. God would thus create 'through' the Word in the sense that the Word forms the template for the creation to come. The debts to Platonism are evident here. But once one conflated God's Word and Wisdom, and read Proverbs 8 in a thoroughly christological way, the possibility arose of seeing the wisdom displayed in creation as somehow being resident within, or equivalent to, Christ himself. Augustine hints at such an association of Word and World in his *Lectures on John 1.9*:

> If, then, on account of some great building a human design receives praise, do you wish to see what a design of God is the Lord Jesus Christ, that is, the Word of God? Mark this fabric of the world. View what was made by the Word, and then thou wilt understand what is the nature of the world. Mark these two bodies of the world, the heavens and the earth. Who will unfold in words the beauty of the heavens? Who will unfold in words the fruitfulness of the earth? Who will worthily extol the changes of the seasons? Who will worthily extol the power of seeds? You see what things I do not mention, lest

> in giving a long list I should perhaps tell of less than you can call up to your own minds. From this fabric, then, judge the nature of the Word by which it was made: and not it alone; for all these things are seen, because they have to do with the bodily sense.

Maximus the Confessor was willing to take things much further. He saw the closest connection between Christ as *logos* and the *logoi* of created beings—with *logoi* best translated as 'God's purposes for things', though one would not go amiss in seeing them as analogous to the Platonic Ideas.[36] As he puts it in *Ambiguum* 7: 'Because he held together in himself the *logoi* before they came to be, by his gracious will he created all things visible and invisible out of nonbeing.'[37] Pseudo-Dionysius provided him the vivid image of Christ the *logos* as the centre of a wheel, with the *logoi* radiating out from him like spokes. Maximus did not shy away from the intimate union of *logos* and *logoi*. In the same passage he writes that the wise person 'will know that the many *logoi* are the one *Logos* to whom all things are related and who exists in himself without confusion, the essential and individually distinctive God, the *Logos* of God the Father.'[38] Indeed, Maximus held that the *logos* is incarnated not only in the birth of Jesus as a human being, but also in the 'incarnation' or coming-to-realization of all the Ideas: again, 'Always and in all God's *Logos* and God wills to effect the mystery of His own embodiment.'[39]

How one feels about all this will depend in large measure on the extent to which one welcomes Plato's influence on Christian theology. We will explore this question in detail in chapter 6, and elaborate on Maximus' teachings in that regard. But it is certainly legitimate to search carefully for the right words if we wish to speak of Christ's role in creation as in any sense paradigmatic. The danger of substituting *paradigm* for *person* is a real one, as is the danger of simply collapsing God into the world. The solution does not necessarily entail tossing anything smacking of Platonism overboard. Let us consider Edwards' articulation of Christology in his 'Discourse on the Trinity':

> God's idea of himself is absolutely perfect, and therefore is an express and perfect image of him, exactly like him in every respect. There is nothing in the pattern but what is in the representation—substance, life, power, nor anything

36. Lars Thunberg, *Microcosm and Mediator: The Theological Anthropology of Maximus the Confessor* (Eng. rev. A. M. Allchin; Copenhagen: Munksgaard, 1965), p. 79.

37. Maximus, *Amb.* 7, trans. in Paul Blowers and Robert Wilken, *On the Cosmic Mystery of Jesus Christ* (Crestwood, NY: St Vladimir's Seminary Press, 2003), pp. 54–55. Maximus cites Col. 1:15–17 immediately before this quotation.

38. Maximus, *Amb.* 7; Blowers and Wilken, *Cosmic Mystery*, p. 54; cf. Thunberg, *Microcosm*, p. 81.

39. Maximus, *Amb.* 7.

> else—and that in a most absolute perfection of similitude; otherwise it is not a perfect idea. But that which is the express perfect image of God, and in every respect like him, is God to all intents and purposes, because there is nothing wanting; there is nothing in the Deity that renders it the Deity but what has something exactly answering of it in this image, which will therefore also render that the Deity.[40]

On the one hand, Edwards is happy to speak of 'God's idea of himself'; the word 'idea' permeates the 'Discourse'. But this idea of God is not a part of the deity, as I might be said to 'have an idea in my head': he is the perfect and personal image of God in his entirety, as it were. If we work with this understanding of God (and Edwards is hardly idiosyncratic here), then we can speak if we wish of the ideas for things being *in* Christ, but only because they are God's ideas for things residing in his image. As Colossians 2:3 says in a different context, Christ is the one '*in whom* are hid all the treasures of wisdom and knowledge.' The relationship of God and his ideas for things still needs parsing, but it will be done as a general theological problem rather than a narrowly christological one.

Christ for the world

Athanasius took pains to argue that Christ as Word and Wisdom is one with the Father and to that extent stands over and against the creation. But he was equally willing to see Christ in solidarity *with* the creation via the incarnation. It was just this, in fact, which led him to a creative solution to the dilemma lodged at the heart of Proverbs 8: 'The LORD *created* me at the beginning of his work' (v. 22). These are treacherous shoals for a high Christology, and it is possible the New Testament writers steered clear of Proverbs 8 for precisely this reason. One could seek a lexical solution to the problem: the Hebrew verb *qnh*, rendered 'created' (*ektisen*) in the LXX, could equally be rendered 'possess', 'lay hold of', or even 'beget'.[41] Athanasius, in keeping with much of the tradition, instead takes the Greek text as it stands[42] (woodenly): 'The Lord created me the beginning of his ways towards his works.' But he interprets it as a cryptic reference to the incarnation:

> so, as 'being always with the Father,' He Himself is Framer of the creation, and His works are evidently later than Himself, and 'He created' signifies, not His beginning of being, but the Economy which took place for the works, which He

40. Edwards, 'Discourse on the Trinity', *Works*, 21:115.

41. For the last, see C. F. Burney, 'Christ as the APXH of Creation', *JTS* 27 (1926): pp. 160–77.

42. For examples of analogous approaches to Prov. 8 in e.g. the Gregorys, Hilary, and Augustine, see Blowers, *Drama*, p. 204.

> effected in the flesh. For it became Him, being other than the works, nay rather their Framer, to take upon Himself their renovation, that, whereas He is created for us, all things may be now created in Him. For when He said 'He created,' He immediately added the reason, naming 'the works,' that His creation for the works might signify His becoming man for their renovation (*C. Ar.* 2.53).

If the reading seems a bit strained, Athanasius admits that proverbs typically require some finesse in interpretation. Nonetheless, his unpacking of the enigmatic Greek phrase 'towards his works' is ingenious, and the theological depth of his rendering is profound. The incarnation may be viewed from a remedial angle here,[43] but the word choice of 'renovation' (*ananeōsis*) is significant: redemption is not a renunciation of primal creation, but rather its renewal. There is for Athanasius, then, the deepest connection between the creation wrought by the Word in the beginning, and the renewal wrought by the Word in the incarnation.

Others have followed in his train. We have noted Maximus' dictum that 'Always and in all God's Logos and God wills to effect the mystery of His own embodiment.' Sergei Bulgakov speaks in a similar way when he describes the incarnation as the 'interior basis of creation', which we quoted in our introduction:

> The Incarnation is the interior basis of creation, its final cause. God did not create the world to hold it at a distance from him, at that insurmountable metaphysical distance that separates the Creator from the creation, but in order to surmount that distance and unite himself completely with the world; not only from the outside, as Creator, nor even as providence, but from within: 'the Word became flesh'. That is why the Incarnation is already predetermined in human kind.[44]

We do not have to answer the vexing question of *cur deus homo?* to affirm the importance of the incarnation for Christ's role in the creation of the world. Even in Athanasius' remedial scheme, Christ's incarnate agency in redemption represents the completion of God's creation project. He is the second Adam, the true human who finally brings God's desired dominion to the cosmos. Recall that Paul had already in 1 Corinthians 15 juxtaposed Christ's eschatological triumph from Psalm 110—all things will be put 'under his feet'—with the 'under his feet' of the creation hymn Psalm 8. Whatever was in view when the job started, it is finished by the embodied

---

43. Cf. Athanasius, *C. Ar.* 2.51: 'but when the works were created and need arose afterwards of the Economy for their restoration, then it was that the Word took upon Himself this condescension and assimilation to the works'.

44. Trans. Louth, 'The Place of *Theosis* in Orthodox Theology', p. 36.

Messiah: *this Jesus*, 'who was taken up from you into heaven, will come in the same way as you saw him go into heaven' (Acts 1:11).[45]

If we may be permitted a brief sojourn into the modern period, Wolfhart Pannenberg brings a great insight into this aspect of Christology when he lays weight on the self-differentiation of the Son as the basis of existence for all other things. He argues that the Son's eternal relationship with the Father 'must include at the least the *possibility* of his moving out of the unity of the divine life into existence in the form of a creature.'[46] He continues:

> In this sense we may view the Son's mediation in creation not only as a structural model (and in this way the Logos) of the determination of all creaturely being for fellowship with God by acceptance of its distinction from him, but also as the origin of the existence of creaturely reality. With this we must presuppose that in his moving out of the unity of the divine life, as in all else, the Son is obedient to the Father. The Son alone is not the creator of the world. He moves out of the deity in execution of the mission that he is given by the Father. Hence the Christian church confesses the Father as the creator of the world, not the Son, for the only content of the work of the Son is to serve the Father and to bring in his kingdom. The Father thus acts as creator through the Son.[47]

While 'moving out of the deity' may be a debatable turn of phrase, Pannenberg's suggestion has great force: the Son's free self-distinction from the Father creates a space, so to speak, for the existence of other things distinct from the Father. Pannenberg's acknowledged debt to Hegel is arguably far less here than his debt to John's gospel.

The world for Christ

If Christ is made incarnate for the sake of the world, however, it is also true that the world exists for the sake of Christ. Colossians 1:16 says that the world was created both through Christ and *for* him. Edwards comments:

> The world is made for Christ: The world was made for the Son of God especially. For God made the world for himself from love to himself; but God

45. Pannenberg at times seems simply to count Jesus' eschatological work as the work of primal creation; see e.g. his note in *Jesus, God and Man* (Philadelphia: Westminster, 1968), p. 391: 'Christ's mediation of creation is not to be thought of primarily in terms of the temporal beginning of the world. It is rather to be understood in terms of the whole of the world process that receives its unity and meaning in the light of its end that has appeared in advance in the history of Jesus.' But compare this with his statements in *Systematic Theology* 2:28: 'The final ordering of creatures to the manifestation of Jesus Christ presupposes that creatures already have the origin of their existence and nature in the Son.' See McDonough, *Christ as Creator*, pp. 248–51.

46. Aquinas, *ST* 2:29.

47. Aquinas, *ST* 2:29–30.

> loves himself only in a reflex act He views himself and so loves himself; so he makes the world for himself, viewed and reflected on, and that is the same with himself repeated or begotten in his own idea: and that is his Son. When God considers of making anything for himself, he presents himself before himself and views himself as his end; and that viewing himself is the same as reflecting on himself or having an idea of himself. And to make the world for the Godhead thus viewed and understood is to make the world for the Godhead begotten: and that is to make the world for the Son of God.[48]

Lest we imagine this is only a raw display of power, the manufacturing of something to dominate, Edwards immediately adds:

> The love of God as it flows forth *ad extra* is wholly determined and directed by divine wisdom, so that those only are the objects of it that divine wisdom chooses. So that the creation of the world is to gratify divine love as that is exercised by divine wisdom. But Christ is divine wisdom, so that the world is made to gratify divine love as exercised by Christ, or to gratify the love that is in Christ's heart, or to provide a spouse for Christ—those creatures which wisdom chooses for the object of divine love as Christ's elect spouse, and especially those elect creatures that wisdom chiefly pitches upon and makes the end of the rest.[49]

Jesus' messianic rule in the world in the last days may thus be seen as the logical fulfilment of his messianic creation of the world in the first days. Edwards helps us to see that the achievement of God's purposes in the Son does not consist solely in the establishment of a well-ordered world: God desires to join in loving union with the world through the Messiah.

Spirit

As noted, 1 Corinthians 8:6 does not directly address the role of the Spirit in creation, though the epistle is a rich source of pneumatology in many other respects. Thankfully, the rest of the Scriptures more than fill the void here. While there was some debate in the early church as to the identity of the spirit/wind hovering over the waters in Genesis 1:2, there was a strong inclination to read this as the third person of the Trinity.[50] Psalm 33:6 was an obvious place to turn for an affirmation of Trinitarian creation: 'By the word of the Lord the heavens were made, and all their host by the breath (*ruach*/spirit) of his mouth.'[51] As the 'breath' of God, the Spirit's activity was particular visible in animate creatures:

48. Edwards, 'Discourse on the Trinity', *Works*, 21:143.
49. Edwards, 'Discourse on the Trinity', *Works*, 21:143.
50. Blowers, *Drama*, pp. 113–18.
51. See the citation of Ps. 33:6 in e.g. Ambrose, *Spir*. 2.5.35.

These all look to thee,
    to give them their food in due season.
When thou givest to them, they gather it up;
    when thou openest thy hand, they are filled with good things.
When thou hidest thy face, they are dismayed;
    when thou takest away their breath, they die
    and return to their dust.
When thou sendest forth thy Spirit, they are created;
    and thou renewest the face of the ground (Ps. 104:27–30).

Texts concerning the Spirit's role in new creation are abundant, particularly in the New Testament: 'it is the spirit that gives life' (John 6:63) and empowers the church to live for God (Acts 1:8; Rom. 8:1–17); he is the Spirit of adoption who enables us to call God Father (Gal. 4:6); he is the one who calls us to come to the glory of the New Jerusalem (Rev. 22:17).

Recent years have seen an upsurge of interest in the Spirit's activity in creation. Recall the subtitle of Moltmann's landmark book *God in Creation: A New Theology of Creation and the Spirit of God*. Colin Gunton argues that through the Spirit God establishes things in their particularity; they are enabled to realize their *telos* through the Spirit.[52] John Polkinghorne, meanwhile, judiciously probes the activity of the Spirit from the standpoint of science. He carefully suggests that we may get a glimmer of the Spirit's work in the *information* that has been found to be an integral element in the organization of biological systems in the world.[53]

It is not as if modern theologians like Moltmann, Gunton, and Polkinghorne are working *ex nihilo* in their musings on the Spirit's role in creation. In addition to the biblical material adduced above, they can draw on a well-stocked larder from their forebears. With respect to the early church, Paul Blowers has isolated four activities 'consistently (but not exclusively) associated with the Spirit' in ancient thought: animating, sanctifying, beautifying, and perfecting.[54] We might summarize by saying that the Spirit is the *reality* of God who in turn gives reality in all its splendour to all creatures.

As animator, the Spirit might be said to be the 'energy' of created things. Thus Edwards: 'The name of the third person in the Trinity, viz. the Holy Spirit, confirms it. It naturally expresses the divine nature as subsisting in pure act and perfect energy, and as flowing out and breathing forth in infinitely sweet and vigorous affection. It is confirmed both by his

---

52. Gunton, *One, Three, Many*, pp. 180–209.

53. John Polkinghorne, 'The Hidden Work of the Spirit in Creation', in *The Spirit in Creation and New Creation* (ed. Michael Welker; Grand Rapids: Eerdmans, 2012), pp. 3–10.

54. Blowers, *Drama*, p. 292.

being called the Spirit, and by his being denominated Holy.'[55] Edwards was not one to shy away from the active engagement of God with the creation, such that at times his thought seems to border on emanationism.[56] For this reason we must be careful not to suggest that the Spirit as 'energy' equals mass times the speed of light squared, or that under the right conditions he could be converted into matter. At the same time, the Spirit is God in his most intimate connection to the creation. Paul captures this paradox in Romans 8:15–16: 'When we cry, "Abba! Father!" it is the Spirit himself bearing witness with our spirit that we are children of God.' It is 'we' doing the crying, yet this act is equally ascribed to the Spirit. It seems to be an analogue to the unity-within-diversity that characterizes inner-Trinitarian relationships.

Sanctifying would clearly be a chief concern of the *Holy* Spirit of God, particularly with respect to humanity. But the related notion of *beautifying*—for what is sanctifying but the beautification of the soul?—is more broadly applicable. The Spirit does not merely confer brute existence; he moves things towards their divinely appointed form. Ambrose gives a suggestive reading of Genesis 1:2 along these lines:

> So when the Spirit was moving upon the water, the creation was without grace; but after this world being created underwent the operation of the Spirit, it gained all the beauty of that grace, wherewith the world is illuminated. And that the grace of the universe cannot abide without the Holy Spirit the prophet declared when he said: '*You will take away Your Spirit, and they will fail and be turned again into their dust. Send forth Your Spirit, and they shall be made, and You will renew all the face of the earth.*' Not only, then, did he teach that no creature can stand without the Holy Spirit, but also that the Spirit is the Creator of the whole creation.[57]

Edwards echoes the sentiment:

> He quickens and beautifies all things. So we read that 'the Spirit of God moved upon the face of the waters' [*Genesis 1:2*], or of the chaos, to bring it out of its confusion, into harmony and beauty. So we read, *Job 26:13*, that God 'by his spirit garnished the heavens.' Now whose office can it be so properly to actuate and enliven all things, as his who is the eternal and essential act and energy of God? And whose office can it be so properly to give all things their sweetness and beauty, as he who is himself the beauty and joy of the Creator?[58]

---

55. Edwards, 'Discourse on the Trinity', *Works*, 21:123.

56. See Oliver Crisp, *Jonathan Edwards on God and Creation* (New York: OUP, 2012), pp. 44ff.

57. Ambrose, *Spir.* 2.5.33; see Blowers, *Drama*, pp. 117–18.

58. Edwards, 'Discourse on the Trinity', *Works*, 21:124.

It is precisely this beauty which represents the *perfecting* of the creature, as the Spirit weaves each one into the cosmic tapestry. This consists in simultaneously differentiating each thing into its own unique form, and uniting these items into a coherent whole. The Spirit realizes God's desire for each thing. To the extent this reflects the Spirit's role as the 'energizing force' of God, however, we must recognize that this is God's power, and indeed God's power that has been bequeathed to the Son for the purpose of forming the world. Thus the persons of the Trinity work in perfect harmony to perfect the world.

3

Why Make a World?

Why Did God Create?

Jonathan Edwards' treatise 'Concerning the End for Which God Created the World' offers a welcoming point of entry for addressing this question. His proposition is that God creates the world for his own glory: 'That if God himself be in any respect properly capable of being his own end in the creation of the world, then it is reasonable to suppose that he had respect to *himself* as his last and highest end in this work; because he is worthy in himself to be so, being infinitely the greatest and best of beings.'[1] Edwards is very much in the theological mainstream with this assertion. To take but two examples, Aquinas writes in *ST* 1:20: 'Thus, then, He wills both Himself to be, and other things to be; but Himself as the end, and other things as ordained to that end; inasmuch as it befits the divine goodness that other things should be partakers therein'; the sentiment is echoed by Duns Scotus: 'God loves himself as goal.'[2]

What distinguishes Edwards' account is the thoroughness with which he argues his case. He amasses a persuasive amount of biblical evidence to support his thesis. He begins with a cluster of texts concerning the divine eternity: God is the 'first and the last' and the 'Alpha and Omega.'[3] While one might stress the (supra-)temporal dimensions of these terms, Edwards plausibly reads them as declarations of divine purpose: 'It is manifest that the Scriptures speak, on all occasions, as though God made himself his end in all his works: and as though the same Being, who is the first cause of all things, were the supreme and last end of all things.' Isaiah 48:11 is even more

1. Jonathan Edwards, 'Concerning the End for Which God Created the World' 1.1.4, *The Works of Jonathan Edwards* (26 vols; New Haven: Yale University Press, 1997–2009), 8:422.

2. Scotus, *De primo principio* 4, n. 9, in Richard Cross, *Duns Scotus on God* (Aldershot: Ashgate, 2005), p. 87.

3. Edwards, *Works*, 8:467; Isa. 44:6; 48:12; Rev. 1:8, 11, 17; 21:6, 13.

straightforward: 'For my own sake, for my own sake, I do it, for how should my name be profaned? My glory I will not give to another.' It is matched by Paul's doxological summary in Romans 11:36, 'For from him and through him and to him are all things. To him be glory for ever. Amen.' Edwards notes that '[i]n the preceding context the Apostle observes the marvellous disposals of divine wisdom, for causing all things to be to him in their final issue and result, as they are from him at first, and governed by him.'[4]

Another appealing aspect of Edwards' presentation is that his central assertion is as much the beginning of the discussion as the end. He distinguishes between the 'chief end' of a matter, which is the final goal aimed at; and an 'ultimate end', which constitutes of anything 'which the agent seeks in what he does for its own sake'.[5] (He can make the same point in different terms by speaking of an 'original' ultimate end and a 'consequential' and 'subordinate' ultimate end.) Thus even if the chief end of the creation is God's own glory, there are any number of intrinsically desirable or ultimate ends entailed in God's creation of the world. God's pursuit of his glory is thus not the megalomaniacal pursuit of 'world domination' which nullifies all else; the good of creatures is secured by a God who will act in the best interest of all precisely by acting in the best interests of the only one who can be trusted to know what a 'best interest' really is—God himself.[6]

Indeed, it is precisely the loving outflow or 'emanation' of his glory that forms the basis for the creation and redemption of the world. In his conclusion, Edwards returns again and again to God's *communication* of his glory:

> The thing signified by that name, 'the glory of God,' when spoken of as the supreme and ultimate end of the work of creation, and of all God's works, is the emanation and true external expression of God's internal glory and fullness; meaning by his fullness, what has already been explained. Or in other words, God's internal glory extant, in a true and just exhibition, or external existence of it . . . There is included in this the exercise of God's perfections to produce a proper effect, in opposition to their lying eternally dormant and ineffectual: as his power being eternally without any act or fruit of that power; his wisdom eternally ineffectual in any wise production, or prudent disposal of anything,

4. Edwards, *Works*, 8:476.

5. Edwards, *Works*, 8:405.

6. See e.g. Edwards, *Works*, 8:534: 'Thus 'tis easy to conceive how God should seek the good of the creature, consisting in the creature's knowledge and holiness, and even his happiness, from a supreme regard to himself; as his happiness arises from that which is an image and participation of God's own beauty; and consists in the creature's exercising a supreme regard to God and complacence in him; in beholding God's glory, in esteeming and loving it, and rejoicing in it, and in his exercising and testifying love and supreme respect to God: which is the same thing with the creature's exalting God as his chief good, and making him his supreme end.'

> etc. The manifestation of his internal glory to created understandings. The communication of the infinite fullness of God to the creature. The creature's high esteem of God, love to God, and complacence and joy in God; and the proper exercises and expressions of these.[7]

Far from being a 'self-serving act', in the popular sense of the term, God's communication of his ineffable glory is the supreme joy of the creature.[8]

Edwards' basic point is secure, but there remains much to explore with respect to God's motivation for creation. We will look at two in detail. First, is creation enacted primarily as a platform for Christ's redemptive work? And second, does God create freely, or is creation in any sense a necessity?

Creation for redemption or redemption for creation?

Since Irenaeus, theologians have regularly asserted that God creates precisely with a view towards redemption. We may choose three representative quotations. Irenaeus writes:

> Hence also was Adam himself termed by Paul 'the figure of Him that was to come,' because the Word, the Maker of all things, had formed beforehand for Himself the future dispensation of the human race, connected with the Son of God; God having predestined that the first man should be of an animal nature, with this view, that he might be saved by the spiritual One. For inasmuch as He had a pre-existence as a saving Being, it was necessary that what might be saved should also be called into existence, in order that the Being who saves should not exist in vain.[9]

Edwards writes in a similar vein:

> There were many things done in order to the Work of Redemption before that [sc. the fall of man]. Some things were done before the world was created, yea

7. Edwards, *Works*, 8:528.

8. Cf. Tertullian, *Marc.* 2.4: 'So then, the Creator's primary goodness is that by which it was God's will not to be eternally in hiding, that is, that there had to be something to which as God he might become known. For what good is so great as the knowledge and enjoyment of God?' Tertullian, *Adversus Marcionem* (trans. Ernest Evans; Oxford: OUP, 1972).

9. Irenaeus, *Haer.* 3.22.3. Leo Scheffczyk, *Creation and Providence* (trans. Richard Strachan; New York: Herder & Herder, 1970), p. 70, comments: 'Here the origin of the world and man is made so dependent on redemption and the pre-existence of the Redeemer that man and his world are seen to have been created in view of the Redeemer and for his sake. Thus the Son in whom all was created is at the same time acknowledged to be the formal cause and the goal of Creation.'

> from all eternity. The persons of the Trinity were as it were confederated in a design and a covenant of redemption, in which covenant the Father appointed the Son and the Son had undertaken their work, and all things to be accomplished in their work were stipulated and agreed. And besides these there were things done at the creation of the world in order to that work before man fell. For the world itself seems to have been created in order to it. The work of creation was in order to God's works of providence. So that if it be inquired which of these two kinds of works is the greatest, the works of creation or God's works of providence, I answer providence because God's works of providence are the end of God's works of creation as the building of an house or the forming an engine or machine is for its use.[10]

Finally we have Barth, using the language of covenant:

> Creation is one long preparation, and therefore the being and existence of the creature one long readiness, for what God will intend and do with in the history of the covenant. Its nature is simply its equipment for grace. Its creatureliness is pure promise, expectation and prophecy of that which is in His grace, in the execution of the will of His eternal love, and finally and supremely in the consummation of the giving of His Son, God plans for man and will not delay to accomplish for his benefit.[11]

He sums things up even more crisply in *Church Dogmatics* (*CD*) III/3: 'Because *servatio*, therefore *creatio* and therefore *conservatio*.'[12]

Would we want to say, then, that the world is created *in order to be redeemed*, which is one way of construing the statements above? Putting things this way could have the unfortunate consequence of suggesting that God makes a defective product only in order to fix it, like an automobile manufacturer deliberately fabricating bad cars in order to make money repairing them later on. On the other hand, if we view redemption as simply an unforeseen remedial measure, we are left with God employing (as Barth says) 'a wretched expedient in face of the obvious failure of a plan in relation to man which had originally had quite a different intention and form.'[13] The

10. Edwards, 'History of Redemption', *Works*, 9:118; cf. Robert W. Jenson, *Systematic Theology* (2 vols; New York: OUP, 1997–99), 2:20.

11. Karl Barth, *Church Dogmatics* (4 vols; Edinburgh: T&T Clark, 1956–75), III/1, p. 232. See John B. Webster, *Barth's Ethics of Reconciliation* (Cambridge: CUP, 1995), pp. 62–65; and Kathryn Tanner, 'Creation and Providence', in *The Cambridge Companion to Karl Barth* (ed. John B. Webster; Cambridge: CUP, 2000), pp. 111–26.

12. Barth, *CD* III/3, p. 80. See Jenson, *Systematic Theology*, 2:20. Compare the statement of Calvin in *Comm Gal.* 4:19: 'For we were born that we might be new creatures in [Christ]'; Peter Wyatt, *Jesus Christ and Creation in the Theology of John Calvin* (Allison Park, PA: Pickwick, 1996), p. 60.

13. Barth, *CD* IV/1, p. 64, see Jenson, *Systematic Theology*, 2:20.

fact that this redemption involves the monumental act of the incarnation of the Son makes the dilemma even more troubling.

The first step to a resolution is to acknowledge the utility of the traditional sequential scheme of creation–redemption–consummation. The flow of the biblical story is typically rendered this way: God creates the world; humanity falls into sin; God begins enacting the plan of redemption with Abraham and Israel; he brings it into definitive shape in the incarnation, crucifixion, and resurrection of Christ, and he will consummate it upon Christ's return. The scheme is especially elegant when we think of redemption as a new creation, which brings the primal creation project to its *telos*.[14] If humanity even in Eden has *somewhere to go*—namely, to the consummate glory of God's city—the divine plan is not fractured even if the route to the city takes some unusual turns.

The incarnation as such can be integrated into this framework without making it seem a 'wretched expedient'. In this view, God always planned to join with the creation in the flesh of the Son, in keeping with Maximus' maxim: 'Always and in all God's Logos and God wills to effect the mystery of His own embodiment.'[15] The idea that the world was in this sense created not only by, but for, the Son has significant analogues in early Jewish thought, notably *b. Sanhedrin* 98b: 'Rab said: The world was created only on David's account. Samuel said: On Moses' account; R. Johanan said: For the sake of the Messiah.' For Barth, this takes the shape of the world created for the sake of the covenant: at the core of *CD* III/1 are the paired contentions that 'creation is the external basis of the covenant' and 'the covenant is the internal basis of creation'.[16]

When we think of *redemption*, however, we must of necessity speak of sin and the atonement wrought by 'the Lamb who was slain from the creation of the world' (Rev. 13:8 NIV). Is the purpose of creation, then, to bring about a situation in which Jesus might be crucified? Support for this might be found in John 12, where the cross is held forth as the moment of

14. As Edwards does in *Miscellany* 702, *Works*, 18:286: 'And the creation of man in particular seems to have been in such a manner, as it was that it might shadow the manner of his greater creation, viz. his new creation'; see Amy Plantinga Pauw, *The Supreme Harmony of All: The Trinitarian Theology of Jonathan Edwards* (Grand Rapids: Eerdmans, 2002), p. 130.

15. Maximus, *Amb.* 7; see discussion in Torstein Tollefsen, *The Christocentric Cosmology of St Maximus the Confessor* (Oxford: OUP, 2012), p. 80.

16. See Tanner's lucid summary in 'Creation and Providence', p. 120: 'The unconditional grace found in Christ—the fact that God steps into our place as God's covenant partners to do and be that of which we are otherwise utterly incapable, the fact that in Christ we become faithful partners of God through God's own act alone—is matched by a creation without presuppositions, a creation that presupposes nothing but a free act of God's love.'

Jesus' glorification, or 1 Corinthians 1, where it is the revelation of God's wisdom and power. If creation is itself seen as an act of kenosis on the part of God (see chapter 5 below), is not the cross the ultimate kenosis, and thus the fitting entrance to the consummate new creation? The resurrected Jesus is worshipped in Revelation 5 precisely as the Lamb *who was slain* and who purchased for God with his blood people from every tribe and tongue and people and nation (5:9). The crucifixion lays the foundation for the New Jerusalem.

While no conceptual scheme can easily solve the problem of evil and the consequent suffering of Christ on the cross,[17] we may at least affirm that the ultimate goal of creation is the expression of the glory of God, which (as Edwards insists) involves the good of his creatures. Thus resurrection and eternal life must be the final word: 'Behold, I make all things new' (Rev. 21:5).[18] While the crucifixion may need to be included in God's plan for the world, it would still be best seen as the supreme moment of *de-creation* in which God dismantles the old broken world so that it might rise anew to glorious life.[19]

As a formula, then, 'creation for the sake of redemption' raises more questions than it answers. It is better perhaps to affirm that God creates the world not merely to exist, but to flourish, and that he will do whatever it takes to enable it to flourish: from the ongoing works of providence which sustain the creation, to the strange work of the cross which sets the world to right, to the consummate work of flooding the world with his glory. Rather than reinforce the sense that creation and redemption have little to do with one another, we may instead celebrate the unity of God's plan of creation and new creation: 'Thus we see that the great and last end of God's works which is so variously expressed in Scripture, is indeed but *one*; and this *one* end is most properly and comprehensively called, "the glory of God".'[20]

Freedom and necessity

As we will see, the basic assertion that God created the world in *freedom*, as an act of his *will*, rather than from *necessity*, is one of the most persistent motifs in the theological tradition. But each one of the italicized terms is doubly problematic. First, the fact that these are abstractions, rather than

17. See Jenson's cogent remarks in *Systematic Theology*, 2:20–24.

18. As Richard Bauckham points out (*The Theology of the Book of Revelation* [Cambridge: CUP, 1993], pp. 25–26), this is one of the rare occasions in Revelation where God himself speaks.

19. See below, chapter 7.

20. Edwards, 'Concerning the End', *Works*, 8:531.

discrete objects in the world, means that their definitions will be mutable (within a certain range of association). Thus in each case we must realize there is no real answer to the question of what 'freedom' or 'will' or 'necessity' *is* in an absolute sense; there is only the question of what we want those words to *do* in a certain context. This intrinsic ambiguity is exponentially heightened when we attempt to apply these words to God. Here the problem of analogous language is chiselled to a fine point: we have enough trouble thinking about these things as limited, corrupt creatures whose misbegotten desires might be thwarted by the recalcitrant world around us; how can we speak adequately of freedom, will, and necessity with respect to the pure and unfettered Being of God Almighty?

Yet some things have to be said as well as we can say them. We would not want to suggest that something outside God *makes* him create, and opposing that claim will involve some working notions of 'freedom', 'will', and 'necessity'. Theologians have also been reluctant to say that the world simply flows out of God as an extension of his divine substance (though for some of a Neoplatonic bent this has proved a more difficult trap to avoid). We might say that the theological work *just is* coming up with adequate definitions for these terms: what do we really mean when we say God creates freely?

The Scriptures themselves are of course not much given to fine philosophical parsing of such things, but they do regularly speak of God 'doing what he wants' with respect to creation (a serviceable definition of freedom provided we do not make too quick a leap from the sort of things we want to the sort of things God might want). The serenity of Genesis 1 and Psalm 104 fits well with the declaration in Psalm 115:3 that 'Our God is in the heavens; he does whatever he pleases.' Isaiah 43:13 makes the same point: 'I am God, and also henceforth I am He; there is none who can deliver from my hand; I work and who can hinder it?'

Revelation 4:11 comes closest to anticipating the language to be used by future theologians, as it speaks expressly of God's will: 'for thou didst create all things, and by thy will they existed and were created.'[21] We might again cite James 1:18: 'Of his own will (Gk. *boulētheis*) he brought us forth by the word of truth so that we should be a kind of first fruits of his creatures.' While the verse is probably a reference to the recreation that comes through the gospel, the connection with primal creation is evident. We

21. The somewhat awkward ending of Rev. 4:11, 'they were and were created', led to some scribal scrambling to guard against an apparent challenge to *creatio ex nihilo* (viz. 'they already existed [= were] and were created'); thus we get variants like 'they came into being, and were [thereby] created', 'they exist, and they were created', and simply 'they were', though the last may be due to parablepsis (the word for 'they were' consists of the same four letters as the end of 'they were created').

might then suggest that for James primal creation is likewise a matter of God's benevolent choice.

Subsequent theologians were happy to take the basic idea that 'God does as he pleases' as the foundation for their subsequent reflection. Thus Gregory of Nyssa says, 'remember that God made us not out of necessity, but out of a good choice'.[22] Maximus the Confessor echoes him: 'If God made all things by his will (which no one denies), and it is always pious and right to say that God knows his own will, and that he made each creature by an act of will, then God knows existing things as he knows the products of his own will, since he also made existing things by an act of will'.[23] Tertullian so prizes God's freedom he writes: 'It is liberty, not necessity, which suits the character of God. I would much rather that He should have even willed to create evil of Himself, than that He should have lacked ability to hinder its creation'.[24]

But the level of technical scrutiny into this divine freedom went far beyond what was on offer in the Bible, and with good reason. The idea that God would choose to create is an important safeguard for the integrity of the creation, with particular relevance to the status of human agents who themselves possess a will. A necessary creation could certainly be deemed a threat to God's honour—one might say that such a creation would have 'just as much right to be there' as God himself. The problem is exacerbated by the fact that 'Necessity' in the *Timaeus* was associated with pre-existing, recalcitrant matter—a clear challenge to the traditional doctrine of *creatio ex nihilo*.

The early fathers in particular were operating in a philosophical world where the collapse of God into the world was very much a live intellectual option. The Neoplatonists attempted to make some sort of distinction between the One and everything else, with the result that many subsequent Christian thinkers adopted their conceptual apparatus to a greater or lesser degree.[25] But the emanationist strategy of Plotinus and his followers seemed

22. Gregory of Nyssa, 'Homily 6', *On the Beatitudes*, trans. in Anthony Meredith, *Gregory of Nyssa* (London: Routledge, 1999), p. 94.

23. Maximus, *Amb.* 7, trans. in Paul Blowers and Robert Wilken, *On the Cosmic Mystery of Jesus Christ* (Crestwood, NY: St Vladimir's Seminary Press), p. 62. See discussion in Lars Thunberg, *Microcosm and Mediator: The Theological Anthropology of Maximus the Confessor* (Eng. rev. A. M. Allchin; Copenhagen: Munksgaard, 1965), pp. 69–70. Cf. Jacob of Serugy: 'He would not be envious to have companions beside Him./ For this reason, although there was no necessity, He created creatures'; trans. in Paul M. Blowers, *Drama of the Divine Economy: Creator and Creation in Early Christian Theology and Piety* (Oxford: OUP, 2012), p. 173.

24. Tertullian, *Herm.* 16.

25. See below, chapter 6; Eriugena might be an example of the 'greater' and Augustine of the 'lesser'.

to concede too much to necessity: one would not say the sun chooses to shine; shining is what it inevitably does.[26] This leads to the further problem that one has to either ascribe deity to everything that is in the world (since they are in effect parts of God) or imagine that the divine essence somehow loses its purity as it attenuates. Neither of these are promising options.

At the same time, most theologians have not wanted to imply that the creation of the world was a completely arbitrary act with no relation to the divine love or wisdom. In what follows, we will therefore need to attend not only to the technical definitions of freedom or will on display, but also to the consequences those definitions have for the nature of created being.

Augustine approached the question of freedom, necessity, and creation with his customary nuance.[27] On the one hand, he would never want to say that something outside God is forcing him to act in a certain manner. 'And by the words, "God saw that it was good," it is sufficiently intimated that God made what was made not from any necessity, nor for the sake of supplying any want, but solely from His own goodness, *i.e.*, because it was good.'[28] To speak of God's 'inability' to sin as a limitation on his freedom is absurd: 'If only that one is free, which is able to will two things, that is, good and evil, God is not free, since he cannot will evil . . . are you going to praise God in such a way that you take way his freedom? Or should you not rather understand that there is a certain blessed necessity by which God cannot be unjust?'[29] If there is any *necessity* with God, then, it stems solely from his own character and thus is 'blessed'.[30]

Augustine could also speak about God's perfect freedom in terms of the divine will. All our discursive reasoning must come to a halt when confronted with the absolute will of God:

---

26. Cf. the incisive critique of David Burrell (*Freedom and Creation in Three Traditions* [Notre Dame: University of Notre Dame Press, 1993], p. 98): 'the models of emanation make the intermediate causes to be instruments of the pervasive power of the first, for the connections must obtain with logical necessity if the model is to prove useful at all.'

27. See Jesse Couenhoven, *Stricken by Sin, Cured by Christ: Agency, Necessity, and Culpability in Augustinian Theology* (New York: OUP, 2013), pp. 66–70.

28. Augustine, *Civ.* 12.24; cf. Augustine, *Gen. Litt.* 1.7.13: ne facienda opera sua per indigentiae necessitatem potius quam per abundantiam beneficentiae Deus amare putaretur.

29. Augustine, *Op. Imp.* 1.100, in Couenhoven, *Cured by Christ*, p. 68. Cf. Anselm's view that freedom is not the ability to sin, but to preserve justice, in Allan B. Wolter and William A. Frank, *Duns Scotus on the Will and Morality* (Washington, DC: Catholic University of America Press, 2012), p. 55.

30. Cf. Blowers' (*Drama*, p. 174) comments on Irenaeus, who sometimes 'seems naively to hint of "necessitarianism in the divine essence" . . . but Irenaeus' principal point is characteristically soteriological: God is paradoxically constrained to create by his own freedom and redemptive goodness.'

> They seek to know the causes of the will of God though the will of God is itself the cause of all that exists. For if the will of God has a cause, there is something that surpasses the will of God—and this we may not believe. Hence, one who asks, 'Why did God make heaven and earth?' should be told, 'Because he willed to.' For the will of God is the cause of heaven and earth, and the will of God, therefore, is greater than heaven and earth.[31]

Aquinas follows suit in Question 19 of the *Summa Theologica* (*ST*). He knows from Romans 12:2 that God has a will; but unlike the human will, which seeks after what it does not have, God's will is one with his essence: 'A will of which the principal object is a good outside itself, must be moved by another; but the object of the divine will is His goodness, which is His essence. Hence, since the will of God is His essence, it is not moved by another than itself, but by itself alone' (*ST* 1.19.1). The creature, then, cannot impose itself on God: 'Hence, since the goodness of God is perfect, and can exist without other things inasmuch as no perfection can accrue to Him from them, it follows that His willing things apart from Himself is not absolutely necessary' (*ST* 1.19.3). Can we term this 'free will' on the part of God? Aquinas is happy to call it that. God of course is not 'free' to sin, but he can choose in other respects:

> Since the evil of sin consists in turning away from the divine goodness, by which God wills all things, as above shown (*De Fide* ii, 3), it is manifestly impossible for Him to will the evil of sin; yet He can make choice of one of two opposites, inasmuch as He can will a thing to be, or not to be. In the same way we ourselves, without sin, can will to sit down, and not will to sit down (*ST* 1.19.10).

Once God commits himself to a particular thing, of course, we can speak of a certain kind of 'necessity'—'Yet it can be necessary by supposition, for supposing that He wills a thing, then He is unable not to will it, as His will cannot change (*ST* 1.19.3)'—but this is hardly an imposition from without.[32]

Duns Scotus is of particular importance to the discussion of the divine will, since he is a seminal figure in the voluntarist controversies of the High Middle Ages. Scotus provides a crisp argument against the notion that God creates necessarily:

> Something is willed necessarily only if it is that without which that which is willed about the goal cannot remain. God loves himself as goal, and whatever he loves concerning himself as goal can remain if nothing other than himself exists, for what is necessary of itself depends on nothing. Therefore from his

31. Augustine, *Gen. Man.* 1.2, pp. 51–52.

32. For discussion, see Rahim Acar, *Talking about God and Talking about Creation: Avicenna's and Thomas Aquinas' Positions* (Leiden: Brill, 2005), pp. 162–68.

> volition [viz. of himself] he does not will anything else necessarily; therefore neither does he cause necessarily.[33]

Aquinas had noted that 'will follows upon intellect' (*ST* 1.19.1). Scotus develops this such that we should first think of God *knowing* what he wants to do as an act of cognition; the divine will actualizes what has been cognized.[34]

Scotus lays great store by the divine will. He held, for instance, that God could have created the world otherwise than he has.[35] With respect to the age-old question as to whether God wills things because they are good, or things are good because he wills them so, Scotus does not hesitate to choose the latter: 'everything other than God is good because it is willed by God and not vice versa.'[36] But this is not a radical voluntarism of the sort we find later in William of Ockham. Scotus, for instance, maintains that 'loving God' is a 'necessary' ethical imperative prior to God's will. What Scotus is getting at is that good things in the world have no eternal existence (even as immaterial ideas) which can lay some claim on God; they are finite. To say otherwise would turn creation on its head and make God subservient to the creature.[37] Scotus also employed the distinction between God's 'absolute power' (*potentia absoluta*) and his 'ordained power' (*potentia ordinate*), the latter of which seems to correspond to Aquinas' notion that once God ordains something a certain type of necessity is invoked. While some have read Scotus as unduly exalting God's absolute power, he argues carefully that should God choose by virtue of his absolute power to override something he has previously ordained, this would only be by way of employing another ordained order in its place. In other words, he does not simply suspend all ordained order and suddenly act 'directly' by way of absolute power.[38]

---

33. *De primo principio* 4, n. 9, in Cross, *Duns Scotus*, p. 87. Cf. in the closing of *De primo principio*: 'At one and the same time you possess the power to freely and contingently will each thing that can be caused and by willing it through your volition cause it to be.' In Wolter, *Duns Scotus*, p. 8.

34. Mary Beth Ingham and Mechthild Dreyer, *The Philosophical Vision of John Duns Scotus: An Introduction* (Washington, DC: Catholic University of America Press, 2004), p. 100. They describe his view of the will as the 'capacity for free self-determination'. Compare the similar definition of Leibnitz: 'What then is the ultimate reason of the divine will? The divine intellect. For God wills those things that He understands to be best and most harmonious, and selects them, as it were, from an infinite number of all possibles.' (Robert M. Adams, 'Leibnitz's Theories of Contingency', in *Leibniz: Critical and Interpretive Essays* [ed. M. Hooker; Manchester: Manchester University Press, 1982], p. 245.) Later in the piece Leibnitz will equate freedom with intelligence, spontaneity, and contingency.

35. Wolter, *Duns Scotus*, p. 19.

36. Wolter, *Duns Scotus*, p. 18.

37. On all this, see Wolter, *Duns Scotus*, pp. 18–19.

38. See Hester G. Gelber, *It Could Have Been Otherwise: Contingency and Necessity in Dominican Theology at Oxford, 1300–1350* (Leiden: Brill, 2004), p. 315: 'Because God

Augustine, Aquinas, and Scotus provide but three instances of the consistent teaching of the church that God creates in freedom. The question arose, however, as to whether the divine *love* creates a certain kind of necessity. The question was particularly acute because the motive of love was not simply derivable from the biblical text. It was also a feature of Plato's *Timaeus*:

> Let me tell you then why the creator made this world of generation. He was good, and the good can never have any jealousy of anything. And being free from jealousy, he desired that all things should be as like himself as they could be. This is in the truest sense the origin of creation and of the world, as we shall do well in believing on the testimony of wise men: God desired that all things should be good and nothing bad, so far as this was attainable.[39]

From at least Philo onward, these lines from the *Timaeus* offered the hope of a genuine rapprochement between the Bible and the best Greek thinking. But could a constitutionally good and generous Creator fail to create—and if not, are we then forced to say that he created *necessarily*?

Aquinas addressed the question directly:

> It is accordingly clear that from the love which God has for His own goodness there is no necessity in the divine will for willing this or that concerning a creature. Nor is there any necessity in it as regards the whole of creation, since the divine goodness is perfect in itself, and would be so even though no creature existed, because God has no need of our goods, as is said in the Psalm (15:2). For the divine goodness is not an end of the kind which is produced by the means to the end, but rather one by which the things which are directed to it are produced and perfected. For this reason Avicenna says that only God's action is purely liberal, because nothing accrues to Him from what He wills or does regarding any creature.[40]

Barth approaches the matter in the same way, underscoring the fact that God's love can never be separated from his freedom—hence his famous

---

has the power to endow a created statute with governing power, his absolute power transcends any particular order of created law. He can establish a new legal order if he so desires. But such a use of absolute power is not a form of direct action in the world, only a form of action mediated through successive ordained systems.' Leibnitz makes a similar point in *Discourse on Metaphysics* 7 (trans. G. R. Montgomery; Chicago: Open Court, 1908), p. 12.

39. Plato, *Tim.* 29d–30a, in *The Dialogues of Plato*, vol. 3 (trans. Benjamin Jowett, London: OUP, 1892).

40. Aquinas, *Quaestiones Disputatae de Veritate* 23.4 (trans. Robert W. Schmidt; Chicago: Regnery, 1954); see Merold Westphal, *Transcendence and Self-Transcendence: On God and the Soul* (Bloomington: Indiana University Press, 2004), p. 129; for a comparison of Thomas and Avicenna on creation, see Acar, *Talking about God*.

dictum that God is 'the one who loves in freedom'. We should not imagine God as subsisting essentially as the Free One, and then somewhat arbitrarily opting to treat creatures in a loving way, 'so that the final and decisive word in our doctrine of God is the affirmation of God as the impersonal absolute.'[41] God instead creates in the love and freedom by which he defines himself:

> The divine meaning and necessity which the creature reveals, which as such it denotes and attests, is God's free love, i.e. the love of God in which He wills and posits another by Himself and is Himself for it—the free love in which He accomplishes this willing and this positing in His own power and by His own independent resolve. It is in the same free love that He Himself is God, i.e. the Father in the Son and the Son in the Father by the Holy Spirit. Again, it is the same free love that He has resolved in Himself from all eternity on His fellowship with man in the person of His own Son. As this free love is revealed, i.e., made visible outside His own being, His hidden glory is revealed. And this is creation to the extent that it makes the creature the exponent, sign and witness of the divine meaning and necessity.[42]

Freedom for the creature

The freedom of God to create also underwrites the freedom of the creature. There has been a great deal of theological discussion on the free will (or otherwise) of human beings, but this was often embedded in discussions of contingency in general. Gregory of Nyssa, for example, sees human freedom as the counterpart to God's freedom, and the chief characteristic of our being in the image of God: 'but pre-eminent among all is the fact that we are free from necessity, and not in bondage to any natural power, but have decision in our own power as we please; for virtue is a voluntary thing, subject to no dominion: that which is the result of compulsion and force cannot be virtue.'[43] Aquinas broadens this out to the created order as a whole:

> Now God wills some things to be done necessarily, some contingently, to the right ordering of things, for the building up of the universe. Therefore to some effects He has attached necessary causes, that cannot fail; but to others defectible and contingent causes, from which arise contingent effects. Hence it is not because the proximate causes are contingent that the effects willed by God happen contingently, but because God prepared contingent causes for them, it being His will that they should happen contingently (*ST* 1.19.8).

---

41. Barth, *CD* II/1, p. 345; see Webster, *Reconciliation*, p. 45.
42. Barth, *CD* III/1, p. 230.
43. Gregory of Nyssa, *De Hom. Opif.* 16.11.

With regards to the human will, Aquinas teaches that God has made the will to *necessarily* seek happiness—that is what the will does—but the particulars of how to seek that happiness are left open.[44] All things, however, are 'ordered to God', and true freedom consists in aligning our lives with God's perfect goodness.[45] Such freedom therefore flows out of the reason and the will, in contrast to the radical autonomy of Ockham, where freedom *precedes* reason and will.[46]

Scotus, meanwhile, makes the point that a contingent world is 'nobler' than a necessary one, since it flows from God's choice rather than from necessity.[47] Here the relationship between the divine intellect and the divine will becomes critical:

> Hence, when the divine intellect understands *This is to be done* before an act of the will, it understands it as neutral, just as when it understands *Stars are even in number*. However, when it is produced into being by an act of the will, then it is understood by the divine intellect as a true object according to one or the other component of a contradiction. Therefore we have to assign the cause of contingency in things to the divine will.[48]

Scotus' emphasis on the divine will also had salutary consequences for scientific investigation. In a necessary world, one could simply reason out

44. Cf. Aquinas, *ST* 1–2.10.4: 'As Dionysius says (Div. Nom. iv) "it belongs to Divine providence, not to destroy but to preserve the nature of things." Wherefore it moves all things in accordance with their conditions; so that from necessary causes through the Divine motion, effects follow of necessity; but from contingent causes, effects follow contingently. Since, therefore, the will is an active principle, not determinate to one thing, but having an indifferent relation to many things, God so moves it, that He does not determine it of necessity to one thing, but its movement remains contingent and not necessary, except in those things to which it is moved naturally.' See Brian J. Shanley, 'Beyond Libertarianism and Compatibilism: Thomas Aquinas on Created Freedom', in *Freedom and the Human Person* (ed. Richard L. Velkley; Washington, DC: Catholic University of America Press, 2007), p.86; cf. *Summa contra Gentiles*, 3.88.4. Shanley, 'Thomas Aquinas', p. 85, summarizes: 'God alone can move the will without coercion precisely because he is its creator; if any other cause were to move the will, it would violate its freedom.'

45. See Shanley, 'Thomas Aquinas', p. 76: According to Thomas, 'we are free precisely because we are naturally and so necessarily ordered to the perfect good who is God . . . Choice must be understood as grounded in the nature of the will as ordered to rest in the perfect good.'

46. Servais Pinckaers, *The Sources of Christian Ethics* (trans. Mary Thomas Noble; Edinburgh: T&T Clark, 1995), p. 331.

47. See Ingham and Dreyer, *Philosophical Vision*, pp. 202–3: 'The fact that the Creator could have realized any number of other worlds makes the existence of this world an act of divine love and generosity . . . Thus, the existence of the created order reveals not divine arbitrary exercise of freedom, but, rather, a glimpse into the divine intent.'

48. John Duns Scotus, *Contingency and Freedom: Lectura I 39* (trans. A. Vos. Jaczn et al.; Dordrecht: Kluwer, 1994), text, p. 106; comments, p. 105.

everything from first principles. In a contingent world, by contrast, things *might have been different*, and therefore phenomena need to be examined in and of themselves to ascertain just what they are.

But an emphasis on divine freedom is not without its own traps. William of Ockham famously exalted the divine will above the divine intellect, thinking that the presence of Platonic ideas could not but introduce a necessitarian strain into Christian thinking.[49] In and of itself this might not seem too grave a cause for concern: Ockham commends faith as the primary gateway to understanding God, and thus undercuts what might be deemed the too-close connection between faith and reason in scholastic theology. Nor is it unbiblical to emphasize the inscrutability of God's will: 'For my thoughts are not your thoughts, neither are your ways my ways, says the Lord' (Isa. 55:8). But Ockham takes a very long walk away from the medieval synthesis; he is not simply arguing for a relatively more modest epistemology. While Ockham is far from denying that God is good, for instance, he denies that this goodness will have a necessary connection with goodness here on earth. William Mann summarizes the problem:

> Because he holds both the separability thesis and the thesis that God's essence is to be perfectly good, Ockham must think that God's being perfectly good has no necessary consequences concerning goodness in the created world. There is nothing overtly contradictory about Ockham's position, but it leaves unexplained how God's perfect goodness makes any difference to the goodness of the created world. Because God's will determines what counts as created goodness and because God's perfect goodness places no constraints on what he could have willed for creatures, Ockham's position assigns God's perfect goodness to a kind of explanatory limbo.[50]

Ockham's proffered examples do little to encourage the reader that the will of God is anything but arbitrary, in the worst sense of the word: in response to Scotus, he argues that if God so chose, he could make hating him a good act.[51] Whether Ockham's voluntarism set the stage for secularism in the West may be debated, but his work illustrates the problems which arise when divine freedom is divorced from divine character, at least with respect to the created order.

Difficulties can also multiply when 'freedom' as a principle becomes the font of reality, as it does for the mystic Jacob Boehme and his spiritual

---

49. See Stanley J. Grenz, *The Named God and the Question of Being: A Trinitarian Theo-Ontology* (Louisville, KY: Westminster John Knox, 2005), pp. 58–64.

50. See William E. Mann, 'The Best of All Possible Worlds', in *Being and Goodness: The Concept of the Good in Metaphysics and Philosophical Theology* (ed. Scott McDonald; Ithaca: Cornell University Press, 1990), pp. 250–77.

51. See Mann, 'The Best of All Possible Worlds', pp. 256–57.

descendant Nicholas Berdyaev. For Boehme, the positing of a primal *Ungrund*, a nothingness that is 'the groundless eye of eternity', preserves the dynamism of the divine life, grounds absolute freedom for creatures, and gives a rationale for the presence of evil in the world.[52] But the theological cost is devastating: the chaos that permits, or that indeed *is*, absolute freedom, is made either an element within God, or something that comes prior to God. While Berdyaev extols Boehme's philosophy as a boldly Christian stroke against a theology held captive by Greek rationalism, Boehme's teaching on the *Ungrund* is far more reminiscent of Hesiod's *Theogony* than the opening chapters of Genesis. Boehme's voluntarism, which as Berdyaev notes had a profound effect on later German philosophy, seems far more toxic than that of Ockham.

By way of summary, it seems difficult to improve on Barth's description of God as the 'one who loves in freedom'. The divine love is certainly involved in the creation of the world, but the notion that this involves some problematic 'necessity' rests on a fundamental misunderstanding: the negative aspects of necessity involve an agent being under some *compulsion* to do something. But this is excluded by definition from God. In the same way, the imagined difficulties of accounting for creation and the divine will seem to spring from a similarly illegitimate transfer of things involved in human choosing.[53] Human choice is a matter of making decisions based on the possibilities afforded by the created order. God is not confronted with anything in his creative activity: neither matter nor space nor time serve as preconditions for his creating, nor is there any 'this' or 'that'—not even *ideas* of this or that—which could precipitate a divine existential crisis as to which way he ought to go. Thus some aspects of voluntarist thinking make sense: nothing impinges on God. He is free to fulfil his own desires.

But God's will is not a control centre in the deity cordoned off from his other attributes. What he wills, he wills as the supremely good, wise, and loving God.[54] Thus the imagery of overflowing love, while open to the abuse

---

52. See the comments in Nikolai Berdyaev, *The Beginning and the End* (trans. R. M. French; New York: Harper, 1952), pp. 104–17, and more extensively in his essay 'The Doctrine of the *Ungrund* and Freedom in Jacob Boehme'.

53. See e.g. Burrell, *Three Traditions*, pp. 116–17: 'the creator has a specific intentional relation to those things which the creator intends to create; a relation hardly clarified by "choice" or "exemplification"'.

54. Cf. Jürgen Moltmann, *God in Creation: A New Theology of Creation and the Spirit of God* (Minneapolis: Fortress, 1993), p. 76: 'in his love God can choose; but he chooses only that which corresponds to his essential goodness, in order to communicate that goodness as his creation and in his creation. God's almighty power is demonstrated only inasmuch as all the operations of that power are determined by his eternal nature itself. God therefore does what for him is axiomatic—what is divine. In doing this he is entirely free, and in this freedom he is entirely himself'.

of emanationism, remains a valid way of expressing the inexhaustible beneficence and generosity of God (see James 1:17–18). Barth writes that God is not obliged to create beings with whom he could be in fellowship: 'He does not have to do it, because in Himself without us, and therefore without this, He has that which He seeks and creates between Himself and us.' But in the very next sentence he adds, 'It implies so to speak an overflow of His essence that He turns to us.'[55] God's 'choosing' is thus in one sense simply another way of describing the metaphysical gap that separates God from everything else; but the 'choosing' will be a loving choice which will bridge that gap in the person of the Son. Thus to say, 'God created the world', is to speak both to the gap between God and the world, and to the connection between God and the world. Many subsequent problems—such as the balance between predestination and free will, or the question of whether God is 'inside' or 'outside' the world—can be helpfully viewed through this prism of 'both–and' rather than 'either–or'.[56]

It may be that the decisive mark of freedom, then, is not 'choosing' per se, though that is indeed a constituent element of human freedom and (perhaps, with some qualifications) divine freedom. It is rather a certain *joy* in action, whereby an agent exults in doing what it is meant to do. For God, this consists in acting in his essential goodness, wisdom, and love. For the creature, it consists in being what God created it to be.

The best of all possible worlds?

If God creates freely, does it follow that he therefore must intend to create 'the best of all possible worlds'? Most readers will be familiar with the mantra of the eternally optimistic Pangloss in Voltaire's *Candide*: 'All's for

55. Barth, *CD* II/1, p. 273, in Webster, *Reconciliation*, p. 43. We may compare Edwards, 'Concerning the End', *Works*, 8:433–34: 'As there is an infinite fullness of all possible good in God, a fullness of every perfection, of all excellency and beauty, and of infinite happiness. And as this fullness is capable of communication or emanation ad extra; so it seems a thing amiable and valuable in itself that it should be communicated or flow forth, that this infinite fountain of good should send forth abundant streams, that this infinite fountain of light should, diffusing its excellent fullness, pour forth light all around.' Of course Edwards' occasionalism may lead him closer to a Neoplatonic scheme of emanation than Barth, but Edwards will still maintain a distinction between God and the world. See Oliver Crisp, *Jonathan Edwards on God and Creation* (New York: OUP, 2012), pp. 84–86.

56. Cf. Edwards, 'Concerning the End': 'The notion of God's creating the world in order to receive anything properly from the creature is not only contrary to the nature of God, but inconsistent with the notion of creation; which implies a being's receiving its existence, and all that belongs to its being, out of nothing. And this implies the most perfect, absolute and universal derivation and dependence.' *Works*, 8:421.

the best, in the best of all possible worlds.' It seems a self-evident absurdity: how can a world that includes horrific suffering (like the Lisbon earthquake of 1755, one of the inspirations for *Candide*) be the 'best possible world', as Gottfried Leibnitz had argued? Pangloss can be dismissed as a jabbering ninny, but the underlying theological problem concerning God's will cannot be so easily set aside. If God is good, he must desire what is best for the world; if he is wise, he will know which world is best out of all possible worlds; and if he is omnipotent, he will be able to bring that world into being. Thus, the world we inhabit must be the best of all possible worlds, appearances to the contrary notwithstanding. Seldom has a proposal looked so unassailable in theory, and so dismal in practice.

We may begin by looking at Leibnitz' own account. While his theory is certainly subject to criticism, we should not mistake him for Pangloss. Leibnitz is not arguing that everything in the present world is a self-evident good, and he was flexible in his approach to the problem over the course of his life.[57] Leibnitz recognizes that the reasons for God's actions (e.g. in permitting sin) will often remain obscure to us, particularly on this side of the beatific vision.[58] Indeed, the excellence of the world does not consist in a dull and easily parsed uniformity, but rather in the complex web of connections God has established between things. As Leibnitz puts it, the 'most perfect' world order is 'one which is at the same time the simplest in hypotheses and the richest in phenomena'—a definition with at least passing resemblance to what a modern physicist might put forward.

Despite the acknowledged difficulty of the task, Leibnitz feels compelled to give some answer to those who slight God's handiwork: '[Nor] am I able to approve of the opinions of certain modern writers who boldly maintain that that which God has made is not perfect in the highest degree, and that he might have done better.'[59] At least in the *Discourse on Metaphysics*, Leibnitz is driven in the direction of a 'best possible world' as much by his piety and reverence for Scripture as by strict philosophical concerns. In this regard he is very much in line with Edwards.

At the heart of Leibnitz' apologetic are the notions of *complexity* and *development*, which we might see as *x* and *y* axes. On the vertical axis, the world at any given moment is a complex network whose logic may be difficult to discern, but whose coherence may be deduced from its evident beauty, and presumed from the excellence of its Creator. Thus Leibnitz: 'Only God, who can comprehend the infinitely complex in one act, can see

57. See C. D. Broad, *Leibnitz: An Introduction* (ed. C. Lewy; Cambridge: CUP, 1975), pp. 32–34; for his willingness to revisit the details of his theory, see Adams, 'Leibnitz's Theories of Contingency', pp. 129ff.

58. Discourse on *Metaphysics* 5 (trans. Montgomery), p. 8.

59. Discourse on *Metaphysics* 3 (trans. Montgomery), p. 5.

how the predicate is contained in the subject and can understand *a priori* the reason for a contingent fact.'[60] On the horizontal axis, this complex of events is always moving forward into new configurations—often ones emerging from the free choice of created beings—and these new configurations will in turn necessitate a re-evaluation of what has gone before. A bad act may remain intrinsically bad, while ultimately serving a good purpose in the unfolding of the world. C. L. Broad sums up Leibnitz' thinking with regards to what may be the most serious challenge to his theory, the sin of Adam:

> We must distinguish, as Leibnitz says, between God's antecedent and his consequent volitions. God's antecedent volition was for an obedient Adam, i.e. he would have preferred an obedient Adam to a disobedient one if he could have chosen simply between alternatives. But he could not. He had to choose between a total state of affairs containing a disobedient Adam, and other total states of affairs containing no Adam or an obedient one. As he saw that the former was *on the whole* better than any of the latter, his *consequent* volition was for a disobedient Adam. E.g. without a fall there could have been no redemption and perhaps no incarnation. And God may have seen the value of the redemption and the incarnation outweighed the disvalue of the fall.[61]

In all this, Leibnitz is hardly sitting on a lonely theological island. We have noted his affinities with Edwards. While medieval scholastics in general rejected a strict 'best of all possible worlds' view,[62] Aquinas (whom Leibnitz respected despite the cavils of his contemporaries)[63] comes close to Leibnitz in his discussion of God's will in *ST* 1.19.6; and even in his demurrals he anticipates some of Leibnitz' key points:

> The universe, the present creation being supposed, cannot be better, on account of the most beautiful order given to things by God; in which the good of the universe consists. For if any one thing were bettered, the proportion of order would be destroyed; as if one string were stretched more than it ought to be, the melody of the harp would be destroyed. Yet God could make other things, or add something to the present creation; and then there would be another and a better universe (*ST* 1.25.6).

As we assess the merits of Leibnitz' contention, we must first ask whether a 'possible world' is even a meaningful category for consideration with respect to God's creation. If we take Duns Scotus as our point of departure, 'possible

60. Quote in Broad, *Leibnitz*, p. 32.
61. Broad, *Leibnitz*, p. 34.
62. See Wolter, *Duns Scotus*, p. 16.
63. *Discourse on Metaphysics* 11 (trans. Montgomery), p. 19.

worlds' do seem possible: God might have created things otherwise, and so we could envision different sorts of worlds. But David Burrell finds in Aquinas a caution against an excessive interest in possibility over against actuality. While we can imagine this or that being different about the world, we should not imagine that God prior to creation confronts a host of 'possible worlds' clamouring to be actualized:

> It is not as though God knows all there is to know about an individual (and for some, even a 'possible' one) by inspecting, as it were, God's own idea of that individual, but rather that God knows the individuals whom God brings into existence, since 'God's knowledge extends as far as God's causality' (*ST* 1.14.11) . . . there is no prior reference field (like that of 'all possible worlds') to which God necessarily belongs.[64]

Even if 'possible worlds' be granted, however, we must still face the problem of how such worlds could be graded. At first blush it seems evident that they can. Following Aquinas' note in *ST* 1.19.6, we could argue that a world with 100,000,000 upright citizens would be quantitatively 'better' than one with 99,999,999 such citizens. But where does one stop? No created universe can match the infinite glory of God, and so one would have to posit an 'infinite progress' of successively more excellent worlds. 'Best possible' becomes meaningless when set over and against God's infinite glory.

But this very fact might salvage a chastened version of Leibnitz' proposal. Let us focus not on 'possible worlds' as a technical term, but on Leibnitz' intent to counter those who chide God for 'not doing better'—a serious charge in light of God's declaration in Genesis 1 that things were 'very good'. If 'better' is a term with no upper limit, then Leibnitz' dynamic view of the cosmos may be acceptable. If the world is viewed as a snapshot at any moment in its fallen state, it is evidently not the best imaginable one in any sense of the word. If, by contrast, the world is taken as an eschatologically oriented drama—a divine comedy—then it is indeed arguable that this *will prove to have been* a most excellent universe. Those who hold that creation is in some sense for the sake of the redemption wrought in Christ argue in analogous fashion to Leibnitz: it is supremely good for God to have displayed his love in the sacrifice of his Son for sinful humanity.

Freedom and consummation

Up to this point, we have mainly been considering God's freedom from the standpoint of 'pre-creation'. Is his freedom still operative now that the world

64. Burrell, *Three Traditions*, pp. 34–35.

is in existence? The question is sharpened when we recognize that God has made certain commitments to the world: Reformed theology (with considerable biblical warrant) has placed the notion of covenant at the heart of God's dealings with the world, but at the philosophical level the same reality is in view with the idea of *potentia ordinata* or Aquinas' 'necessity of supposition'. If God binds himself to the world in such a way, is he no longer free?

Part of the answer lies in a return to definitions: if we define 'freedom' simply as choosing arbitrarily between options, then God is not 'free' to renounce his promises. As Hebrews 6:17–18 has it: 'So when God desired to show more convincingly to the heirs of the promise the unchangeable character of his purpose, he interposed with an oath, so that through two unchangeable things, in which it is impossible that God should prove false, we who have fled for refuge might have strong encouragement to seize the hope set before us.' But if freedom is instead defined as God's ability to pursue his own glory, or to uphold justice, then God's works of providence and consummation are indeed done in his perfect freedom. This includes the freedom to enact 'miracles', which so unsettled some early modern thinkers as an unsightly and arbitrary intrusion into what ought to be a fine-tuned universe. Scotus' proposal of 'successive ordained systems'[65] seems sufficient to meet that challenge. God remains free to act *quietly* and maintain the universe on its typical course. He is equally free to work more *loudly* and, for instance, introduce a physical restoration which could not simply be extrapolated from the current state of affairs, but which is nonetheless in harmony with his previously ordained purposes. Thus Lazarus is miraculously raised from the dead, but he is raised *as Lazarus*, bearing all the physical features and relationships which he possessed before his demise.

We might say that God is free to be himself, and therefore to do what he pleases to bring the world into conformity to his desires. This is the foundation of Christian hope. Revelation's description of God as 'the one who is and was and is to come' takes on special significance in this regard. The Greek formula to which it bears obvious resemblance—'Zeus was, Zeus is, Zeus will be'[66]—might be taken to reinforce the notion that the gods provide a stable foundation for the ongoing life of the world. John's reworking stresses the dynamic coming of God to the world, at a time and manner of his choosing. Whatever events might be necessary as part of the eschatological programme, and whatever rhythms those events might follow ('time, times, and half a time'; sevens seals, seven trumpets, seven bowls), it remains the case that 'But of that day or that hour no one knows' (Mark 13:32).

65. See again Gelber, *Dominican Theology*, p. 315.

66. This was said to be sung of Zeus at the oracle of Dodona, according to Pausanias, *Descr.* 10.12.10.

The arrival of the consummate new creation rests in God's freedom. So, too, does its unimaginable richness and beauty. God has committed himself to sharing his glory with the world, but even the prophets and apostles can only offer hints as to what that will look like: 'But, as it is written, "What no eye has seen, nor ear heard, nor the heart of man conceived, what God has prepared for those who love him"' (1 Cor. 2:9).

4

From Eternity to Here: Time and Creation

We have explored why God would create the world at all. But since the earliest centuries of the church another question has been posed: why would God create at one particular time versus another? The question may seem trivial in and of itself, but it carries with it considerable theological freight: if there is no reason God creates at point *x* versus point *y*, this might lead one to conclude that the world itself is eternal. This might in turn compromise our understanding of God's sovereignty. The matter of *when* God creates also raises the issue of how an infinite God can somehow engender a finite world. In later chapters we will consider how the creation project moves along the temporal spectrum once things get going. For now we will ask the more foundational question: how do we get from Eternity to Here?

Time and Eternity

The most remarkable thing about eternity is the fact we can talk about it intelligibly at all. As numerous thinkers have pointed out, eternity is not merely the extension of the temporal spectrum backwards and forwards unto infinity. This is difficult enough to imagine, but at least it involves putting one foot after the other from some starting point. Eternity proper is something more: it has been described as the possession of all times all at once (*totum simul*), or as a kind of timelessness; it is sometimes associated with a transcendent religious state, a rapture within which the customary boundaries of time and space dissolve.[1] Men and women receive only fleeting glimpses of such a state of affairs, but it has been presumed by many inside and outside the church to be God's state of Being.

The Bible does not address the question of God, time, and creation with philosophical precision, but it offered plenty of working space for future theologians seeking a fusion of scriptural tradition and enlightened reason.

1. See Richard Sorabji, *Time, Creation and the Continuum: Theories in Antiquity and the Early Middle Ages* (London: Duckworth, 1983), pp. 157–63 on Plotinus' mystical experiences of timelessness.

According to Genesis 1 the world has a beginning (at least as an ordered cosmos), while God is simply there. This is no small thing in Mediterranean culture where gods typically emerged from the elements or were the offspring of other gods. In Hesiod's *Theogony*, for instance, personal gods only appear after Chaos, Earth, and Tartarus, and the current world ruler Zeus has to wait some four hundred lines before he finally makes it onto the stage. Whether God's enigmatic self-designation in the Hebrew text of Exodus 3:14—'I am who I am'—is a strict statement of his 'eternity' is a much debated point, but at the very least it *permits* one to think along those lines.

The same can be said for the portrait of God in Psalm 90:1–4:

> LORD, thou hast been our dwelling place in all generations.
> Before the mountains were brought forth,
> or ever thou hadst formed the earth and the world,
> from everlasting to everlasting thou art God.
> Thou turnest man back to the dust,
> and sayest, 'Turn back, O children of men!'
> For a thousand years in thy sight
> are but as yesterday when it is past,
> or as a watch in the night.

As in Genesis, God is presumed to be there before anything else, and there is no concern that his being is going to diminish in the future. 'From everlasting to everlasting' (Heb. *Me'olam ad-'olam*) might be more strictly rendered 'from age to age'; this could indicate merely an enduring duration along the temporal spectrum without implying a qualitatively distinct 'timelessness'.[2] But such a minimal reading hardly seems the most likely one in light of the note about God being there before the hills in order stood.

Early Jewish and Christian interpreters began to explore in greater depth questions of God, time, and eternity. The translators of the Septuagint, faced with 'I am that I am' in Exodus 3:14, opted for the grammatically defensible and philosophically loaded translation *egō eimi ho ōn*, 'I am the one who is.'[3] The rendering is not only technically permissible, it expresses in crisp fashion the ontological dimension of the Hebrew original: while Exodus is clearly not offering up a technical explanation of God's eternity, it does at least suggest that in contrast to the world he has created, God just is. The designation made it into the New Testament as part of the formula 'the one who is and was and is to come' in the book of Revelation (1:4; cf. 4:8; 11:17; 16:5).

---

2. The word *'olam* expresses long duration; in later Judaism it came to be a designation for the world itself.

3. On the translation and its effects, see Sean M. McDonough, *YHWH at Patmos: Rev. 1:4 in Its Hellenistic and Early Jewish Setting* (Tübingen: Mohr Siebeck, 1999), pp. 131–41.

The phrase is an integral part of the Apocalypse's portrait of God enthroned above the world and its history, directing things with surety to accomplish his purposes. (The reworking of the formula in Rev. 4:8 to 'the one who was and is and is to come' highlights God's role as Creator.) While John does not draw out all the possible implications of the designation for God's aseity, it is interesting to note that the Beast in Revelation 17 is described as the one who 'was, and is not, and is to ascend from the bottomless pit and go to perdition' (17:8). This is an obvious parody of the divine name, and one wonders if the statement that the Beast 'is not' goes beyond the ups and downs of various Roman emperors and speaks to the ontological deficiencies of evil as such.[4] If this is true, then the affirmation that God is 'the one who is' makes a correspondingly strong statement on God's absolute being.

The New Testament does adopt the Greek word *aiōn* (Plato's 'eternity') for *'olam*, but the ambiguity of the Hebrew designation remains. As in the Hebrew bible, the word is often best rendered 'age' in the sense of an 'era'. Thus Jesus can speak of the end or consummation of 'the age' (Matt. 13:39, 40, 49), and Hebrews 1 affirms that God made 'the ages' (*tous aiōnos*) through Christ. It also appears as the functional equivalent of *ad-'olam*, 'forever' or 'in perpetuity', for instance in John 8:35, 'the slave does not continue in the house for ever'. For more dramatic effect another *aiōn* could be added on, namely Galatians 1:5, 'to whom be glory for ever and ever' or 'to the ages of ages', *eis tous aiōnas tōn aiōnōn*. There is a clearer sense here than in the OT of a contrast between the present evil age and the glorious age to come, but there is no sense that this coming age is somehow non-durational.

The idea of a non-durational eternity enters the picture with the philosophical discussions of eternity, which begin with Plato's predecessor Parmenides.[5] The philosopher takes a journey to the edge of the world, reaching the gates of Day and Night where he meets the goddess Justice. She tells him of the 'two ways' of understanding:

> The first, namely, that It is, and that it is impossible for anything not to be, is the way of conviction, for truth is its companion . . . The other, namely, that It is not, and that something must needs not be,—that, I tell thee, is a wholly untrustworthy path. For you cannot know what is not—that is impossible—nor utter it; For it is the same thing that can be thought and that can be.[6]

4. Bauckham argues plausibly that the 'is not' refers to the *Nero redivivus* myth, which held that while Nero had disappeared for the nonce ('is not') he would later return to wreak havoc on the Roman Empire. See Richard Bauckham, *The Climax of Prophecy: Studies on the Book of Revelation* (London: T&T Clark, 2007), pp. 396–452.

5. On the question of time and eternity in the ancient world, including early Christianity, see above all Sorabji, *Time*.

6. Plato, *Parmenides*, 2.3–3.1.

Scholars have long debated the precise meaning of these cryptic words. They signify at least a declaration about what can and cannot be predicated: we can only speak of what is, not of what is not.[7] But the distinction between the 'way of Being' and the 'way of Seeming' seems to move into deeper ontological territory, the homeland of what will become known as the Platonic distinction between the world of true Being and the world of unstable Becoming. Whatever Parmenides might have intended, this disjunction of the eternal, invisible world and the transient world of change was to lodge itself in the heart of Greek philosophy and subsequently in the heart of Christian theology. At the centre of Parmenides' discourse is the notion of time and being: 'One path only is left for us to speak of, namely, that It is. In it are very many tokens that what is, is uncreated and indestructible, alone, complete, immovable and without end. Nor was it ever, nor will it be; for now it is, all at once, a continuous one' (8.1–5). What began as a simple statement on predication turns out in Parmenides' eyes to have profound ontological implications. In an intellectualizing tour de force, Parmenides thus dismisses change and motion from genuine being: that which truly is *just is*. 'Coming into being and passing away have been driven afar' (8.27–28), as he puts it.

The Way of Being remains obscure and abstracted in Parmenides, but Plato follows in his trajectory, and it is in any case Plato's vision of time and eternity which becomes formative for the Christian tradition. Plato adopts Parmenides' foundational insight on being and time, clarifying it in some places and developing it in others. If the idea of restricting true being to the present tense seems obscure, for example, we may think of mathematics: does it make any sense to say that 'one plus one was two', or 'one plus one will be two'? Mathematical truths simply are. In the same way, when we say of something that it is 'true' or 'beautiful', we are judging the object in question by an enduring standard of Truth or Beauty. If this idea of Truth or Beauty comes to be or passes away, its value as a standard crumbles.

This brings us to Plato's discussion of time and eternity, which finds its most influential expression in the *Timaeus*. Plato gets round to the notion of eternity in *Timaeus* 37c ff. His debt to Parmenides is evident:

> Wherefore he resolved to have a moving image of eternity, and when he set in order the heaven, he made this image eternal but moving according to number, while eternity itself rests in unity; and this image we call time. For there were no days and nights and months and years before the heaven was created, but when he constructed the heaven he created them also. They are all parts of time, and the past and future are created species of time, which we unconsciously but wrongly transfer to the eternal essence; for we say that he 'was,' he 'is,' he 'will be,' but the truth is that 'is' alone is properly attributed to him, and

7. See e.g. G. E. L. Owen, 'Eleatic Questions', *Classical Quarterly* n.s. 10 (1960): pp. 90ff.

> that 'was' and 'will be' only to be spoken of becoming in time, for they are motions, but that which is immovably the same cannot become older or younger by time, nor ever did or has become, or hereafter will be, older or younger, nor is subject at all to any of those states which affect moving and sensible things and of which generation is the cause.

As in Genesis, the heavenly bodies serve as timekeepers for the cosmos, though Plato adds the important notion that the endless celestial cycles are intended to give a dim image of eternity. We also see here the roots of Augustine's notion that the world is created 'with time' rather than 'in time'.

While in many respects Aristotle's views are something of an inversion of Plato, on the question of eternity they shared considerable common ground. In his *De Caelo*, he provides an argument that life outside the heavens must be eternal:

> It is therefore evident that there is also no place or void or time outside the heaven. For in every place body can be present; and void is said to be that in which the presence of body, though not actual, is possible; and time is the number of movement. But in the absence of natural body there is no movement, and outside the heaven, as we have shown, body neither exists nor can come to exist. It is clear then that there is neither place, nor void, nor time, outside the heaven. Hence whatever is there, is of such a nature as not to occupy any place, nor does time age it; nor is there any change in any of the things which lie beyond the outermost motion; they continue through their entire duration unalterable and unmodified, living the best and most self-sufficient of lives. As a matter of fact, this word 'duration' possessed a divine significance for the ancients, for the fulfilment which includes the period of life of any creature, outside of which no natural development can fall, has been called its duration. On the same principle the fulfilment of the whole heaven, the fulfilment which includes all time and infinity, is 'duration'—a name based upon the fact that it is always—duration immortal and divine. From it derive the being and life which other things, some more or less articulately but others feebly, enjoy.[8]

That 'divinity' resides within this timeless realm is made clear later on in the same work:

> So, too, in its discussions concerning the divine, popular philosophy often propounds the view that whatever is divine, whatever is primary and supreme, is necessarily unchangeable. This fact confirms what we have said. For there is nothing else stronger than it to move it—since that would mean more divine—and it has no defect and lacks none of its proper excellences.[9]

---

8. Aristotle, *Cael.* 279a17–28, in *On the Heavens* (trans. John Leofric Stocks; Oxford: Clarendon, 1922).

9. Aristotle, *Cael.* 279a22–279b1, in *On the Heavens* (trans. Stocks).

The broad conceptual parallels between Genesis and the *Timaeus* made a Christian rapprochement with Plato likely. The Septuagint rendering of Exodus 3:14 made it a virtual certainty. The link between God as 'the one who is', and Plato's description of the really real as 'that which is', had far-reaching effects. Philo made ample use of Exodus 3:14 LXX, and it is possible the formulation lay at the foundation of his entire project to reconcile Torah and Greek philosophy. The designation was ideally suited to Philo's apophaticism: though God is essentially unnameable, 'the One who is' is as good a label as we can find, 'so that they may learn the difference between what is and what is not, and also the further lesson that no name at all can be properly used of Me, to Whom alone existence belongs.'[10] As the eternally existent one, he is the ground for all other existence: 'For, as He alone really is, He is undoubtedly also the Maker, since He brought into being what was not.'[11]

But the Greek philosophical tradition also bequeathed at least two problems on the church in its reflection on God, time, and creation. First, the close connection between 'the One who is' and 'that which is' masked a fundamental divide: the first posits a personal being, while the second posits a principle or conglomeration of principles. Strict timelessness might make sense of a mathematical formula like 'one plus one is two', but it is much more difficult to map this kind of non-durational eternity onto a person. Second, the overwhelming majority of Greek followers of Plato understood him to be speaking somewhat mythologically of the 'creation' of a world that is in fact eternal. The language of the Demiurge is simply a way of describing the rationality of the world as it presents itself to us; it is not meant to be taken as an actual creation account.[12] Christian theologians were inclined to believe in a personal God who created the world in the beginning, but it was difficult to resist the urge to pull God towards the principial side of the ledger. Likewise, their affection for the philosophical tradition meant they had to expend a considerable amount of energy explaining how they could embrace so many aspects of that tradition while rejecting the important tenet of the eternality of the world.

Augustine's treatment of time is a watershed in the church's philosophical development. He is obviously dependent on Plato for key points, but he places Plato's motifs squarely in the context of an encounter with a fully personal God. This is nowhere more evident than in the celebrated passage on time in the *Confessions*. Here above all the *confessional* nature of the text

---

10. Plato, *Mos.*, 1.74–76.

11. Plato, *Mos.*, 2.100.

12. Thomas Johansen argues convincingly that the Demiurge ought to be viewed as an embodiment of the idea of craftsmanship; see Thomas K. Johansen, *Plato's Natural Philosophy: A Study of the Timaeus-Critias* (Cambridge: CUP, 2004).

must be kept in mind: whatever Augustine purports to say about God and time at the technical level, it is spoken as a prayer to a God Augustine knows and loves. He is wrestling with the question of how a God who must be beyond time (as argued in the closing sections of chapter 10) can encounter a man like himself bound within time:

> Is it possible, O Lord, that, since thou art in eternity, thou art ignorant of what I am saying to thee? Or, dost thou see in time an event at the time it occurs? If not, then why am I recounting such a tale of things to thee? Certainly not in order to acquaint thee with them through me; but, instead, that through them I may stir up my own love and the love of my readers toward thee, so that all may say, 'Great is the Lord and greatly to be praised' (11.1.1.).

The answer can only be found in a thoroughgoing account of the relationship of God and the world as a whole. Even here Augustine finds things slipping away from him: God has spoken through Moses that he made all things in the beginning, but Moses himself is unavailable to provide any explanation for the enigmatic features of his text (11.3.5). But since God himself never slips away, Augustine can approach him with his questions. God's enduring Word has spoken the whole fleeting world into existence:

> Thou dost call us, then, to understand the Word—the God who is God with thee—which is spoken eternally and by which all things are spoken eternally. For what was first spoken was not finished, and then something else spoken until the whole series was spoken; but all things, at the same time and forever. For, otherwise, we should have time and change and not a true eternity, nor a true immortality (11.7.9).

What then is a 'true eternity' for Augustine? It centres on the idea of *changelessness*, a pervasive theme in *Confessions* 11. Heaven and earth 'cry aloud that they were made, for they change and vary'; by contrast, 'Whatever there is that has not been made, and yet has being, has nothing in it that was not there before' (*Conf.* 11.4). Augustine speaks of God's 'eternal reason where nothing begins or ceases' (*Conf.* 11.8) and notes that God's Word does not pass away like human words: 'For what was first spoken was not finished, and then something else spoken until the whole series was spoken; but all things, at the same time and forever. For, otherwise, we should have time and change and not a true eternity, nor a true immortality' (*Conf.* 11.7).[13]

---

13. Cf. Gregory Nazienzen, *Or. Bas.* 38.7: 'For in Himself He sums up and contains all Being, having neither beginning in the past nor end in the future; like some great Sea of Being, limitless and unbounded, transcending all conception of time and nature, only adumbrated by the mind, and that very dimly and scantily.'

Eternity thus conceived gives Augustine a means to address those who argue that the world must be eternal, since it is the product of God's eternal will:

> Those who say these things do not yet understand thee, O Wisdom of God, O Light of souls. They do not yet understand how the things are made that are made by and in thee. They endeavor to comprehend eternal things, but their heart still flies about in the past and future motions of created things, and is still unstable. Who shall hold it and fix it so that it may come to rest for a little; and then, by degrees, glimpse the glory of that eternity which abides forever; and then, comparing eternity with the temporal process in which nothing abides, they may see that they are incommensurable? They would see that a long time does not become long, except from the many separate events that occur in its passage, which cannot be simultaneous. In the Eternal, on the other hand, nothing passes away, but the whole is simultaneously present (*Conf.* 11.11).[14]

He summarizes his thoughts in *City of God* chapter 11, where he puts forth the influential notion that time is created along with the world:

> For if eternity and time are rightly distinguished by this, that time does not exist without some movement and transition, while in eternity there is no change, who does not see that there could have been no time had not some creature been made, which by some motion could give birth to change,—the various parts of which motion and change, as they cannot be simultaneous, succeed one another,—and thus, in these shorter or longer intervals of duration, time would begin? Since then, God, in whose eternity is no change at all, is the Creator and Ordainer of time, I do not see how He can be said to have created the world after spaces of time had elapsed, unless it be said that prior to the world there was some creature by whose movement time could pass. And if the sacred and infallible Scriptures say that in the beginning God created the heavens and the earth, in order that it may be understood that He had made nothing previously,—for if He had made anything before the rest, this thing would rather be said to have been made 'in the beginning,'—then assuredly the world was made, not in time, but simultaneously with time.

Augustine has caught his fair share of grief for importing Platonic notions of eternity into the Christian faith, and even his staunchest supporters may

14. Cf. Gregory of Nyssa, *C. Eun.* 2.26: 'It is clear, even with a moderate insight into the nature of things, that there is nothing by which we can measure the divine and blessed Life. It is not in time, but time flows from it; whereas the creation, starting from a manifest beginning, journeys onward to its proper end through spaces of time; so that it is possible, as Solomon somewhere says, to detect in it a beginning, an end, and a middle; and mark the sequence of its history by divisions of time. But the supreme and blessed life has no time-extension accompanying its course, and therefore no span nor measure.'

wonder if he takes things a bit far in arguing, for instance, that the saints in eternity will share in the *totum simul* of God's eternity.[15] But Augustine seems fundamentally correct in positing a qualitative difference between the time of the world and the 'time' of the Creator of the world. Platonism merely provided him with more philosophical precision in articulating the biblical truth that God is 'the one who is and was and is to come', the one 'declaring the end from the beginning, and from ancient times things not yet done' (Isa. 46:10).[16]

Aquinas relies on Boethius and Augustine for his views on the eternity of God (see e.g. *ST* Q10). More noteworthy is his discussion of the eternity of the world, which occasioned considerable debate in the Middle Ages.[17] The controversy arose from statements by some of his would-be disciples, who were over-persuaded by Thomas's thoughtful treatment of the philosophical arguments in favour of the world's eternity. Since Thomas had entwined himself with Aristotle, he could not dismiss the Philosopher's views out of hand. Aquinas could also appreciate the challenge posed by a Primary Cause who fails to cause something at any given point.

Whether Aquinas successfully squares Aristotle with his own views is a matter beyond our immediate concerns. But his insights on the question of why God should create at one point rather than another are well considered. He points out, in keeping with Augustine, that such a question rests upon a false premise:

> But the universal agent who produces the thing and time also, is not correctly described as acting now, and not before, according to an imaginary succession of time succeeding time, as if time were presupposed to His action; but He must be considered as giving time to His effect as much as and when He willed, and according to what was fitting to demonstrate His power (*ST* 1.46.1).

This point is undergirded by Aquinas' premise that creation does not involve change, which safeguards God's aseity and distinguishes temporal being from God's eternity.[18]

---

15. See discussion below.

16. For contemporary support of Augustine's basic approach, see e.g. G. J. Whitrow, *The Natural Philosophy of Time* (Oxford: Clarendon, 1980), pp. 32–33. Cf. also Gregory Nazienzen's perceptive description of eternity (*Or. Bas.* 38.8): 'But what time, measured by the course of the sun, is to us, that Eternity is to the Everlasting, namely, a sort of time-like movement and interval co-extensive with their existence.'

17. For some compelling insights on views of the eternity of God and the world prior to Aquinas, note the contribution of John Philoponus, as detailed in Sorabji, *Time*, pp. 214–24, 228–31.

18. See David B. Burrell, *Faith and Freedom: An Interfaith Perspective* (Malden: Blackwell, 2004), p. 198.

If Aquinas had left matters here, subsequent trouble might have been avoided. But he goes on to argue that the non-eternity of the world is a matter of faith, and not demonstration (*ST* 1.46.2). This could make it sound as if the belief is therefore somewhat arbitrary or inconsequential, a supposition strengthened by the inclusion here of the (essentially unrefuted) opinions of philosophers who held that the world is 'created' in the sense that it depends utterly on God and unfolds in time—but not in the sense that it is created 'in the beginning'. But Thomas provides a compelling argument as to why assertions about the world's duration must be matters of faith.

> The reason of this is that the newness of the world cannot be demonstrated on the part of the world itself. For the principle of demonstration is the essence of a thing. Now everything according to its species is abstracted from 'here' and 'now'; whence it is said that universals are everywhere and always. Hence it cannot be demonstrated that man, or heaven, or a stone were not always. Likewise neither can it be demonstrated on the part of the efficient cause, which acts by will. For the will of God cannot be investigated by reason, except as regards those things which God must will of necessity; and what He wills about creatures is not among these, as was said above (Q[19], A[3]). But the divine will can be manifested by revelation, on which faith rests. Hence that the world began to exist is an object of faith, but not of demonstration or science. And it is useful to consider this, lest anyone, presuming to demonstrate what is of faith, should bring forward reasons that are not cogent, so as to give occasion to unbelievers to laugh, thinking that on such grounds we believe things that are of faith (*ST* Q46, 2).

Aquinas makes at least two profound points here. The first is that we cannot burst the bounds of the world relying solely on our reasoning; it is like asking someone to speak *from personal experience* about what the world was like before they were born. In fact, we might want to say that in our finiteness we cannot even recognize that there *is* any boundary, since this would imply an ability to see the timeline, its beginning (or end), and the space beyond it.[19] We are thus led to (erroneously) imagine that the world is infinite, setting up a hall of mirrors in our mind that gives the illusion of

19. See again Gregory of Nyssa, I. 2.26: 'Every discursive effort of thought to go back beyond the ages will ascend only so far as to see that that which it seeks can never be passed through: time and its contents seem the measure and the limit of the movement and the working of human thought, but that which lies beyond remains outside its reach; it is a world where it may not tread, unsullied by any object that can be comprehended by man. No form, no place, no size, no reckoning of time, or anything else knowable, is there: and so it is inevitable that our apprehensive faculty, seeking as it does always some object to grasp, must fall back from any side of this incomprehensible existence, and seek in the ages and in the creation which they hold its kindred and congenial sphere.'

infinitude in what is actually a bounded temporal zone. More importantly, since God creates not out of necessity but by his will, there is no accounting for the creation except by recourse to God's own revelation.

Barth begins his discussion of the topic by affirming that God is eternal, and that this eternity is essential to his freedom. He describes eternity as 'the simultaneity of beginning, middle, and end'; for God 'beginning, succession and end are not three but one, not separate as a first, a second and a third occasion'. It is thus not simply 'an infinite extension of time both backwards and forwards'.[20] In keeping with Psalm 90, God's eternity has immense practical application as a guarantee of his constancy, which grounds our trust in him. In all this Barth is merely giving an elegant restatement of the theological tradition and its distinction between time and eternity.

Where Barth advances the discussion considerably is in his positive conception of God and time—though in his own eyes he is simply trying to recapture the view he finds in Scripture:

> It is to be noted again that, in distinction from the concept of eternity which later dominated the Church, the Bible is interested predominantly, if not exclusively, in this primary and positive quality of eternity, and scarcely or not at all in the secondary quality which is its character as non-temporality. It is not to be explained as naïve, Semitic realism, but by a conception that is incomparably more profound and goes to the heart of the matter, if in the Bible an abstract qualification of eternity as non-temporality emerges explicitly only on the very circumference of its consideration.[21]

According to Barth, Boethius had provided an elegant summary of such a positive view of eternity—'Total, simultaneous and complete possession of unlimited life'—but the more static concepts of Augustine typically held sway in the church, leading to a 'Babylonian captivity' of eternity as 'an abstract opposite of time'.[22] Barth is particularly troubled by the legacy of the language of 'timelessness', which cuts God off from the temporal creation, leaving time homeless. Since 'God's eternity is itself beginning, succession and end', he is the prototype for creaturely time: 'God has time because and as He has eternity'.[23] More pointedly, God has *time for us*. The words of the psalmist, 'My times are in thy hand' (Ps. 31:15), should be taken in the strongest possible sense:

20. Karl Barth, *Church Dogmatics* (4 vols; Edinburgh: T&T Clark, 1956–75), II/1, p. 608.

21. Barth, *CD* II/1, p. 610.

22. Barth, *CD* II/1, p. 611.

23. Barth, *CD* II/1, p. 611.

> God's hands, the workings of His omnipotence, are not themselves timeless but supremely temporal, so that our time can really be in them, and can be not merely apparent but real time. As the tree on the river's bank is always beside it, yet does not flow with it; as the Pole Star is at the zenith of the vault of heaven, yet does not move round with it; and as the ocean surrounds the land on all sides and yet is not land itself—so the eternal God co-exists with the time created by Him.[24]

God is genuinely engaged with the world, and this should provide the starting point for our reasoning about time. Nowhere is the engagement more evident than in the incarnation:

> The fact that the Word became flesh undoubtedly means that, without ceasing to be eternity, in its very power as eternity, eternity became time. Yes, it became time. What happens in Jesus Christ is not simply that God gives us time, our created time, as the form of our own existence and world, as is the case in creation and in the whole ruling of the world by God as its Lord. In Jesus Christ it comes about that God takes time to Himself, that He Himself, the eternal One, becomes temporal, that He is present for us in the form of our own existence and our own world, not simply embracing our time and ruling it, but submitting Himself to it, and permitting created time to become and be the form of His eternity.[25]

We are not, then, stranded in the sea of time, alienated from the eternal God. In Christ God has made a home for himself within time, such that we can now feel at home in time as well.

Summary

The traditional lines of discussion of time and eternity continue to the present day: it is never easy to parse the relationship in a way that preserves both divine aseity and divine engagement with the world.[26] Einstein's theory of relativity has added an interesting wrinkle to the matter, though Christianity's premise of a contingent universe kept it from becoming a problem along the lines of Darwinian evolution. In any case, divine eternity lies beyond the

24. Barth, *CD* II/1, p. 613–14.

25. Barth, *CD* II/1, p. 216.

26. For the defence of God's eternity, see e.g. Paul Helm, *Eternal God: A Study of God without Time* (Oxford: Clarendon, 1988) and Brian Leftow, *Time and Eternity* (Ithaca: Cornell University Press, 1991). Full-blown process theology has not proved especially durable, but recent debates surrounding the 'openness' of God show the discussion is not closed. For a helpful assortment of essays, see Christian Tapp and Edmund Runggaldier, eds, *God, Eternity, and Time* (Farnham: Ashgate, 2011).

pale of purely scientific inquiry, and 'time' as commonly conceived retains its usefulness for day-to-day living.[27]

Following Barth, we might wish to speak of God as 'time-full' rather than time-less. This will permit us to retain the necessary classical distinction between the eternal God and the transient world, but without implying that God somehow lacks something the world has, or that the experience of creaturely duration remains a mystery for him. In even more homely fashion, we might say that God is both the rainbow overarching all time, and the rain that drops down at every instant of time.

As for the time of the world, the church has understandably viewed a coeternal universe as a threat to God's aseity. The threat was especially sharp viewed against the backdrop of a Greco-Roman culture in which the world as a whole served as the matrix of the gods, or contained within itself the predicates attributed in the Bible to God alone. The world *as it exists in God's mind* presented a different set of challenges for Christian Platonists: the Platonic Ideas are constitutionally timeless, and once they are located within God's mind or his *logos*, or are more or less *equated* with the *logos*, it becomes difficult to disentangle them from the divine eternity. If theologians have not manufactured a perfect solution to the problem, there has at least been a consistent effort to distinguish the kind of eternity that obtains in the case of the Trinity and the kind of eternity that obtains with the Ideas.

The example of Aquinas shows, however, that claims for the eternity of the cosmos itself cannot be wished away; the spectre of the otiose God looms over the tradition. Augustine's sophisticated take on time and eternity is probably sufficient to dispel that ghost, but the challenges faced by Aquinas can help us appreciate the limitations of our understanding of the world. It is tempting to think that we can independently reason our way back beyond the beginning of things, skirting Gibraltar until we reach the sea of infinity beyond. But as creatures no such easy passage is assured, and so it is prima facie sensible to imagine that the world has been around forever, since it is all we naturally know. There is no independent point of reference by which we might measure its duration. It is no wonder that Parmenides and Plato cannot adequately depict the Ideas without resorting to the functional equivalents of biblical apocalyptic visions: prophetic figures burst the bonds of time and space to deliver an account of transcendental enduring realities.

Once the validity of such visionary insights is granted, however, the eternity of the world is no longer a necessary deduction. While the language

27. The notion of absolute time is defended by William Lane Craig, 'Divine Eternity and Einstein's Special Theory of Relativity', in *God, Eternity, and Time* (ed. Tapp and Runggaldier), pp. 145–55. The reality of time in general receives a penetrating apology in David Braine, *The Reality of Time and the Existence of God: The Project of Proving God's Existence* (Oxford: Clarendon, 1988).

of 'before the world began' or 'after the end of history' may not be fully adequate to express the nature of eternity—it inevitably conjures up a *time* line, with flimsy partitions thrown up at 'the beginning' and 'the end'—it does point in the right direction.

How Old, and How Long?

Compared to the fundamental questions of time and eternity raised in the previous section, the issue of how long the world has been around is at first blush not of tremendous theological import: the answers will range from 'about 10,000 years ago' to 'billions and billions of years ago', depending on one's theological and scientific taste. If anything, there is greater variability as to the time God will finish the world off (or 'up', if one wants to be positive): anything from 'tomorrow' to 'billions and billions of years hence' to 'never' might be offered up. But the quantity of time embraced by the world is related to the quality of time that obtains in the created order, and so the question merits a brief treatment.

A long time

In some fundamentalist circles, the phrase 'young earth creationism' has served as a dividing line between an orthodox and heterodox understanding of creation. We are less concerned here with the questionable scientific basis for the plus-or-minus 10,000-year figure, and more concerned with the deployment of the comparative 'young' as a diagnostic for correct belief. The irony is that in their effort to be more 'biblical', the proponents of a 'young' earth run counter to some currents within the Bible itself. Consider again the opening verses of Psalm 90: 'Lord, thou hast been our dwelling place in all generations. Before the mountains were brought forth, or ever thou hadst formed the earth and the world, from everlasting to everlasting thou art God.' The sentiment here seems to be that the mountains are *very, very* old, and God was around even before them. The mountains dwarf us not only physically, but also temporally, and we are meant to glean from this some sense of God's eternality. Seen from this perspective, the mind-numbing figures put forth by modern geology serve the theological interests of Psalm 90 quite well. John McPhee, in his magisterial survey of American geology, *Annals of the Former World*, muses:

> Human time, regarded in the perspective of geologic time, is much too thin to be discerned—the mark invisible at the end of the ruler. If geologic time could somehow be seen in the perspective of human time, on the other hand,

> sea level would be rising and falling hundreds of feet, ice would come pouring over continents and as quickly go away. Yucatans and Floridas would be under the sun one moment and underwater the next, oceans would swing open like doors, mountains would grow like clouds and come down like melting sherbet, continents would crawl like amoebae, rivers would arrive and disappear like rainstreaks down an umbrella, lakes would go away like puddles after rain, and volcanoes would light the earth as if it were a garden full of fireflies. At the end of the program, man shows up—his ticket in his hand.[28]

The existential import of these questions of time and eternity is driven home in similar fashion in the beginning of Augustine's *Confessions*. Augustine's reflections on his infancy lead seamlessly to thoughts of God's infinitude:

> And, behold, my infancy died long ago, but I am still living. But thou, O Lord, whose life is forever and in whom nothing dies—since before the world was, indeed, before all that can be called 'before,' thou wast, and thou art the God and Lord of all thy creatures; and with thee abide all the stable causes of all unstable things, the unchanging sources of all changeable things, and the eternal reasons of all non-rational and temporal things—tell me, thy suppliant, O God, tell me, O merciful One, in pity tell a pitiful creature whether my infancy followed yet an earlier age of my life that had already passed away before it. Was it such another age which I spent in my mother's womb? For something of that sort has been suggested to me, and I have myself seen pregnant women. But what, O God, my Joy, preceded that period of life? Was I, indeed, anywhere, or anybody? No one can explain these things to me, neither father nor mother, nor the experience of others, nor my own memory. Dost thou laugh at me for asking such things? Or dost thou command me to praise and confess unto thee only what I know?[29]

So much for looking backward towards the time of creation. When it comes to looking forward to the time of consummation, Paul appears to offer different counsel. We might see creation happening a long time ago, but the remaining time is short:

> I mean, brethren, the appointed time has grown very short; from now on, let those who have wives live as though they had none, and those who mourn as though they were not mourning, and those who rejoice as though they were not rejoicing, and those who buy as though they had no goods, and those who deal with the world as though they had no dealings with it. For the form of this world is passing away (1 Cor. 7:29–31).

---

28. John McPhee, *Annals of the Former World* (New York: Farrar, Straus & Giroux, 1998), p. 171. The title is taken from the writing of the pioneering Scottish geologist James Hutton, whose discoveries were to play a major role in challenging traditional chronologies drawn from Genesis.

29. Augustine, *Conf.* 1.6.

One could take this to mean that Paul felt the world was going to end in so short a time that there was no point in investing in it. While it is possible Paul felt this way, the emphasis here is much more on the quality of whatever time remains rather than its quantity.[30] The expression rendered 'the appointed time has grown very short' (Gk. *ho kairos sunestalmenos estin*) is notoriously difficult to understand. It might refer to the 'shortening' of the time of eschatological suffering, in accord with texts like Mark 13 and the 'three and a half times' of Daniel 12:7 (which could represent a truncation of an expected seven-unit 'week' of tribulation). Even then, the absolute amount of time would not be at issue; it is simply shorter than it otherwise would have been. Anthony Thiselton's translation 'limits have been placed on the critical time' might fit with this view.[31] More important for us is the concluding remark in verse 31 that 'the form of this world is passing away'. While the *schēma* or 'form' here is somewhat vague (Thiselton suggests 'the external structures of this world are slipping away'), the sense is of a world-system that is unable to bear the weight of the coming glory—a system that has taken its stand against God and his crucified Messiah (cf. 1 Cor. 2:6) and thus lives in the shadow of looming judgement. The various ills that beset the church are 'relativizing question marks which hang over a world order which has no future'.[32]

Time after time

Do we somehow 'escape' time in the eschaton? The Neoplatonic exitus–reditus scheme would point in that direction, and it could be Christianized by recourse to the analogous structure of 1 Corinthians 15: if all things proceed from the Father through Christ, and return to him through Christ, might not the end of all things entail a sharing in the divine timelessness? If in *theosis* we ultimately become partakers of the divine nature, would this not logically involve partaking in his eternity? Augustine seems to think so. In book 12 of the *Confessions*, he looks forward to the eschatological state in which we are embraced in God's changelessness: 'Do you deny this: that there is a certain sublime created order which cleaves with such a chaste

30. Another possibility is that Paul is referring to the inadvisability of marriage in light of some historical crisis in mid-first-century Corinth. See Bruce W. Winter, *After Paul Left Corinth: The Influence of Secular Ethics and Social Change* (Grand Rapids: Eerdmans, 2001), pp. 241–68. This is possible, but we do not want to miss the deeper theological point Paul is making.

31. Anthony C. Thiselton, *The First Epistle to the Corinthians: A Commentary on the Greek Text* (Grand Rapids: Eerdmans, 2000), p. 566.

32. Thiselton, *Corinthians*, p. 581.

love to the true and truly eternal God that, although it is not coeternal with him, yet it does not separate itself from him, and does not flow away into any mutation of change or process but abides in true contemplation of him alone?'[33]

Augustine's formulation can receive only a qualified endorsement. The *Confessions*, as we have noted, are dominated by the existential crisis precipitated by a world that is always slipping through our fingers towards death and dissolution. The stability and solidity of the so-called 'eternal state' stand in deliberate contrast to the parlous world in which we now dwell. This accords well with certain aspects of John's apocalyptic vision. In contrast to the fits and starts of earthly worship, the heavenly creatures never cease to praise God day and night (4:8, though even here we note the presence of earthly time indicators 'day' and 'night'). Temporal boundaries appear to be obliterated at the end of chapter 5, when John in his visionary state witnesses 'all creation which is in heaven and on the earth and under the earth and on the sea and all the things in them' worshipping the One who sits on the throne and the Lamb (5:13, my translation). The climactic vision of the New Jerusalem lays great stress on the ills that 'will no longer be': death, mourning, crying out and grief are all no more, because the 'first things have passed away' (21:4, my translation). The chief timekeepers of the current world order appear to be relieved of their duties: 'And the city has no need of sun or moon to shine upon it, for the glory of God is its light, and its lamp is the Lamb' (21:23).[34] The notion of *rest* predominates (cf. 14:13 and the promised Sabbath rest of Heb. 4:9).

But ascribing divine eternity to even redeemed creatures raises numerous questions. One can only with great difficulty grope towards a sense of how God abides in eternity, especially if one describes that in terms of 'timelessness'—how is it possible for an entity created in time to mirror that experience of absolute life? Even if a person were to persist perpetually

---

33. Augustine, *Conf.* 12.15; cf. Augustine, *Conf.* 12.13, which implies that our coming knowledge of God mirrors his eternity: 'Thus, for the time being I understand that "heaven of heavens" to mean the intelligible heaven, where to understand is to know all at once—not "in part," not "darkly," not "through a glass"—but as a simultaneous whole, in full sight, "face to face." It is not this thing now and then another thing, but (as we said) knowledge all at once without any temporal change.' See discussion in Matthew Lamb, 'Eternity Creates and Redeems Time: A Key to Augustine's Confessions within a Theology of History', in *Divine Creation in Ancient, Medieval, and Early Modern Thought: Essays Presented to the Rev'd Dr Robert D. Crouse* (ed. Michael Treschow et al.; Leiden: Brill, 2007), pp. 117–40, p. 136.

34. One piece of apparent evidence which should be dismissed is the conclusion of Rev. 10:6, sometimes translated 'time (*chronos*) will be no more'. This should almost certainly be rendered 'there will be delay no longer'; see e.g. G. K. Beale, *The Book of Revelation: A Commentary on the Greek Text* (Grand Rapids: Eerdmans, 1999), p. 539.

from the moment of their birth, there is still the bottomless deficit of its prior state of non-being. 'Eternity minus *x*' is no longer eternity. Augustine perceptively links human memory and eternity, but surveying the temporal spectrum of the past is qualitatively different from God's *totum simul.* There is also the related pastoral issue of how we could experience non-durational life (assuming that is even a coherent concept) as a blessing rather than a curse. Revelation does emphasize the *resting* of the saints in the New Jerusalem, and this was no doubt a comforting word to the beleaguered churches of Asia Minor; but it never commits to a strict view of timelessness. The more dynamic and philosophically defensible idea of continual progress put forward by Origen and Gregory expands upon the vision of the Apocalypse, but in such a way as to organically develop Revelation's seeds of hope.[35]

35. See below, chapter 6.

5

Where Are We?

The question of God and time brings with it the question of God and space. If the question 'When did God create?' is not the best way of putting things, the question 'Where did God create?' seems patently absurd. Do we imagine he could have made it 'a little bit to the left' or 'slightly higher up'? The universe simply is where it is. Need anything more be said?

In fact more does need to be said, because we still must face the issue of where the creation stands *with respect to God*. Does God need to 'open up' a space within himself for the creation in a kind of *kenosis*? Is he confronted with anything antecedent to creation—a *nihil* to be filled, or a chaos to be subdued? Is it proper to say the creation is *in* God? Is God by contrast *in* creation? Or ought those two things in fact to be seen in contrast at all? Does God live in 'heaven' or 'paradise' in a way that he does not (at least at present) live on earth? The range of questions is vast, and we will address them as best we can in the limited space available.

Nature and Grace

It is difficult to know where to place the obviously relevant question of nature and grace, a duality which has shaped much of the theological tradition. While these abstract terms might be seen as modes of divine operation, we begin with a very brief note here because they seem to resolve into two putative *spheres* of divine operation: God is at work *here*, but not *there*; or both here and there, but in different ways. The decision then becomes how to demarcate these spheres, and how to decide what goes into which.

But it is precisely from this tendency to think in terms of two spheres that mischief arises. Nature and grace are mismatched terms. It is more helpful to think of one 'sphere', namely created reality. 'Nature' seems a perfectly adequate label to place on created reality. We would then have one place of divine operation. One may then wish to distinguish differing modes of divine operation: the quiet work of sustaining things in their 'natural' course, and the noisier work of intervening in created reality in novel ways.

Kenosis?

In recent years, there has been a trend towards viewing creation as an act of kenosis, or self-emptying, on the part of God.[1] One might say that God *withdraws* a part of himself to make room for the created order, or that he opens up room *within* himself for the creation. One might speak more generally of the presence of the Other (particularly when the consummate Other is recalcitrant humanity) as a remarkable intrusion into the divine serenity, and one that thus entails some degree of suffering on the part of the Creator. There is surely something to be said for this line of thinking. The idea of withdrawal, of making room, can be taken as a colourful way of saying that God allows the creation to be itself. In the same way, Moltmann's description of God as our *living space* is a charming image of our intimate connection with God. We are not simply a part of God's family; we dwell in his house. We are not left outside.

While all this is true, one must still ask whether the designation *kenosis* is of the most preferable. Certainly this is not the Scripture's habitual way of speaking. Creation is typically seen as the supreme demonstration of God's power. If spatial metaphors are to be invoked, the tradition thinks of creation as a *going out*, an act of effulgence rather than a withdrawal. This ex-pressive power is captured best in Psalm 104:1–4:

> O Lord my God, thou art very great!
> Thou art clothed with honor and majesty,
> who coverest thyself with light as with a garment,
> who hast stretched out the heavens like a tent,
> who hast laid the beams of thy chambers on the waters,
> who makest the clouds thy chariot,
> who ridest on the wings of the wind,
> who makest the winds thy messengers,
> fire and flame thy ministers.

The light of verse 2 appears to be the mode in which God goes out from himself to create the world (and to this extent may have been taken as a token of Christ's role in creation), and equally the luminous expression of his power that can unfurl the heavens and call into being the fiery angels.

We can also ask whether the spatial metaphor implicit in kenosis is being worked too hard. This is an unhappy situation in at least two respects. First, it intrudes a fairly strong idea of space, and restricted space at that,

---

1. This is perhaps most closely associated with Moltmann, though see the array of thinkers in *The Work of Love: Creation as Kenosis* (ed. J. C. Polkinghorne; Grand Rapids: Eerdmans, 2001).

into the being of God. We may ask whether it is helpful to even speak of space within God at all; but if we do, could we not imagine God as constitutionally roomy, with more than enough space to accommodate any creation he likes? Must he diminish himself in some way to create space? Second, the idea of kenosis may be coupled with the Newtonian sense of space as a monumental container into which things are then put. Does it work when one sees the universe within the framework of space-time, the dynamic system occasioned by the mutual interpenetration of matter and energy?

Finally, the invocation of the cross and the kenosis of Christ is problematic. There is a paradoxical glory to the crucifixion and humiliation of Jesus, nowhere more evident than in John 12 and the 'lifting up' of Jesus.[2] This is the pathway to new creation torn open by the willed act of Jesus. But as we have intimated earlier, the cross may be viewed as the ultimate act of de-creation.[3] In it, the entire old world order is swallowed up in a purgative act that sets the stage for recreation.

Matter Arising: The Doctrine of *Creatio Ex Nihilo*

Because the doctrine of *creatio ex nihilo* stands at the threshold between the 'pre-creational' state and the emergence of everything else, we might equally treat it in our chapter on the process of creation. We have placed it here, in the broadly pre-creation section of the book, as a reminder that God is confronted with nothing in his act of creation. It is not simply the case that there is no matter there to be beaten into shape: there is no 'there' there in which matter might dwell. We say this not in the first instance from the perspective of modern science and the notion of the space-time continuum. It is rather a theological assertion predicated on the absolute uniqueness of the infinite God.

Since the Bible does not come out and say, 'God did not use pre-existent matter in creating the world', one can always make something of a case that the Bible does not teach *creatio ex nihilo*. Nor can it be said definitively that the Hebrew verb *bara'* or the words 'In the beginning God created the heavens and the earth' can only refer to creation out of nothing. At the same time, there is nothing to preclude such a reading. 'In the beginning God created the heavens and the earth' is a pretty laconic introduction, and no amount of form- or redaction-critical insights, or comparisons with ancient mythology, can demonstrate that matter must have been lying to

2. See Richard Bauckham, *Jesus and the God of Israel: God Crucified and Other Studies on the New Testament's Christology of Divine Identity* (Grand Rapids: Eerdmans, 2009), pp. 33–37.

3. See chapter 8 below.

God's hand. The Ancient Near Eastern backgrounds can take us only so far: the Genesis text departs from the parallel texts in all sorts of other ways, so why not in this one as well? The tradition of the church has generally been that *creatio ex nihilo* is at the very least a reasonable extrapolation from the text of Genesis, and there is no good reason to disagree with the consensus.

The emergence of the doctrine proper is riddled with the same ambiguity; everything depends on what criteria one wishes to employ to discern the presence of *creatio ex nihilo*. Using fairly stringent criteria, Gerhard May puts the formation of the doctrine in second-century Christian disputes with Gnosticism.[4] J. C. O'Neill by contrast argues for the early emergence of the doctrine, citing texts like *2 Maccabees* 7:28: 'I beseech you, my child, to look at the heaven and the earth and see everything that is in them, and recognize that God did not make them out of things that existed. Thus also mankind comes into being.' Paul speaks in a similar fashion: in Romans 4:17 he describes God as the one who 'gives life to the dead and calls into existence the things that do not exist', and in 1 Corinthians 1:28 he declares that God chose 'things that are not, to bring to nothing things that are'.[5] Greeks had been debating at least since the writing of the *Timaeus* whether the world had a true beginning or not, so one could argue that the statements in Maccabees and Paul are the first Jewish-Christian stirrings of the affirmation that the world did have an absolute beginning. But the texts are terse enough to permit alternative explanations: they could refer to the fact that unshaped stuff remains 'nothing' until God fashions it into a given object. To take an everyday example, a given human being is 'nothing' until they are conceived, but the stuff from which this person will be made is already abroad in the world. On balance, I lean towards O'Neill's account; and if nothing else, we cannot assume that Paul or the author of Maccabees must have believed in eternally pre-existent matter.

Given the uncertainty of its origins, and its debatable biblical warrant, one might wonder why *creatio ex nihilo* has had such a privileged place in Christian teaching on creation. The key lies in how this teaching reinforces other doctrines. As May points out, the 'driving motive which underlies the Christian doctrine of *creatio ex nihilo* is the attempt to do justice to the absolute sovereignty and unlimited freedom of the biblical God acting in history'.[6] We see this illustrated throughout the early church.

Tertullian gives a very thorough defence of *creatio ex nihilo* in his *Against Hermogenes*. He first denies that God made the world from his

4. Gerhard May, *Creatio ex Nihilo* (trans. A. S. Worrall; London: T&T Clark, 2004).

5. While the reference in 1 Corinthians is probably to the status of the Corinthian believers—the 'nothings' of Roman society—an allusion to the creation seems likely in light of the parallels with Romans and *2 Maccabees*.

6. May, *Creatio ex Nihilo*, p. viii.

own substance, since he is indissoluble (*Herm.* 2). Positing eternal matter just makes matters worse: now we would have two gods, since eternity is a necessarily divine property (4). In fact, by Hermogenes' own logic—and despite his protestations that matter is eternal but inferior to God—matter proves itself superior to God:

> Nay more, he even prefers Matter to God, and rather subjects God to it, when he will have it that God made all things out of Matter. For if He drew His resources from it for the creation of the world, Matter is already found to be the superior, inasmuch as it furnished Him with the means of effecting His works; and God is thereby clearly subjected to Matter, of which the substance was indispensable to Him. For there is no one but requires that which he makes use of; no one but is subject to the thing which he requires, for the very purpose of being able to make use of it (8).

On the positive side, Tertullian argues that God's uniqueness demands creation from nothing:

> This rule is required by the nature of the One-only God, who is One-only in no other way than as the sole God; and in no other way sole, than as having nothing else (co-existent) with Him. So also He will be first, because all things are after Him; and all things are after Him, because all things are by Him; and all things are by Him, because they are of nothing: so that reason coincides with the Scripture, which says: 'Who hath known the mind of the Lord? or who hath been His counsellor? or with whom took He counsel? or who hath shown to Him the way of wisdom and knowledge? Who hath first given to Him, and it shall be recompensed to him again?' Surely none! Because there was present with Him no power, no material, no nature which belonged to any other than Himself (17).

If we want to talk about anything being 'with God' before the creation, we can only speak of his own wisdom: 'Of this He made all things, making them through It, and making them with It' (18). Tertullian identifies this Wisdom with the Spirit, and makes ample use of Proverbs 8 in this regard; he goes on to associate the wisdom of God with his Word (operating in the capacity of Wisdom), thus giving a fully Trinitarian expression of the act of creation.

Tertullian may seem to wander close to the edge of orthodoxy here, since the unwary reader might imagine that God's wisdom is somehow an instrument in the same way pre-existent matter is supposed to be: a malleable substance subsequently shaped into a cosmos.[7] But this is merely a

7. Irenaeus runs into a similar problem when he speaks of God drawing matter 'from himself' in *Haer.* 2.30.9. As with Tertullian, the context indicates that Irenaeus is talking about the ultimate origin of matter, and does not mean to suggest it is somehow

function of the rhetoric: Tertullian is essentially saying, 'If we want to speak about God "using" anything in the act of creation, he only needs to "use" his own Wisdom—he doesn't need anything else at all.' As he clarifies later (20): 'For it was in Wisdom that He made all things at first, because by meditating and arranging His plans therein, He had in fact already done (the work of creation).' The structure is analogous to that of Irenaeus: God alone makes the world, through his Son and Spirit. As for the substance *from which* God makes the world, it is conspicuous in Genesis by its absence:

> Now, since we have here clearly told us who the Maker was, that is, God, and what He made, even all things, and through whom He made them, even His Word, would not the order of the narrative have required that the source out of which all things were made by God through the Word should likewise be declared, if they had been in fact made out of anything? What, therefore, did not exist, the Scripture was unable to mention; and by not mentioning it, it has given us a clear proof that there was no such thing: for if there had been, the Scripture would have mentioned it (20).

Such an argument from silence has its problems, as Tertullian acknowledges in the ensuing chapter. But if nothing else, he is reinforcing the point made above that Genesis 1 does not *demand* pre-existing matter.

Of particular interest to us is Tertullian's move to ground *creatio ex nihilo* in eschatology. He argues that in the end God 'will bring back all things to nothing' (34). He cites a litany of what we will later term 'de-creation' texts, including Revelation 21:1, 'the first heaven and the first earth had passed away'; and Psalm 102:25–26: 'Of old thou didst lay the foundation of the earth, and the heavens are the work of thy hands. They will perish, but thou dost endure; they will all wear out like a garment. Thou changest them like raiment, and they pass away.' The fact that God is willing to reduce the world to nothing shows that it arose from nothing in the first place: 'I return therefore to the principle which defines that all things which have come from nothing shall return at last to nothing. For God would not have made any perishable thing out of what was eternal, that is to say, out of Matter' (34).

Gregory of Nyssa affirms the doctrine of *creatio ex nihilo*, not least because of the incommensurability of the eternal, invisible God and the ever-changing nature of the creation. But he acknowledges the difficulties in accounting for how the material creation could emerge from the immaterial God:

> What method is there for the production of matter from the immaterial, or of the nature that has dimensions from that which is unextended? for if these

part of God; see Paul M. Blowers, *Drama of the Divine Economy: Creator and Creation in Early Christian Theology and Piety* (Oxford: OUP, 2012), p. 179.

> things are believed to have their existence from that source, they clearly come into existence after being in Him in some mysterious way; but if material existence was in Him, how can He be immaterial while including matter in Himself? and similarly with all the other marks by which the material nature is differentiated; if quantity exists in God, how is God without quantity? if the compound nature exists in Him, how is He simple, without parts and without combination? so that the argument forces us to think either that He is material, because matter has its existence from Him as a source; or, if one avoids this, it is necessary to suppose that matter was imported by Him *ab extra* for the making of the universe.[8]

Gregory's solution to the dilemma in the *De Hominis Opificio* and his *Hexaemeron* is extremely subtle and has occasioned much debate.[9] He appears to put forward a radical idealism, wherein material objects are taken to be concatenations of intelligible qualities such as colour, weight, resistance, and so on:[10]

> By his wise and powerful will, being capable of everything, he established for the creation of things all the things through which matter is constituted: light, heavy, dense, rare, soft, resistant, fluid, dry, cold, hot, colour, shape, outline, extension. All of these are in themselves thoughts and bare concepts; none is matter on its own. But when they combine, they turn into matter.[11]

Since God is an intelligible being himself, Gregory reasons, there is therefore no problem in imagining that objects in the world *understood as concatenations of ideas* 'have their existence from the incorporeal nature, the intellectual nature on the one hand giving being to the intellectual potentialities, and the mutual concurrence of these bringing to its genesis the material nature.'[12]

8. Gregory of Nyssa, *De Hom. Opif.* 23.3.

9. For a helpful summary, see Blowers, *Drama*, pp. 179–80; cf. Richard Sorabji, *Time, Creation and the Continuum: Theories in Antiquity and the Early Middle Ages* (London: Duckworth, 1983), pp. 287–94.

10. This brings Gregory very close to the radical idealism later adopted by Berkeley, though he does not spell things out in nearly as much detail as Berkeley was to do. See Sorabji, *Time*, pp. 290–94.

11. Gregory of Nyssa, *Hex.* (PG 44:69c ff.), trans. in Sorabji, *Time*, p. 290. Cf. Gregory of Nyssa, *De Hom. Opif.* 24.2: 'If, then, colour is a thing intelligible, and resistance also is intelligible, and so with quantity and the rest of the like properties, while if each of these should be withdrawn from the substratum, the whole idea of the body is dissolved; it would seem to follow that we may suppose the concurrence of those things, the absence of which we found to be a cause of the dissolution of the body, to produce the material nature: for as that is not a body which has not colour, and figure, and resistance, and extension, and weight, and the other properties, while each of these in its proper existence is found to be not the body but something else besides the body, so, conversely, whenever the specified attributes concur they produce bodily existence.'

12. Gregory of Nyssa, *De Hom. Opif.* 24.2.

This is an ingenious approach to the problem, but one wonders if it really arrives at a solution. Taking a cue from Samuel Johnson's response to Berkeley, we might ask whether 'idea' and 'object' can be collapsed into one another so neatly: the word 'idea' is useful precisely for things in our mind that do not have size or colour or weight (except metaphorically); objects in the world are those things we can strike against or measure or see. There is also the theological cost to be reckoned: if creation consists at a minimum in having something other than God around, how does a world of conglomerated divine ideas count as 'creation'? Is it not simply God by another name, or in a different guise? We seem to be moving back towards some sort of emanationism. It is a cousin to the notion of the divine energy or *élan vital* which differentiates itself into a world order ultimately indistinguishable from the divinity.

Augustine gives as concise an expression of the doctrine as one could hope for in *De Vera Religione* 35–36: 'From what did he make them [all things]? From nothing (*ex nihilo*) . . . Therefore, if the world was made out of some unformed matter, that matter was made out of absolutely nothing (*omnino de nihilo*).'[13] He elaborates on this in *Confessions* 13.33:

> For [thy works] were made from nothing by thee, and not from thyself, and not from any matter that is not thine, or that was created beforehand. They were created from concreated matter—that is, matter that was created by thee at the same time that thou didst form its formlessness, without any interval of time. Yet, since the matter of heaven and earth is one thing and the form of heaven and earth is another thing, thou didst create matter out of absolutely nothing (*de omnino nihilo*), but the form of the world thou didst form from formless matter (*de informi materia*). But both were done at the same time, so that form followed matter with no delaying interval.[14]

13. Augustine, *Ver. Rel.* 35–36; see Carol Harrison, *Beauty and Revelation in the Thought of Saint Augustine* (Oxford: OUP, 1992), p. 41.

14. See C. Harrison, *Beauty*, p. 99. Augustine contrasts God with human craftsmen in *Conf.* 11.5: 'But how didst thou make the heaven and the earth, and what was the tool of such a mighty work as thine? For it was not like a human worker fashioning body from body, according to the fancy of his mind, able somehow or other to impose on it a form which the mind perceived in itself by its inner eye (yet how should even he be able to do this, if thou hadst not made that mind?). He imposes the form on something already existing and having some sort of being, such as clay, or stone or wood or gold or such like (and where would these things come from if thou hadst not furnished them?). For thou madest his body for the artisan, and thou madest the mind which directs the limbs; thou madest the matter from which he makes anything; thou didst create the capacity by which he understands his art and sees within his mind what he may do with the things before him; thou gavest him his bodily sense by which, as if he had an interpreter, he may communicate from mind to matter what he proposes to do

Creation from nothing had an obvious appeal to Augustine as he sought to extricate himself from the errors of the Manichaeans. The fact that God was not stuck with bad materials meant that Augustine could affirm the goodness of creation, while the fact that the creation was *not God* allowed one to make sense of the vicissitudes of life and reserve the utmost praise for God alone:

> So, too, all things that God has made are very good, but they are not good in the same way that God is good, because he is their maker, while they are made. Nor did he give birth to them out of himself so that they are what he is; rather he made them out of nothing so that they are equal neither to him by whom they have been made nor to his Son through whom they have been made.[15]

Aquinas addresses the matter of *creatio ex nihilo* thus:

> We must consider not only the emanation of a particular being from a particular agent, but also the emanation of all being from the universal cause, which is God; and this emanation we designate by the name of creation. Now what proceeds by particular emanation, is not presupposed to that emanation; as when a man is generated, he was not before, but man is made from 'not-man,' and white from 'not-white.' Hence if the emanation of the whole universal being from the first principle be considered, it is impossible that any being should be presupposed before this emanation. For nothing is the same as no being. Therefore as the generation of a man is from the 'not-being' which is 'not-man,' so creation, which is the emanation of all being, is from the 'not-being' which is 'nothing' (*ST* 1.45.1).

Aquinas' use of the term 'emanation' need not imply that the creation is somehow an extension of God, materially tied into the divine essence. Like his predecessors, Thomas is speaking of the ultimate origin of all things, and he avails himself of the language to hand to express that truth.

While the arrival of modern science posed a serious challenge to the six-day creation in the relatively recent past, *creatio ex nihilo* has fared rather better. Some of this is due to the popularity of the Big Bang Theory, which made the idea of a beginning to the universe seem more scientifically plausible. Whether the theory provides more than psychological support for *creatio ex nihilo* is another matter: given a zero-point for the present universe, there is still the question of whether there was some stuff lying about from a prior universe. If nothing else, however, the Big Bang Theory, coupled with ever-increasing insights into the curious nature of 'matter', does get us away

---

and report back to his mind what has been done, that the mind may consult with the Truth which presideth over it as to whether what is done is well done.'

15. Augustine, *Gen. Man.* 1.2, p. 51.

from the notion that God would require a cosmos-size basket of material which he could then pound into the proper shape.

We can therefore find Barth still affirming *creatio ex nihilo* in the presence of modern scientific understanding and critical analysis of Genesis.[16] It is true that his subsequent discussion of 'nothingness' has some unusual features, which we will attend to later.[17] Nonetheless, his discussion is predicated upon the utter uniqueness of God, who faces nothing prior to his act of creation but his own will.

The usefulness of the doctrine of *creatio ex nihilo* may be viewed from several different angles. From the perspective of honour and shame, which was of immense importance in the ancient world, eternal matter could be deemed a raw threat to God's unique glory. Arguments for God's existence based on causality, such as those of Duns Scotus, would be drained of their force if an uncaused reality, matter, existed alongside God. God is thus reduced to the status of 'co-creator', one member of a cosmic partnership. The fact that in many versions of this theology matter is an uncooperative element prone to gumming up the works only makes matters worse: the putatively almighty craftsman God is in fact saddled with second-rate materials that constantly frustrate his purposes.

If on the other hand matter or the world does not exist eternally on its own, one might still argue that the world somehow emanates from God's very being. This eliminates the anxiety surrounding the question of how the infinite God contacts the finite cosmos. It also provides on the surface a plausible rationale for the presence of evil or imperfection in the world: as the divine essence diffuses outward, it naturally becomes attenuated—rather like a lump of dough that starts to develop holes after it is stretched too thin, or a fragrance that becomes less and less perceptible the further it is from the source.

It is easy to see, however, that this strategy holds no prospect of success, and thus *creatio ex nihilo* remains a necessary teaching. As a theodicy emanationism has a remarkably short shelf life: the initial attractiveness of the 'attenuated divine essence' quickly wilts under the question: what sort of God would be subject to this sort of diminution? The doctrine of divine simplicity may be subject to misunderstanding, but it proves its utility here: God cannot be broken up into bits, with some of him over here, and some of him over there; he does not exist in a state of disorganization or disrepair. He must be *whole*, and thus in some sense he must stand over and against the world, even as in other respects he can stand with, and even via the incarnation in, the world. If, then, there must be a gap between God and

16. See e.g. Karl Barth, *Church Dogmatics* (4 vols; Edinburgh: T&T Clark, 1956–75), III/1, p. 4.

17. For a summary, see Matthew Rose, *Ethics in Barth: God, Metaphysics and Morals* (Farnham: Ashgate, 2010), pp. 177–80.

the world, and the world (even in some inchoate state) cannot be simply posited as existing 'out there' apart from God, waiting for his creative word, one logical alternative is *creatio ex nihilo*.[18]

In or Out?

Nothing, then, is there before God creates it. But having created the world, where does God stand with respect to it? Is he 'inside' or 'outside' the creation? If we are to answer these questions, it is crucial to consider first the linguistic and theological use of prepositions in general. Prepositions may be likened to the rivets of language. Though small in themselves, they do important work maintaining structures of thought. But they can also bear only so much stress. One fundamental limitation is that prepositions inevitably carry within themselves some sort of spatial or temporal connotation. This is not much of a problem when you are thinking something *up* or looking *into* an issue. But when you try to solve major theological issues by means of prepositions, the strain begins to show.

This is glaringly evident in the case of the relationship of God and the creation. There may be problems with Neoplatonically tinged descriptions of God as 'beyond Being'—but this at least has the merit of reminding us that God is not simply one more item on the cosmic inventory list. He is in this sense at least 'outside' the cosmos. But even thinking of God being 'outside' the cosmos tends to put us in the position of a (further) outside observer looking at the bounded cosmos over here, and God over there. No wonder that Aristotle resorted to paradoxical language when discussing the heavenly realm: it is a place that is no place, *atopos*: 'It is obvious that there is neither place nor void nor time outside the heaven, since it has been demonstrated that there neither is nor can be body there.'[19] It does not matter if we talk about inside or outside—there is theological danger on every side. We must

---

18. The doctrine also had far-reaching effects on the notion of the soul's relationship to God. In Plato and (probably) Origen, the soul was deemed pre-existent and thus had a kind of natural connection to deity. Once the absolute ontological gap between God and everything else is recognized, the hope of encountering God solely by an act of contemplation was erased. This in turn helped precipitate the Arian crisis, since Christ (it would seem) had to be placed on one side or the other of the gap—he could not sit mid-way between the world of being and the world of becoming. On this, see esp. Andrew Louth, *The Origins of the Christian Mystical Tradition from Plato to Denys* (Oxford: Clarendon, 1981), pp. 75ff. One may debate whether pre-Nicene Christians uniformly saw the Logos as an 'intermediate zone' (Louth's terminology)—John himself, for instance, does not regard the *logos* that way in his gospel—but the development of *creatio ex nihilo* did raise the stakes for how one articulated Christology.

19. Aristotle, *Cael.* 279a17.

guard ourselves, then, against pressing the full weight of the relationship between God and the world down onto these unfortunate prepositions. We cannot avoid using them, but we must recognize that the prepositions serve as place-holders for extremely subtle questions of relationship that are inevitably going to contain elements of contiguity and discontinguity.

The problem was addressed at least obliquely by an ancient and widespread Christian formula: 'He contains all things, but He Himself can be contained by no one.'[20] The origins of the saying go at least as far back as Philo: 'For not even the whole universe would be a place fit for God to make his abode, since God is his own place, and He is filled by Himself, and sufficient for Himself, filling and containing all other things in their destitution and barrenness and emptiness, but Himself contained by nothing else, seeing that He is Himself One and the Whole.'[21] Philo himself was probably indebted to previous philosophers for the containing/uncontained motif, and it may ultimately derive from Aristotle's notion that God is the 'place' of all things.[22] Whatever its origin, the saying proved extremely popular. It appears not only in writers like Irenaeus and the Shepherd of Hermas, but also in iconography, like the mosaic of Mary in the Chora Church in Istanbul which describes her as the 'Container of the Uncontainable'.[23] Augustine takes the motif as his point of departure for the *Confessions*:

> Since, then, thou dost fill the heaven and earth, do they contain thee? Or, dost thou fill and overflow them, because they cannot contain thee? And where dost thou pour out what remains of thee after heaven and earth are full? Or, indeed, is there no need that thou, who dost contain all things, shouldst be contained by any, since those things which thou dost fill thou fillest by containing them? For the vessels which thou dost fill do not confine thee, since even if they were broken, thou wouldst not be poured out. And, when thou art poured out on us, thou art not thereby brought down; rather, we are uplifted. Thou art not scattered; rather, thou dost gather us together. But when thou dost fill all things, dost thou fill them with thy whole being? Or, since not even all things together could contain thee altogether, does any one thing contain a single part, and do all things contain that same part at the same time? Do singulars contain thee

20. Irenaeus, *Haer*. 2.30.9; compare the nearly verbatim parallel in Shepherd of Hermas, *Mand*. 1:1: 'containing all things, but he alone is uncontained.'

21. See discussion in Ronald Williamson, *Philo and the Epistle to the Hebrews* (Leiden: Brill, 1970), p. 217, who also notes the motif is present in Philo, *Migr*. 1.31, *Sobr*. 63, *Somn*. 1.185. Philo uses the verb *periechō* rather than *chorō* in Shepherd of Hermas, but the thought is the same.

22. See e.g. Sextus Empiricus, *Math*. 10.33, in Ute Possekel, *Evidence of Greek Philosophical Concepts in the Writings of Ephrem the Syrian* (Louvain: Peeters, 1999), p. 141.

23. Gk. *hē chōra tou achōretou*; note that in the same church Christ is described as 'the place of the living', *hē chōra tōn zōntōn*.

> singly? Do greater things contain more of thee, and smaller things less? Or, is it not rather that thou art wholly present everywhere, yet in such a way that nothing contains thee wholly? (1.3)

The presence of Philo as the proximate origin for the saying may raise suspicions that this is yet another unwelcome intrusion of Greek philosophy into biblical faith. But the Scriptures themselves wrestle in very similar fashion with the dilemma of how to speak of God and the space of the world. Isaiah is well aware of the paradox that God is simultaneously exalted above all things, and near to even the lowliest of his people: 'For thus says the high and lofty One who inhabits eternity, whose name is Holy: "I dwell in the high and holy place, and also with him who is of a contrite and humble spirit, to revive the spirit of the humble, and to revive the heart of the contrite"' (Isa. 57:15).[24] Job experiences this first hand: God comes in the terror of a storm-theophany and uses the immensity and complexity of the cosmos to silence him. If Job cannot understand or control the created order, how can he presume to judge the Creator of all?

Ezekiel 1 offers especially vivid insights, at multiple levels. As William Brownlee has noted, the theophany in Ezekiel 1 portrays the cosmos in miniature, with the sovereign Lord seated above the dome of the world.[25] The key to recognizing this is the presence of the Hebrew word *raqiach* or 'firmament' in verse 22 (cf. v. 26): 'Over the heads of the living creatures there was the likeness of a firmament, shining like crystal, spread out above their heads.' With the *firmament* thus in place, the remainder of the vision makes more sense: the living creatures below the firmament would represent the animate creation, while the flashing lights and wheels within wheels presumably signify astronomical phenomena.

Equally pertinent is the description of the Lord himself. That his throne sits upon the cosmic dome is already a sign of his exaltation above all visible realms. But the description of his appearance hints at an even greater transcendence (Ezek. 1:28): 'Such was the appearance of the likeness of the glory of the LORD.' The three qualifiers—Ezekiel sees only the *appearance* of the *likeness* of the *glory* of the Lord—suggest that even God's radiant manifestation in the heavenly places does not capture his infinite splendour. We thus have a picture of the truth espoused by Solomon in 1 Kings 8:27: 'But will God indeed dwell on the earth? Behold, heaven and the highest heaven cannot contain thee; how much less this house which I have built!'

---

24. Compare the equally well-known verse in Isa. 55:8–9: 'For my thoughts are not your thoughts, neither are your ways my ways, says the LORD. For as the heavens are higher than the earth, so are my ways higher than your ways and my thoughts than your thoughts.'

25. See William Brownlee, *Ezekiel 1–19* (Waco, TX: Word, 1986), pp. 27ff.

Yet this utterly transcendent God is with his people. The appearance of God's glory by the river Chebar is remarkable, in that it defies Ancient Near Eastern conventions that a deity's power would be restricted to its home country, and it might defy Ezekiel's priestly expectation that the glory of God would properly manifest itself in the temple—the temple whence the glory had already fled before the Babylonian invasion. That God should come to earth at all is condescension enough; that he should return to his disgraced people in the midst of their exile is yet more stunning. It also augurs well for Israel's future. Ezekiel's vision of the world-creating and world-ruling God in chapter 1 is matched by his vision of the world-renewing God of chapters 37–48, who settles into his world and spreads the life-giving waters of his Spirit to revive the face of the land.[26]

Ezekiel's imagery, strange as it may seem, is perhaps the best way to gesture towards the uncapture-able truth that God is both 'inside' and 'outside' the world, and that the world is both 'inside' and 'outside' God. To put it another way: we do not want to say that the world is a part of God, but nor do we want to say that the world is apart from God. As Augustine says in a slightly different context: 'Therefore He governs all things in such a manner as to allow them to perform and exercise their own proper movements. For although they can be nothing without Him, they are not what He is.'[27] Aquinas likewise argues that the same God who infinitely surpasses all else is at the same time in the closest contact with created entities as the source of their being:

> Now since God is very being by His own essence, created being must be His proper effect; as to ignite is the proper effect of fire. Now God causes this effect in things not only when they first begin to be, but as long as they are preserved in being; as light is caused in the air by the sun as long as the air remains illuminated. Therefore as long as a thing has being, God must be present to it, according to its mode of being. But being is innermost in each thing and most fundamentally inherent in all things since it is formal in respect of everything found in a thing, as was shown above. Hence it must be that God is in all things, and innermostly . . . God is above all things by the excellence of His nature; nevertheless, He is in all things as the cause of the being of all things.[28]

26. Jesus seems to take the river flowing from the temple in Ezek. 47 as a reference to the eschatological gift of the Spirit; see John 7:37–39. Rev. 22:1 may likewise allude to the Spirit via Ezek. 47, see e.g. G. K. Beale, *The Book of Revelation: A Commentary on the Greek Text* (Grand Rapids: Eerdmans, 1999), pp. 1103–6.

27. Augustine, *Civ*. 7.30, cited in Étienne Gilson, *The Christian Philosophy of Saint Augustine* (trans. L. E. M. Lynch; New York: Random House, 1960), p. 238.

28. Aquinas, *ST* 1.8.1. This passage is crucial to the shape of David Burrell's argument on the nature of creation in *Freedom and Creation in Three Traditions* (Notre Dame: University of Notre Dame Press, 1993).

To those who object that God cannot be everywhere, Thomas first cites Jeremiah 23:24, 'I fill heaven and earth', and goes on to demonstrate that God is 'in' all things not as if he were a body somehow conjoined or mingled with other bodies, but rather in the sense that he touches them with his power. Thus he approves of the tradition that 'God by a common mode is in all things by His presence, power and substance.'[29] It may be also said that all things are 'in God', in that they exist through the divine power, and the *ideas* of things are in God (*ST* 1.18.4).[30]

Heaven and Earth

Ezekiel's vision can also serve as a launching-off point for a discussion of the biblical view of the *arrangement* of the cosmos. Throughout the Bible the phrase 'heaven and earth' typically articulates two dimensions of *one created reality*.[31] This derives in part from the tendency to conflate the visible heavens and the idea of 'heaven' as God's dwelling place. Ancient Near Eastern cosmologies could describe the sky as a great cosmic dome whereon the starry deities gathered, and this probably forms part of the conceptual apparatus for the biblical depiction of God surrounded by his heavenly host. This need not be taken with crude literalism, any more than we must believe that the Egyptian artist who depicted the goddess Nut overarching the world thought that the sky was in fact a huge, anatomically correct (super-)human. Locating God amidst the beautifully ordered celestial brightness was a way of speaking about his supreme glory—a glory which was nonetheless in meaningful contact with even terrestrial realities. One might occasionally speak of the *huperouranos*, the 'above heaven', to indicate God's transcendent being, but typically 'heaven' does double duty for the visible heavens and the invisible place of God's presence.[32]

---

29. See Aquinas, *ST* 1.8.2–3.

30. Aquinas draws close here to the concept of the *logos* and the *logoi* in Maximus the Confessor. Thomas appears to move in this direction in order to make sense of John 1:3–4 (quoted in *ST* 1.18.4): 'What was made, in Him was life.' The punctuation and interpretation of the verses in John are notoriously difficult.

31. See Jonathan T. Pennington, *Heaven and Earth in the Gospel of Matthew* (Grand Rapids: Baker, 2009).

32. Nor need we detain ourselves with how many 'levels' there were to the 'biblical' universe. One might speak with the *Apocalypse of Abraham* of seven levels of heaven (presumably the celestial spheres governed by the sun, the moon, and the five known planets) or with Paul of three levels (presumably the lower sky, the starry vault, and the above-heaven; though there are other possibilities; see Joel White, 'Paul's Cosmology: The Witness of Romans, 1 and 2 Corinthians, and Galatians', in *Cosmology and New Testament Theology* (ed. Jonathan T. Pennington and Sean M. McDonough; London: T&T Clark, 2008), pp. 90–106. This is not to mention the various regions ascribed to

We must also reckon here with the prophetic visions of God in heaven. Invitations to the heavenly courtroom might be rare, and transport there unusual, but such ecstasies are a consistent feature of the biblical landscape. In them, one sees a realm that blends features of eternity and time, divine and human, or whatever label we might wish to put on this essential duality. Thus we have the effulgence of the divine presence in the 'one seated on the throne' (Rev. 4) or 'the Ancient of Days' (Dan. 7) or the cosmic chariot-rider (Ezek. 1); the glorious heavenly host surrounding the throne; and the living creatures who *ceaselessly* chant the divine praise (Rev. 4). Time- and earth-bound humans are distinctly not at home in this place. But they are still able to be there in some fashion, and so the question arises in what manner a created being could dwell in an uncreated 'place', however briefly. Moreover, this heaven is clearly time-bound in its presentation: it shares architectural features with Ancient Near Eastern and Graeco-Roman imperial courts—an afternoon's stroll through the British Museum will be enough to demonstrate the links between the hybrid 'living creatures' of Revelation 4 and Ancient Near Eastern iconography.

One may either attempt to argue that the prophetic visions constitute a direct window into the nature of uncreated reality (at which point one must also ask why the appearance of these eternal living creatures *changes* from e.g. Isa. 6 to Rev. 4), or simply acknowledge that the visions depict a dimension of created reality wherein the divine, the angelic, and the human may intersect. Jürgen Moltmann has treated the matter with great care in *God in Creation*. He not only demonstrates the created nature of heaven; he also goes on to explain the theological rationale for this 'dual world':

> The point to remember in the context of belief in creation is that heaven is neither God nor is it divine; it is a part of the created world. But as part of the created world it has to be distinguished from the visible world; for it is only if we make this distinction that the visible world can be understood as a created world existing from God, and open for him who dwells in heaven. 'He who dwells in heaven' is the Creator who indwells his creation. The world-immanence of God therefore makes the world an eccentric world, and divides it into heaven and earth.[33]

---

the Underworld: Hades might be distinguished from Tartarus, as in the *Iliad*; one might speak with John in Revelation of the 'Abyss' below the world (probably a conflation of Hades/Tartarus/Sheol conceptions with the fallen angel-imprisoning floodwaters of Gen. 6); or one might grimly gesture towards the Underworld at large. The basic function of all these cosmological arrangements is pretty consistent: above us there is a realm of unimagined splendour where God dwells, and below us there is a strange and dread place that bespeaks the horrors of separation from the divine realm of light. We are caught in the middle, but destined for either the light or the darkness.

33. Jürgen Moltmann, *God in Creation: A New Theology of Creation and the Spirit of God* (Minneapolis: Fortress, 1993), pp. 158ff.

If God is to be *at home*, as it were, in his creation, he needs a place there—but it must be a distinctive, set apart place to indicate his ineffable otherness. Parallels to the tightly structured space of the temple should be evident.

Particularly important for our theology of creation is the notion that the future created order in some sense exists already in the heavenly realm. In the first-century AD (BC) *Apocalypse of Abraham*, Abraham views a kind of motion picture depicting events from primeval times to the final judgement. A strong predestinarianism governs the vision:

> And I said, 'Eternal, Mighty One! What is this picture of creation?' And he said to me, 'This is my will with regard to what is in the light and it was good before my face. And then, afterward, I gave them a command by my word and they came into existence. Whatever I had decreed was to exist had already been outlined in this and all the previously created (things) you have seen stood before me.'[34]

Abraham's cinematic tour of the world's destiny is a particularly vivid example of widespread Jewish and Christian teaching (with a likely assist from Platonism) that the creation unfolds precisely in accordance with God's plan. We will explore this in more detail when we consider the process by which God creates the world.

At times the future city may be depicted as an already-existing reality. The most famous example is the New Jerusalem in the latter chapters of Revelation, which comes 'down out of heaven from God, prepared as a bride adorned for her husband' (Rev. 21:2). This bears a strong resemblance to the appearance of the glorious Zion in the vision to Ezra in *4 Ezra* 9–10. To this might be added the vision of the Epistle to the Hebrews and its 'heavenly Jerusalem'[35] (12:18–23), the 'city with foundations' to which Abraham looked forward (Heb. 11:10).

One could take these visions in a fairly literal fashion, as the Montanists appear to have done in their assertion that the New Jerusalem was soon to descend onto the little towns of Pepuza and Tymion (left unexplained is how the 3,000-mile cubic city was supposed to fit in those two hamlets).[36] They are better understood as evocative images that speak economically to a very complex reality. On the one hand, one can hardly deny that there is some sort of 'predestinarian' element in the visions. It is not as if God is caught up in perpetual anxiety, wondering if the city of his dreams will ever be realized. The visions of the New or Heavenly Jerusalem speak to

34. *Apoc. Ab.* 22.

35. On Hebrews, see esp. Jon Laansma, 'The Cosmology of Hebrews', in *Cosmology and New Testament Theology* (ed. Pennington and McDonough), pp. 125–43.

36. For details, see William Tabernee, *Fake Prophecy and Polluted Sacraments: Ecclesiastical and Imperial Reactions to Montanism* (Leiden: Brill, 2007), pp. 115–18.

the certain hope God's people have of a permanent and peaceful dwelling place. Nor are the contours of this hope left up in the air: when Jerusalem (or its temple) is measured in Ezekiel, Zechariah, and Revelation, this seems to be an indication that God has a particular configuration in mind for the city, that he is working purposefully rather than haphazardly to bring his kingdom to bear on the world.

Is, then, the city of God a prefabricated urban megalith tossed down from heaven to crush the present creation to bits (cf. Dan. 2)?[37] A closer inspection shows that this is not the case. The city is, after all, still named Jerusalem, indicating some degree of continuity with the present world order. More pointedly, in Revelation the city's gates bear the names of the tribes of Israel, while the foundation stones bear the names of the twelve apostles of the Lamb (Rev. 21:12–14). Even if the primary intent here is to hint that the city represents the people of God,[38] the fact remains that the New Jerusalem is established in and through the work of people *in history*. It is not simply an alien entity descending from the sky: it is rather Augustine's 'pilgrim city',[39] now finding its resting place at last. Thus the New Jerusalem in some sense embeds within itself the historical experiences of the people of God.

If from one angle the New Jerusalem represents the restored people of God, it equally represents a renewed and enhanced Eden. The tree of life, the river in its midst, the ubiquitous gold—all evoke the creation narrative. The promise of paradise is realized. But where has the Garden gone from Genesis 3 to Revelation 21? What is the path from primal creation to new creation? The question is of sufficient weight to merit an involved discussion.

Is Eden out of Time and out of Space?

The book of Ezekiel centres on the departure of the Lord's glory from the land. But what is to be done when the land itself departs? This is the enigma of Eden. Not only have we left it; it has left us. We may begin with Milton, at the end of his epic *Paradise Lost*, and at the end of Adam and Eve's Eden:

> In either hand the hastening Angel caught
> Our Lingering Parents, and to the eastern gate
> Led them direct, and down the cliff as fast

37. Note that even in Dan. 2 the rock that strikes the statue *becomes* a great mountain (2:35), with no specification as to how long that process might take.

38. See R. Gundry, 'The New Jerusalem: People as Place, not Place for People', *NovT* 29.3 (1987): 254–64; but Richard Bauckham is better to say it is people *and* place *and* presence (*The Theology of the Book of Revelation* [Cambridge: CUP, 1993], pp. 132–43).

39. See e.g. Augustine, *Civ.* 19.17: 'The heavenly city, or rather the part of it which sojourns on earth and lives by faith.'

> To the subjected plain—then disappeared.
> They, looking back, all the eastern side beheld
> Of Paradise, so late their happy seat,
> Waved over by that flaming brand; the gate
> With dreadful faces thronged and firey arms.
> Some natural tears they dropped, but wiped them soon;
> The world was all before them, where to choose
> Their place of rest, and Providence their guide.
> They, hand in hand, with wandering steps and slow,
> Through Eden took their solitary way.

The invocation of a poet here is deliberate: if we have any hope of finding out about paradise, it will probably be by the indirect route of poetry rather than the straight road of prose. Even so, our steps will be wandering and slow enough.

Paradise is well and truly lost, such that even saying where it was, let alone where it is, proves difficult. Genesis offers but a few clues: we know where the Tigris and the Euphrates are, but after that the evidence meanders and winds up in the swamps of speculation—so much so, in fact, that some have suggested the rivers are not even *meant* to converge on any earthly map.[40] While we can account for a fair amount of 'here be dragons' vagueness in ancient geography, it would seem remarkably odd for the writer of Genesis to suggest that paradise was just slightly off the beaten path—as if an errant caravan party might stumble upon the cherubim at the gates and the flaming sword. The terse notice of the expulsion of Adam and Eve from the garden indicates only that they are driven outside paradise: 'therefore the Lord God sent him forth from the garden of Eden, to till the ground from which he was taken. He drove out the man; and at the east of the garden of Eden he placed the cherubim, and a flaming sword which turned every way, to guard the way to the tree of life' (Gen. 3:23–24).

The Jewish tradition of interpretation bears this out. In *1 Enoch*, the paradisiacal mountain of God appears to be situated in various places in the distant east or north-east.[41] What is most important for us is that these appear to be places extremely difficult of access, and indeed visible only to Enoch, the visionary par excellence. We must qualify, then, the statement that paradise is utterly lost: it is still accessible *for a few chosen saints* or *in the visionary state*. This tradition continues in the Christian church, most notably in John's vision in Revelation.

---

40. See e.g. Gordon Wenham, *Genesis 1–15* (WBC 1; Nashville: Thomas Nelson, 1987), pp. 66–67.

41. See e.g. Kelley C. Bautch, *A Study of the Geography of 1 Enoch 17–19* (Leiden: Brill, 2003), pp. 64–66.

One could also get a glimpse of Eden in the tabernacle and the temple.[42] It is regularly suggested that Eden is a kind of temple, a holy space with Adam and Eve assigned to the priestly service of *watching* the space to keep it pure. The associations are striking, though describing Eden as a temple might put things the wrong way round. The temple is rather a representation of the reality of Eden amidst God's creation. The paradisiacal carvings on the walls evoke the abundance of the Garden, and the curtain evokes the starry dome of the sky; while the increasingly restricted zones of access remind Israel of the difficulty of getting back to the presence of God. Even the temple, the greatest symbol of God's presence with his people, serves at the same time as a sad reminder of all that has been lost.[43]

Ephrem the Syrian (d. AD 373) provides a particularly striking example of Christian views of Eden in his *Hymns on Paradise*. He begins with charming descriptions of the glory of paradise, a mountain so high that 'the crest of the Flood/reached only its foothills':

> Amidst glorious rays
> it lies resplendent,
> all fragrant with its scents;
> magnificent clouds
> fashion the abodes
> of those who are worthy of it.[44]

The poem is suffused with such imagery, alongside intriguing speculations about the different levels and appurtenances of the paradisiacal mountain. Precisely what is being described, however, is difficult to say: Sebastian Brock suggests that Ephrem's paradise is a kind of conical mountain overarching the earth, with its roots in the encircling ocean; its interior walls are thus our sky.[45]

If the details do not quite seem to add up, however, that is only because they were never meant to. Paradise is not chartable in any earthly geography. It is a transcendent realm. In fact, while Ephrem never disavows the reality

---

42. See e.g. Wenham, *Genesis*, p. 67 for some of the parallels.

43. Gregory K. Beale, *The Temple and the Church's Mission: A Biblical Theology of the Dwelling Place of God* (Downers Grove, IL: IVP, 2004), pp. 66–80.

44. St Ephrem the Syrian, *Hymns on Paradise* (trans. Sebastian Brock; Crestwood, NY: St Vladimir's Seminary Press, 1990), 1.4–5, p. 79.

45. *Hymns on Paradise* (trans. Brock), p. 54. In his commentary on Genesis (2.6, *HP*, p. 201), Ephrem adds a further detail: the rivers leaving paradise 'are swallowed up under the surrounding sea, descending as it were down a tall water pipe; having passed through the ground beneath the sea and reached this earth, the earth then sprouts forth with one of them in the West—the Danube, or Pishon—the Gihon in the South, and the Euphrates and Tigris in the North.'

of paradise, he makes it clear that the imagery he uses is gesturing towards invisible realities far grander than what we can see or even imagine:

> All that you hear told
> about this Paradise,
> so pure and holy,
> is pure and spiritual.
> Let not this description of it
> be judged by one who hears it,
> for descriptions of it
> are not at all subject to judgment,
> since, even though it may appear terrestrial
> because of the terms used,
> it is in its reality
> spiritual and pure . . .
>
> For him who would tell of it
> there is no other means
> but to use the names
> of things that are visible,
> thus depicting for his hearers
> a likeness of things that are hidden.[46]

None of this makes Ephrem (necessarily) a strict Platonist—one could view his work as the hymnic progeny of the book of Hebrews—but the broadly idealistic lines of his thinking are evident enough.[47] His outlook fits comfortably alongside the Cappadocians, and the apophatic tones of his work, though muted, bear some resemblance to those of Dionysus and John Scottus Eriugena.[48] For all that, what is most striking about his poetry is his willingness to evoke the amiable beauties of paradise in very earthy images: 'the bowers of the just/dripping with unguents/and fragrant with scents' (5.6); 'both grass and roots/bring benefit and profit' (7.20); 'Should you wish/to climb up a tree,/with its lower branches/it will provide steps before your

46. *Hymns on Paradise* (trans. Brock), 11.3–5, p. 155.

47. For the influence of Greek thought on Ephrem, see again Possekel, *Philosophical Concepts*.

48. See e.g. 11.6–7: 'If someone concentrates his attention solely/on the metaphors used of God's majesty,/he abuses and misrepresents that majesty,/and thus errs/by means of those metaphors/with which God had clothed himself for his benefit.' See Brock's translation and comments, p. 48. As we will see below, Ephrem's description of the resurrection bodies of the righteous as 'fine and subtle', resembling 'the mind/which is able,/if it so wills, to stretch out and expand' (5.8, *HP*, p. 105), resonates with some of Eriugena's thoughts on the resurrection (though the Irishman will take things in a much more radical direction than Ephrem ever did).

feet' (9.3). His demurrals that these are meant to indicate spiritual realities are genuine, but equally genuine is his affection for the world; throughout the poem, as Brock says, he is 'expressing his awareness of the sacramental character of the created world, and of the potential of everything in the created world to act as a witness and pointer to the Creator'.[49]

We find something quite similar in the Middle English poem *Pearl*, a touching story of a father whose young daughter has died. It gives full voice to the father's anguish, even as he sees his daughter in paradise, and thus captures as do the psalms a living faith and hope which does not dismiss grief:

> Wondrous was made each mountain-side
> With crystal cliffs so clear of hue;
> About them woodlands bright lay wide,
> As Indian dye their boles were blue;
> The leaves did as burnished silver slide
> That thick upon twigs were trembling grew.
> When glades let light upon them glide
> They shone with a shimmer of dazzling hue.
> The gravel on ground that I trod with shoe
> Was of precious pearls of Orient:
> Sunbeams are blear and dark to view
> Compared with that fair wonderment.
> As shredded gold that glistered bright
> She shone in beauty upon the shore;
> Long did my glance on her alight,
> And the longer I looked I knew her more.

He may only spy this glorious place from a distance. When he tries to cross the river to be with his daughter, he is swept out of his dream vision back to earth:

> It pleased me ill outcast to be
> So suddenly from that region fair
> Where living beauty I could see.
> A swoon of longing smote me there,
> And I cried aloud then piteously:
> 'O Pearl, renowned beyond compare!
> How dear was all that you said to me,
> That vision true while I did share.
> If it be true and sooth to swear
> That in garland gay you are set at ease,
> Then happy I, though chained in care,
> That you that Prince indeed do please.'

49. *Hymns on Paradise* (trans. Brock), p. 39.

But Eden is not merely that which has been wrenched from the plane of the world; it is also that which calls out to us in the midst of the present creation. W. B. Yeats may only with difficulty be deemed a Christian theologian, but few have captured this sentiment more compellingly than he did in the prelude to *The Shadowy Waters*:

> Is Eden far away, or do you hide
> From human thought, as hares and mice and coneys
> That run before the reaping-hook and lie
> In the last ridge of the barley? Do our woods
> And winds and ponds cover more quiet woods,
> More shining winds, more star-glimmering ponds?
> Is Eden out of time and out of space?
> And do you gather about us when pale light
> Shining on water and fallen among leaves,
> And winds blowing from flowers, and whirr of feathers
> And the green quiet, have uplifted the heart?

Yeats's poem bears comparison with Psalm 8, which similarly sees the glories of primal creation enduring in the present age: 'O LORD, our Lord, how majestic is thy name in all the earth!' (v. 1).[50]

The tragedy is that the Edenic voice calling out through the natural world fades; the reach exceeds the grasp. This *Sehnsucht* finds particularly clear expression in the Romantics, and nowhere more poignantly than in Wordsworth's 'Intimations of Immortality':

> There was a time when meadow, grove, and stream,
> The earth, and every common sight,
> To me did seem
> Apparelled in celestial light,
> The glory and the freshness of a dream.
> It is not now as it hath been of yore; –
> Turn wheresoe'er I may,
> By night or day,
> The things which I have seen I now can see no more.

50. Calvin Kendall has argued that the Venerable Bede portrays Ireland and England as paradisiacal places of natural abundance 'outside time' in the beginning of his *Ecclesiastical History*; the most obvious example would be the well-known absence of snakes from the island: 'No reptiles are found there, and no snake can live there; for, though snakes are often carried thither out of Britain, as soon as the ship comes near the shore, and the scent of the air reaches them, they die' (1.1). See Calvin Kendall, 'Imitation and the Venerable Bede's Historia Ecclesiastica', in *Saints, Scholars, and Heroes: Studies in Medieval Culture in Honor of Charles W. Jones* (2 vols; ed. Charles Williams Jones, Margot H. King, and Wesley M. Stevens; Collegeville, MN: Hill Monastic Manuscript Library, Saint John's Abbey and University, 1979), 1:180.

Wordsworth is surely circumspect enough to realize that while one might say (as he puts it a few lines later) that 'there hath past away a glory from the earth', it is equally true that it is our perception of that glory that fails. The meadow, grove, and stream are what they were, but the heart grown old can no longer hear the glorious voice issuing through them.[51] The seraphim in Isaiah 6 can rightly declare, 'Holy, Holy, Holy, is the LORD of Hosts, the whole earth is full of his glory' (v. 3). They can equally well offer a more ambiguous version of the trishagion in Revelation 4:8: 'Holy, Holy, Holy, is the Lord God Almighty, who was and is and is to come!' As Richard Bauckham notes, 'We recall that chapter 4 portrays in heaven the rule of God which is yet to come on earth. God's glory is not yet manifested in a world dominated by injustice.'[52]

It is common to place this disenchantment on a particular point on the historical continuum. But there is no consensus as to where one should locate that point. Avihu Zakai is one of many who would place it in the so-called Age of Enlightenment.[53] Stanley Rosenberg, meanwhile, would push it further back; in his scheme the disenchantment stems not from hordes of atheistical French freethinkers, but from Saint Augustine himself.[54] According to Rosenberg, Augustine in his reading of Genesis presented a world that was 'rational and describable', and in so doing de-animized and disenchanted the cosmos.[55] Still others would see the development of Greek philosophy as the time of transition from Mythos to Logos.[56]

This suggests that the relationship of enchantment and disenchantment is not one of demonstrable historical progression, where humanity's childish belief in the magic of the world inexorably gives way to a mature vision of the world as a collection of brute facts. If enchantment is a problem, it is a persistent one. At best, one might leverage Wordsworth's poem to argue

---

51. Yeats again, 'A Song' (in *The Wild Swans at Coole*): 'I thought no more was needed/Youth to prolong/Than dumb-bell and foil/To keep the body young./Oh, who could have foretold/That the heart grows old?'

52. Bauckham, *Theology of Revelation*, p. 46.

53. Avihu Zakai, *Jonathan Edwards's Philosophy of History: The Re-enchantment of the World in the Age of Enlightenment* (Princeton: Princeton University Press, 2003).

54. S. P. Rosenberg, 'Forming the Saeculum: The Desacralization of Nature and the Ability to Understand It in Augustine's Literal Commentary on Genesis', in *Studies in Church History* (ed. P. Clarke and T. Claydon; London: Thomas Nelson & Sons, 2010), 46:1–14.

55. Rosenberg, 'Saeculum', pp. 3, 9.

56. This is the common assumption that gave rise to the collection of essays *From Myth to Reason? Studies in the Development of Greek Thought* (ed. Richard Buxton; Oxford: OUP, 2001). As the question mark in the title indicates, the volume casts doubt on the idea that Greek culture experienced a smooth and easily demonstrated shift from a mythical to a rational way of approaching the world.

that the enchantment–disenchantment dynamic makes itself known in the life experience of particularly sensitive individuals. But even then it would be an open question as to whether the memories of childhood wonder are illusions to be dissolved in the light of day, or precious if fleeting glimpses into the fundamental nature of reality.[57]

The doctrine of creation points in the direction of the latter. Christians routinely speak of 'dying and going to heaven' as the goal of life, and theologians have often been all too ready to foster this notion. Even those like Augustine and Edwards who have a fairly nuanced understanding of the future state tend to use the shorthand 'heaven' in their writings. This carries inevitable overtones of insubstantiality.[58] It is not as if employing the language of 'heaven' is completely misguided, since if nothing else there is a certain dissolving of the boundary between heaven and earth in the eschaton. John can still speak of a duality of the 'new heaven and new earth' (Rev. 21:1), but heaven's most salient feature—the glory of God—floods earth in the end: 'And I saw no temple in the city, for its temple is the Lord God the Almighty and the Lamb. And the city has no need of sun or moon to shine upon it, for the glory of God is its light, and its lamp is the Lamb' (21:22–23).

But maintaining a vision of Paradise Regain'd is the scriptural prescription for thinking about the ultimate future. It reminds us that we are created beings, not pinched-off bits of the divine essence destined to be absorbed back into his immaterial glory. We may conclude with Barth's musing on Eden, our once and future home:

> More cannot be extracted from the passage, because more is not offered, than that it was a real place on earth, distant from and unique in relation to all other earthly places, yet belonging to the same plane, so that real man could be there on the real earth, and to this day cannot overlook or forget but must always remember that among all the known and accessible places on earth there was and is also that unknown and inaccessible place, that in addition to his own place there is also that which is lost to him, and that that place is his home (*CD* III/3, p. 253).

57. See e.g. C. S. Lewis' fictionalized spiritual autobiography *The Pilgrim's Regress*, where the protagonist's early life experiences prove critical for his journey towards faith; C. S. Lewis, *The Pilgrim's Regress; An Allegorical Apology for Christianity, Reason, and Romanticism* (Grand Rapids: Eerdmans, 1959).

58. But cf. Augustine's statement in *Civ*. 22.29: 'Wherefore it may very well be, and it is thoroughly credible, that we shall in the future world see the material forms of the new heavens and the new earth in such a way that we shall most distinctly recognize God everywhere present and governing all things, material as well as spiritual, and shall see Him, not as now we understand the invisible things of God, by the things which are made, Romans 1:20 and see Him darkly, as in a mirror, and in part, and rather by faith than by bodily vision of material appearances, but by means of the bodies we shall wear and which we shall see wherever we turn our eyes.'

6

Plato's Shade: Ideas and the Structure of Creation

While our discussion on God and space focused on the external structure of creation, we could not escape some questions as to the internal structure of creation. Does the model for the visible cosmos somehow reside in God's mind? If so, how do these ideas relate to objects in the world? With this, of course, we run square into the nettlesome legacy of Plato and his influence on Christian theology. *Pace* Dante, Plato's shade has never been content to wander quietly in the first circle of the inferno; he haunts dogmatics to this day. The 'Platonization' of the Bible, and of its creation theology in particular, has long been a term of derision in the Western Church.[1] How much of this criticism proves damning of Plato himself is an open question: as the archetypal 'dead white male', he is regularly presented as the quintessence of a world-denigrating, logo-maniacal intellectualism that stands as the implacable foe of a vigorous doctrine of creation. This obscures the fact that Plato presents his ideas about the Ideas in a very nuanced and evolving fashion, and that his views on the material world go well beyond 'the world is a bad and inferior place' of popular rhetoric. That his work has been taken in this direction—even by those within the church—is without question. But with respect to his central assertion that the visible world in some sense rests upon Ideas, we may justly invoke the dictum *abusus non tollit usum*.

Whatever we make of Plato himself, some sort of 'Platonism' or 'idealism' has regularly served as a resource for Christian reflection on creation.[2] Neither of the terms is without its problems. As we have already noted, 'Platonism' is often in the eye of the beholder, and may have little grounding in the Athenian's actual writings. What is more, the Neoplatonism of Plotinus has arguably been more influential in the church than Plato's own teachings. The word 'idealism' is perhaps even worse, since its meaning can

1. See e.g. Colin E. Gunton, *The Triune Creator: A Historical and Systematic Study* (Edinburgh: T&T Clark, 2001), pp. 28–32.

2. Cf. the comments of Torstein Tollefsen, *The Christocentric Cosmology of St Maximus the Confessor* (Oxford: OUP, 2012), pp. 22–23.

range from the popular 'wanting to live in accordance with noble principles' to the technical philosophical label for believing that *only* ideas really exist (with Bishop Berkeley being its most notable exponent). Nonetheless, there is something coursing through the tradition that wants a label. Since it is Plato who first clearly articulated the immaterial structure of creation, and the Ideas lay at the heart of his system, the terms are appropriate, provided we afford them ample latitude in application.

We will survey a wide range of Christian theologians influenced by the Platonic tradition. We will deal with some major figures (e.g. Augustine, Edwards) relatively briefly, since their thought is explored in depth elsewhere in the book. This will afford us more space to explore lesser-known theologians such as John Scottus Eriugena, Ralph Cudworth, and S. T. Coleridge (the last well known as a poet, but less so as a theologian). The surveys will be brief, but they should suffice to demonstrate that a generally 'Platonic' outlook on life did not go hand in hand with a denigration of the created order.

Philo provides a crucial link between Plato and the Bible's account of creation.[3] Philo had imbibed deeply of the philosophical currents of his day, and he is generally regarded as a Middle Platonist with debts to both the Athenian master and subsequent developments in Greek thinking outside the Academy.[4] The first crucial development for our purposes was the notion that Plato's Ideas somehow resided within God's mind, a notion that would prove hospitable to later Christians seeking to reconcile passages like John 1 and Greek thought. The second was the Stoic notion of a divine *logos* that permeated the world and shaped it into the beautiful cosmos we behold. This same *logos* was present in humanity as reason, and enabled us to connect with the *logos* of the world and understand it.

Philo's most enduring legacy to the church's theology of creation was his two-stage reading of the early chapters of Genesis. With obvious debts to the *Timaeus*, Philo takes the opening verses of Genesis to refer to the creation of the intelligible 'infrastructure' of the universe: 'In the first place therefore, from the model of the world, perceptible only by intellect, the Creator made an incorporeal heaven, and an invisible earth, and the form of air and of empty space.' If ever the phrase 'Platonizing the Bible' has purchase, it is here. This invisible world, moreover, is modelled on the divine *logos*: God has his detailed idea of what he would like to do, then he creates the invisible model, then he creates the visible world according to the model. At other

---

3. See above all David Runia's magisterial *Philo of Alexandria and the Timaeus of Plato* (Leiden: Brill, 1986).

4. On Middle Platonism, see John M. Dillon, *The Middle Platonists, 80 B.C. to A.D. 220* (Ithaca: Cornell University Press, 1977).

times, Philo can envision the *logos* in a more dynamic way as a tool that shapes matter into the desired form, but the essential concept is the same. Scholars debate the extent of Philo's originality in all this—opinions range from Henry Wolfson's assertion that Philo is a defining voice in Western philosophy to A. J. Festugière's dismissal of him as a garden-variety Middle Platonist—but Philo provides (if nothing else) the clearest representation of the Greek philosophical trends which were to leave a lasting mark on the creation theology of the church.

Augustine

The influence of Neoplatonism on Augustine is well documented, as is the subsequent influence of Augustine on all future Christian theology.[5] Augustine underscores his fundamental metaphysical agreement with the Platonists in book 8 of the *City of God*:

> These philosophers, then, whom we see not undeservedly exalted above the rest in fame and glory, have seen that no material body is God, and therefore they have transcended all bodies in seeking for God. They have seen that whatever is changeable is not the most high God, and therefore they have transcended every soul and all changeable spirits in seeking the supreme. They have seen also that, in every changeable thing, the form which makes it that which it is, whatever be its mode or nature, can only be through Him who truly is, because He is unchangeable (8.6).

He commends the Platonists because they 'have preferred the intelligible nature to the sensible' (8.6), and he even avers that Plato probably read Moses in translation, since he agrees with 'I am who I am' (8.11); regardless, Plato could have deduced his views from creation in any case, in keeping with Romans 1:20 (8.12).

Here we may touch upon only a few of the more obvious Platonic and Neoplatonic influences on his thought. Augustine's *Literal Interpretation of Genesis* may seem wildly mis-titled in the eyes of modern readers. It consists of a Platonized reading of the text which would do Philo proud, and his exegesis is far removed from what we would deem a literal or scholarly unpacking of the text. The hermeneutics of what Augustine means by 'literal' need not detain us here. Suffice it to say that, for Augustine, the narrative of the six days was not meant to be taken as an actual extended sequence of

5. 'To Plotinus he is indebted for almost all the matter and for the whole technique of his philosophy.' Étienne Gilson, *The Christian Philosophy of Saint Augustine* (trans. L. E. M. Lynch; New York: Random House, 1960), p. 234.

time describing the formation of the world and its furnishings. God creates in an instant. The story instead points to the creation of the angels (symbolized by 'heaven') and matter (symbolized by 'earth') along with the creation of the Ideas in which earthly things will participate. The details of his reading are often perplexing, but in this work and elsewhere his commitment to the formative role of the Platonic Ideas is evident.[6]

The fact that the intelligible world is prior to and higher than the sensible world does not imply, however, that the visible world is mere rubbish. While the Platonist in him acknowledges that the visible world is a mixture of being and not-being (with raw matter teetering on the verge of nothingness), it is equally true that we begin to apprehend the Ideas, and indeed the glory of God, through the things that have been made. Witness his statement in the *Confessions*:

> For that thou art to be praised is shown from the fact that 'earth, dragons, and all deeps; fire, and hail, snow and vapors, stormy winds fulfilling thy word; mountains, and all hills, fruitful trees, and all cedars; beasts and all cattle; creeping things, and flying fowl; things of the earth, and all people; princes, and all judges of the earth; both young men and maidens, old men and children,' praise thy name! But seeing also that in heaven all thy angels praise thee, O God, praise thee in the heights, 'and all thy hosts, sun and moon, all stars and light, the heavens of heavens, and the waters that are above the heavens,' praise thy name—seeing this, I say, I no longer desire a better world, because my thought ranged over all, and with a sounder judgment I reflected that the things above were better than those below, yet that all creation together was better than the higher things alone (7.13).[7]

As we noted in chapter 4, Plato's influence is also visible in Augustine's treatment of time and eternity. He is not simply a slavish imitator of Plato: Augustine developed some finely formulated insights of his own on the question of time. Recall his observation that the world was created not in time, as if God had to decide at some point on the temporal spectrum when he would create; but instead he created the world 'with time'—time came into being along with the world. Nonetheless, Plato's idea that time is the moving image of eternity certainly captured his imagination. This is evident in his famous doctrine of *totum simul*, the idea that God experiences everything all at once. Whether humans ultimately participate in this experience of eternity is more questionable. While Augustine held to a traditional understanding of the literal resurrection of the body—in contrast to the nuances introduced by the Origenists—he still holds forth the promise

6. See the lucid summary in Gilson, *Philosophy of Augustine*, pp. 197–209.
7. Augustine, *Conf.* 7.13.

of sharing in God's eternity in fairly strict fashion: in heaven, he writes, we 'know all totally and simultaneously without any succession of time'.[8] This is difficult enough to imagine in the case of the ineffable God; Augustine does not explain precisely what this would mean for glorified humanity.

Origen and the Cappadocians

Origen, like the patriarch Jacob, left a rich but troubled patrimony to his descendants. Whatever we might make of his *De Principiis* today, and however well the version we possess mirrors Origen's own beliefs,[9] he and his followers had a very suspect reputation in antiquity. Rather than attempting to unravel this tangled skein, we will devote most of our attention to the writings of the Cappadocians and the theological synthesis of Eastern thought achieved by Maximus the Confessor. Here we will only mention the controversial idea (whether it stems from Origen or his followers) that souls had originally been united with God, but then fell away from this unity and were punished by entrapment in material bodies. Such a belief stems fairly directly from Plato's *Phaedrus* and the fall of the soul from the glories of the intellectual realm.

The Origenist fall of the soul into materiality may seem a strange bit of doctrine. But beneath the odd narrative veneer lies a serious theological problem: if the Ideas for things are eternally present with God, how could their entry into a world of change and multiplicity be accounted a good thing? The question of the One and the Many is arguably the focal point of Greek philosophical speculation, and so it is hardly surprising that Christian theologians attempted to address it as they teased out the philosophical implications of their faith. It was left to Maximus to approach the question in a way that would avoid some of the more obvious defects of the Origenist approach.

Gregory of Nyssa, who was strongly influenced by Plato,[10] reflects something of Origen's spirit in his adoption of the Neoplatonic exitus–reditus scheme: the soul falls away from God into the life of passions, but by the

8. Augustine, *Conf.* 12.13, discussed in Matthew Lamb, 'Eternity Creates and Redeems Time: A Key to Augustine's Confessions within a Theology of History', in *Divine Creation in Ancient, Medieval, and Early Modern Thought: Essays Presented to the Rev'd Dr Robert D. Crouse* (ed. Michael Treschow et al.; Leiden: Brill, 2007), pp. 117–40.

9. See e.g. the defence of the general reliability of Rufinus's translation of Origen in Alan Scott, *Origen and the Life of the Stars* (Oxford: Clarendon, 1991), pp. 168–72.

10. '[T]he greatest pagan influence on Gregory of Nyssa was certainly Plato (and later forms of Platonism)'. Morwenna Ludlow, *Universal Salvation: Eschatology in the Thought of Gregory of Nyssa and Karl Rahner* (Oxford: OUP, 2000), p. 23.

grace of Christ returns to its heavenly home. Gregory, it must be stressed, did not see embodiment as such a problem (though he did think sexual differentiation was a result of a foreseen fall).[11] Even the non-human creation was worthy of celebration. He sets the stage for the creation of humanity with a lyrical evocation of the goodness of the world into which man will enter:

> The earth was full, too, of her produce, bringing forth fruits at the same time with flowers; the meadows were full of all that grows therein, and all the mountain ridges, and summits, and every hillside, and slope, and hollow, were crowned with young grass, and with the varied produce of the trees, just risen from the ground, yet shot up at once into their perfect beauty; and all the beasts that had come into life at God's command were rejoicing, we may suppose, and skipping about, running to and fro in the thickets in herds according to their kind, while every sheltered and shady spot was ringing with the chants of the songbirds. And at sea, we may suppose, the sight to be seen was of the like kind, as it had just settled to quiet and calm in the gathering together of its depths, where havens and harbours spontaneously hollowed out on the coasts made the sea reconciled with the land; and the gentle motion of the waves vied in beauty with the meadows, rippling delicately with light and harmless breezes that skimmed the surface.[12]

Moreover, Gregory has a more dynamic understanding of human destiny than the language of 'return' might suggest. While God may have a kind of Platonic ideal of the human as a pre-existing goal, there is still the need for a journey towards perfection in the created world.[13] Indeed, for Gregory this journey is in a sense unending. Even in the eschaton, the approach to the infinite God can only be continual:

> You see how boundless is the path for those rising up to God, yet how it is that what the soul has comprehended is the beginning of something beyond her? [He who looks at] the divine boundless beauty . . . continues to wonder at God's continuous revelation; he never exhausts his desire to see more because what he awaits is always more magnificent and more divine than anything he has seen.[14]

Does this infinite journey include the body? Gregory speaks at times in classical Platonist fashion as if disembodied life is a superior existence. Our earthly body is like a 'horrid mask' which we take off so that we can 'return to our proper beauty in which we were formed from the beginning . . . For

11. Ludlow, *Universal Salvation*, p. 47.
12. Gregory of Nyssa, *De Hom. Opif.* 1.5.
13. Ludlow, *Universal Salvation*, pp. 48–50.
14. Gregory of Nyssa, in *Cant.* 11, in Ludlow, *Universal Salvation*, p. 63.

the matter of the body is a stranger and foreigner to the bodiless spirit'.[15] We have already seen the radically idealist approach he took to the constitution of matter.

Elsewhere, however, Gregory affirms the resurrection of the body, and offers some remarkable thoughts as to how that takes place. Perhaps under the influence of Methodius' *De Resurrectione*, Gregory asserts that the risen person will have the same 'particles' (*stoicheia*) as before. In this life, the soul makes a kind of stamp or impression on the body, such that the soul at the resurrection can recognize its own particles and reform the body.[16] In close parallel to 1 Corinthians 15, Gregory also counters the contention that a mere replication of the present body would be a catastrophe: while the same matter will be involved, he argues, it will have different qualities.[17]

We find a far more subdued form of Platonism in Basil's *Hexaemeron*. Basil touches only briefly on the noetic realm at the beginning of his discourse:

> It appears, indeed, that even before this world an order of things existed of which our mind can form an idea, but of which we can say nothing, because it is too lofty a subject for men who are but beginners and are still babes in knowledge. The birth of the world was preceded by a condition of things suitable for the exercise of supernatural powers, outstripping the limits of time, eternal and infinite. The Creator and Demiurge of the universe perfected His works in it, spiritual light for the happiness of all who love the Lord, intellectual and invisible natures, all the orderly arrangement of pure intelligences who are beyond the reach of our mind and of whom we cannot even discover the names.[18]

Elsewhere in the *Hexaemeron* Basil is happy to celebrate the beauty of the world as a revelation of divine wisdom and love.

Gregory Nazienzen follows the Philonic tradition of interpreting Genesis in more overt Platonist fashion. In keeping with the *Timaeus*, Nazienzen writes that God was not content to keep his goodness to himself: 'it was necessary that the good be poured forth and spread outward, so that there would be more recipients of its benevolent activity, for this was the summit of goodness.'[19] He goes on to describe the creation of the angels, which are described as 'intelligent spirits' or 'a kind of immaterial or bodiless fire', with

15. Gregory of Nyssa, *De Mortuis* 11.52, 2–4, 9–11, in Ludlow, *Universal Salvation*, p. 66.

16. Ludlow, *Universal Salvation*, pp. 68–69; see Gregory of Nyssa, *De Hom. Opif.* 5.27.2.

17. Ludlow, *Universal Salvation*, pp. 73.

18. Basil, *Hex.* 1.5.

19. Gregory Nazienzen, *Or. Bas.* 38.9.

obvious debts to Hebrews 1. But he summarizes their creation by invoking the *kosmos noētos* of the *Timaeus*: 'So therefore for these reasons the intelligible world was created' (*Or. Bas.* 38.10). This 'first world was beautiful to God', and so he decides to create a 'second material and visible world, that which is composed of heaven and earth and the system and composite of realities existing between them'. The climax of creation consists in weaving together the visible and invisible realms in humanity composed of body and soul: 'The human being is a kind of second world, great in smallness, placed on the earth, another angel, a composite worshipper, a beholder of the visible creation, an initiate into the Intelligible, king of things on earth, subject to what is above, earthly and heavenly, transitory and immortal, visible and intelligible, a mean between greatness and lowliness.'[20] The idea of 'man as microcosm' was a favourite trope in the ancient church, and one which we will explore below in our treatment of humanity. For our purposes, it is critical to see that Gregory's unabashed celebration of intelligible realities could stand alongside an affirmation of the beauty of the visible world. Echoing Basil, he describes the world as

> a system of earth and sky and all that is in the midst of them; an admirable creation indeed when we look at the fair form of every part, but yet more worthy of admiration when we consider the harmony and unison of the whole, and how each part fits in with every other in fair order, and all with the whole, tending to the perfect completion of the world as a Unit. This was to show that He could call into being not only a nature akin to Himself, but also one altogether alien to Him.[21]

Maximus

Maximus the Confessor (580–662) has attracted renewed interest in the West since the mid-twentieth century, not least through the publication of Hans Urs von Balthasar's *Cosmic Liturgy*.[22] Maximus is a major theologian of creation in his own right, as well as a representative of tendencies that go back at least to Origen and Pseudo-Dionysius.[23] As such, he is ideally situated to summarize the broadly Platonist strain in early Eastern cosmology. Like his forebears, the problem of the One and the Many drives his philosophical

20. Gregory Nazienzen, *Or. Bas.* 38.11.

21. Gregory Nazienzen, *Or. Bas.* 45.6

22. Hans Urs von Balthasar, *Cosmic Liturgy: The Universe According to Maximus the Confessor* (trans. Brian E. Daley; San Francisco: Ignatius, 2003).

23. Lars Thunberg, *Microcosm and Mediator: The Theological Anthropology of Maximus the Confessor* (Eng. rev. A. M. Allchin; Copenhagen: Munksgaard, 1965), p. 77.

project. How can it be that such a wildly diverse world constitutes a unified whole? Taken from a more theological angle: how can the one true God give rise to, and remain in relationship with, a world of 'manys'?

In response to this, Maximus offers a sweeping narrative of cosmic redemption climaxing in the *theosis* of man and the world.[24] As we touched on in chapter 2, the narrative is borne along by the person of Christ, who while remaining the one eternal *logos* unites in himself the many *logoi* of things in the world. While we have embraced the translation of *logoi* as 'God's purposes for things', the rendering 'Ideas' would not be far off the mark, and would make the Platonist heritage evident.[25] It is just here that he will seek to redirect some of the wilder tendencies of Christian idealism and point them in a more helpful direction. The wildness may ultimately be traced back to Origen; the path forward will be provided by Chalcedon.

Maximus' solution was to conceive of the *logoi* in a more dynamic fashion than the Origenists had. He affirms that God knows the *logoi* before the creation, but he also affirms that they only come into realization at their proper time. Thus the *logoi* should not be placed on the same ontological plane as God.[26] It is no sin for things that are not-God to come into being and progress towards a goal; this is the reason for their existence. To put it another way: God knows what he wants to do, but the knowing is not so weighty that it eliminates the significance of the doing. As Balthasar says, ideas and existent things exist for Maximus in a 'certain reciprocal dependence, a sort of circular motion, which lays the foundation for existence in the idea, as God's decision, and then assures the eternal endurance of the ideas on the basis of the enduring solidity of existence itself'.[27] Creatures (and it seems Maximus is thinking particularly of personal beings here) are gifted with the capacity to move from being to well-being to eternal being.[28] Thus motion as such is not seen as a 'fall' (as in Origenism), but the realization of God's purposes for things.

But this is only one side of Maximus' attempt to sort out the Ideas and put them in their place. Granted the validity of motion and becoming, he

24. As Torstein Tollefsen writes: 'The doctrine of *logoi* is not only a doctrine of metaphysical principles in a cosmological sense, but it is a multidimensional doctrine bearing on the whole divine economy of creation and redemption.' Tollefsen, *Christocentric Cosmology*, p. 66.

25. Thunberg, *Microcosm*, p. 79.

26. Cf. von Balthasar, 'The contingence of the ideas and that of concrete, individually existing things are only the twofold expression of a single contingence: that of created being.' *Cosmic Liturgy*, p. 164.

27. Von Balthasar, *Cosmic Liturgy*, p. 121.

28. He inherits this manner of speaking from Gregory Nazienzen; cf. *Or. Bas.* 38.3: Christ 'comes into being [in the Incarnation], that the one who has given us being might also grant us well-being', N. V. Harrison, p. 62.

must still demonstrate how the liberated *logoi* keep from spinning out of control in an ever-widening gyre. The Gospel of John and the Letter to the Colossians provided part of the answer: if Jesus is the *logos*, then surely the *logoi* find their coherence in him: 'Because he held together in himself the *logoi* before they came to be, by his gracious will he created all things visible and invisible out of non-being.'[29] But the real challenge is to prevent Christ from simply collapsing into the *logoi*, and becoming nothing more than a kind of impersonal cosmic blueprint. Maximus himself might seem to fall prey to this danger: in the passage just cited he asserts that the wise person 'will know that the many *logoi* are the one Logos to whom all things are related and who exists in himself without confusion, the essential and individually distinctive God, the Logos of God the Father'.[30] Further confusion could be engendered by Maximus' teaching that the *logos* is incarnated not only in the birth of Jesus as a human being, but also in the 'incarnation' or coming-to-realization of all the ideas: again, 'Always and in all God's Logos and God wills to effect the mystery of His own embodiment.'[31]

This is where Chalcedonian Christology comes to Maximus' aid. The Chalcedonian Confession's words refer to the Son: 'one and the same Christ, Son, Lord, only begotten, to be acknowledged in two natures, inconfusedly, unchangeably, indivisibly, inseparably'. But they also point towards a model of being in which two distinct things can co-inhere while maintaining their own identity. The model simply had to be transferred from the two natures of Christ to the natures of the *logos* and the *logoi*. Christ as *logos* maintains a 'super-essential' character, but he is nonetheless able to cohere with the *logoi*, like the hub of a wheel whence the spokes radiate.[32] Things in the world are thus connected both with each other and with God via the *logos*. As Maximus says in his *Mystagogia*: 'God realizes this union among the natures of things without confusing them but in lessening and bringing together their distinction, as was shown, in a relationship and union with himself as cause, principle, and end.'[33]

29. Maximus, *Amb*. 7, trans. in Paul Blowers and Robert Wilken, *On the Cosmic Mystery of Jesus Christ* (Crestwood, NY: St Vladimir's Seminary Press, 2003), pp. 54–55. Maximus cites Col. 1:15–17 immediately before this quotation.

30. Maximus, *Amb*. 7, trans. Blowers and Wilken, *Cosmic Mystery*, p. 54; cf. Thunberg, *Microcosm*, p. 81.

31. Maximus, *Amb*. 7.

32. See Thunberg, *Microcosm*, pp. 77–81. Thunberg writes (p. 81), 'the presence of the *Logos* in the *logoi* is always seen as a kind of incarnation—a parallel to the incarnation in the historical Jesus—and thus as an act of divine condescension.'

33. *Mystagogia* 1, *Maximus Confessor: Selected Writings* (trans. George Berthold; Mahwah, NJ: Paulist, 1985), p. 188.

Idealism in the Medieval West

We have already discussed Augustine, who provided the foundation for Western theology. We may turn next to the early medieval theologian John Scottus Eriugena, who was himself very much indebted to Augustine at key points.[34] Eriugena is of particular interest as one of the most 'Eastern', and indeed one of the most thoroughly Platonic, of Western theologians; it is at times difficult to resist thinking of him as 'John Scottus Origena'. He knew Greek, which was somewhat rare for a Western theologian at that time, and the influence of Gregory of Nyssa, Pseudo-Dionysius, and Maximus is evident throughout his work. The latter two play an especially formative role in his thinking: he embraces wholeheartedly the apophaticism and Neoplatonic exitus–reditus scheme of Dionysius, and undergirds this with Maximus' developed theory of the *logoi*.[35]

Eriugena nonetheless remains a difficult author to summarize. He is a very careful and subtle thinker, with a keen appreciation for the limitations of human language and the difficulty of probing the secrets of creation and recreation. He says numerous times, for instance, that 'God is Nothing'. At one level this is simply an extreme way of saying that God is beyond our comprehension and cannot be slotted in alongside other *things*. (He also employs the slightly less radical formula that God is *superessentialis* or beyond Being.) Whether this is the most helpful way of putting things is of course open to question; but he is trying to do justice to the ineffable nature of God.

This leads us to the second reason his work needs to be approached with appropriate caution. At times, the influence of the Neoplatonic 'exit and return' structure seems to leave him completely unmoored from any biblical anchor. The situation is exacerbated by the fact that he devotes much more time to philosophical rumination than to overt scriptural exegesis. But Eriugena's desire to remain faithful to the biblical revelation should not be underestimated. He says as much in his grand dialogue on nature, the *Periphyseon* (1.64):

> In fact, nothing should be said or thought about God by those who live purely and piously, and zealously seek the truth except what is found in sacred

34. See John J. O'Meara, *Eriugena* (Oxford: Clarendon, 1988), esp. pp. 33ff.

35. Dermot Moran indeed deems him to be a thoroughgoing immaterialist on a par with Bishop Berkeley (*The Philosophy of John Scottus Eriugena: A Study of Idealism in the Middle Ages* [Cambridge: CUP, 1989], p.82). For a spirited critique of his view, see the review of his book by Marcia L. Colish in Isis 82 (1991): pp. 722–24. Moran also proposes, less controversially, that Eriugena has gleaned most of his understanding of Plato and the Neoplatonists through his Christian sources, pp. 104–7.

> Scripture; nor should those who have a belief about God or are discussing Him use any designations and metaphors except the Scriptural ones. Who would presume to say anything of his own devising about the Ineffable Nature beyond what It Itself has attuned Its sacred instruments, the theologians, to say about it?[36]

While Eriugena does of course use metaphors other than those found in Scripture, he is not merely paying lip service to the authority of the Bible. Much of Eriugena's theological project can be seen as an attempt to come to grips with the final clause of 1 Corinthians 15:28: 'Then God will be all in all' (my translation). Most Western exegetes tend to divide this between 'God' and 'all in all', and then endeavour to figure out what is signified by this 'all in all'. The typical conclusion is that it refers to the full extension of God's sovereignty over the cosmos.[37] Eriugena, following the Eastern tradition, sees the words 'God will be all' as a genuine theological problem: how can it be that God will *be* all in the eschaton? The question of God absorbing things back into himself, then, is not merely something he picked up from Neoplatonism—it seems to surface within Scripture itself.

Eriugena's solution is quite interesting. He first notes (with avowed bafflement) that certain of his forebears have said that God in some sense 'creates himself'. How can this be? The Teacher in the dialogue avers: 'Therefore Divine Nature, which is simply Divine Will, is said to be made in all things; for in it being and will are not two different things, but one and the same in creating everything which, it seemed, ought to be made.'[38] The creation thus reflects the nature of the Creator: 'Just as there is no natural good besides Itself [i.e. the Divine Nature], but everything said to be good is good by participation in the one Highest Good, so everything said to exist exists not in itself but by participation in the Truly Existing Nature.'[39] The language of participation betrays the Platonic conceptions at work here; but Eriugena is arguably trying to make sense in Platonic language of Paul's statement in Romans 1:20 (which he alludes to elsewhere) that God's unseeable qualities of eternity and power and divinity can be seen in the things which have been created.[40]

36. Eriugena, *PP* 1.64, trans. in Myra L. Uhlfelder and Jean Potter, *Periphyseon: On the Division of Nature* (Indianapolis: Bobbs-Merrill, 1976), p. 86; cf. his prayer in Eriugena, *PP* 5.38.

37. See Roy E. Ciampa and Brian S. Rosner, *The First Letter to the Corinthians* (Grand Rapids: Eerdmans, 2010). The RSV is even vaguer with the rendering 'that God may be everything to everyone'.

38. Eriugena, *PP* 1.12, trans. in Uhlfelder and Potter, p. 16.

39. Eriugena, *PP* 1.12, trans. in Uhlfelder and Potter, pp. 16–17.

40. See e.g. Eriugena, *PP* 5.38, where Romans 1:20 is deployed with particular reference to Christ, as noted by Willemien Otten in her nuanced account of Eriugena's

It is understandable that Eriugena has been regularly accused of not merely Platonism, but pantheism, particularly when he is given to turns of phrase like this:

> God and the creature are not two things distinct from one another, but one and the same.[41]

> For there is a most general nature in which all things participate, which is created by the one universal Principle. From this nature corporeal creatures are derived and can be likened to streams which, issuing from one all-providing source, pursue their different courses through subterranean channels until they break out above ground in the different forms of the individual objects of nature.[42]

Eriugena is facing the same challenge as Maximus in his teaching on the *logos* and the *logoi*: how does one articulate the close union between God and the world—a concept scripturally rooted in verses like 'God will be all in all' and 'I said, "You are gods" '—without dissolving all boundaries between the two? Eriguena seems to want to affirm some distinction, but he does not always manage to convey that with the utmost clarity.

With respect to the inauguration of the visible world, Eriugena affirms the Philonic reading of Genesis 1:1–2 as the creation of the ideas or 'primordial causes' of all things.[43] While these primordial causes subsist in God's mind, they are distinct from him as things created in the Son, and thus are not properly deemed coeternal with him.[44] He then follows Maximus and his theory of the *logoi* fairly closely. He does suggest with Gregory that the differentiation into different sexes is a result of the fall, but he does not clearly come out in favour of the Origenist teachings that souls as such are pre-existent or that the entire material creation is a result of the fall.[45] (Even here he is probably reading the primal creation account in light of

---

use of Scripture, 'The Parallelism of Nature and Scripture: Reflections on Eriugena's Incarnational Exegesis', in *Iohannes Scottus Eriugena* (ed. Gerd van Riel, Carlos G. Steel, and J. J. McEvoy; Leuven: Leuven University Press, 1996), p. 91.

41. *PP* 3, O'Meara, *Eriugena*, p. 112.

42. *PP* 4.5, O'Meara, *Eriugena*, p. 122. One wonders if traditions of the subterranean streams leaving Eden (such as we saw in Ephrem) may have influenced Eriugena in his choice of imagery here.

43. *PP* 2.35–36; see O'Meara, *Eriugena*, p. 95. 'All things which are seen to arise through generation at times and places in the order of the centuries were made all together and at once in the Word of God' (*PP* 3, O'Meara, *Eriugena*, p. 111).

44. Eriugena, *PP* 2; see Uhlfelder and Potter summary, p. 112.

45. See Moran, *Eriugena*, pp. 116–17. On the question of the pre-existence of souls in the medieval period, see Lodi Nauta, 'The Preexistence of the Soul in Medieval Thought', *RTAM* 63 (1996): pp. 93–135.

the eschatological reality that we will be 'like the angels' [see Matt. 22:30], which he interprets as meaning being without sex. Moreover, prior to the fall, humanity had a celestial, spiritual body like the one it will have in the resurrection.[46]) For what it is worth, he was also said to be a good Hibernian lover of nature.[47]

It is in his eschatological teaching that Eriugena most clearly displays his fusion of Neoplatonism and Christianity. The idea of 'return' is of paramount importance in his thinking of the end. All things are to return to the 'original causes of things'. At one level this is shorthand for the deification of the cosmos, a return to God, the ultimate cause of all things. Eriugena can at times liken this to the return of a drop to a stream of water, an image which does little to commend any sense of ongoing personal identity. Elsewhere, however, Eriugena seems to be thinking of a return to the archetypal forms or ideas which ground existence in the visible world. In this sense, we might say that things become what they were ultimately intended to be. This is not of course in contradiction to deification as such (even if the drop of water metaphor is not of much help in reconciling the two): indeed it is precisely God's pervasive presence that leads things towards their goal.

None of this is particularly in tension with the mainstream Christian tradition. Questions arise when Eriugena attempts to delve more deeply into how this all works out in the end (a task he admittedly undertakes with due caution). Eriugena is bound by Scripture and tradition to affirm the resurrection of the body; but given his Neoplatonic leanings, he was bound to articulate this in a way that steered well clear of mere material restitution.[48] He managed the dilemma, drawing heavily on the Origenist heritage, by positing a number of steps in the return of all things to their causes:

> Return is marked, in effect, by seven steps. First will be the change of the earthly body into vital motion; second, of vital motion into sense; third, of sense into reason; next, of reason into mind, in which the end of all rational creation is established. After this virtual fivefold union of the parts of our nature . . . so that they are not five but one, with the lower always consumed by the higher, not so that they cease to be but so that they are one; there will

46. *PP* 2; see O'Meara, *Eriugena*, p. 99.

47. Dermot Moran, 'Nature, Man, and God in the Philosophy of John Scottus Eriugena', in *The Irish Mind: Exploring Intellectual Traditions* (ed. R. Kearney; Dublin: Wolfhound, 1985), pp. 91–106, 324–32, p. 93.

48. This is particularly true in light of the fact that medieval thinkers were still wrestling with very concrete questions such as how a person's body parts could come together in the eschaton. See Carlos Steel, 'The Return of the Body into the Soul: Philosophical Musings on the Resurrection', in *History and Eschatology in John Scottus Eriugena and His Time* (ed. Michael Dunne and J. J. McEvoy; Leuven: Leuven University Press, 2002), pp. 582–83.

> follow three other steps of ascent, of which one will be the crossing of the soul into the knowledge of all things which are after God; the second, of knowledge into wisdom . . . the third and highest step is the supernatural falling of the most purified souls into God Himself.[49]

It is hard to imagine a more literally *intellectualized* eschatological schema than this, but it is important to notice that Eriugena sees the body as somehow caught up into a higher reality rather than sloughed off in the process of ascent—'not so that they cease to be but so that they are one'.[50] Eriugena pushes at the boundaries of orthodoxy here, but he would no doubt claim to be offering an account of what it means to have a 'spiritual body'. Safer options lay close to hand (in Augustine, for instance), and Eriugena's decision to hew closer to Origen here may constitute a bridge too far in the campaign to unite the Bible and the Greek philosophical tradition.

Eriugena's influence was felt in the so-called 'School of Chartres', a group of Platonist thinkers in twelfth-century France. The quotation marks are necessary in light of the fact that the importance of Chartres itself on these scholars has been much debated.[51] For our purposes, it is sufficient to say that Platonism exercised a profound influence on a significant number of medieval theologians, including Fulbert of Chartres, Bernard of Chartres, William of Conches, Gilbert de la Porrée, Thierry of Chartres, and John of Salisbury. Fulbert is known as the father of the group, though precisely what he taught remains obscure. It does seem clear, however, that he inculcated in his students an appreciation for pagan as well as Christian learning.[52] Bernard, likewise, lies rather hidden in the shadows. John of Salisbury called him 'the best Platonist of his time', and Bernard may have written a commentary on the *Timaeus*. But all we have of his teaching (through John) are scattered lines of verse. Bernard's Platonism is evident even in these brief references:

> I say that the cause of particular existences is to be found
> Not in the intimate union of matter and form
> But rather in the fact that one of these [the form] perdures
> Being called by the Greek *idea*, even as he called matter *hyle*.[53]

---

49. Eriugena, *PP* 5.39, trans. in Uhlfelder and Potter, pp. 357–58.

50. Steel, 'Return of the Body into the Soul', pp. 581ff.

51. See a summary of the debate in Édouard Jeauneau, *Rethinking the School of Chartres* (trans. Claude Paul Desmarais; Toronto: University of Toronto Press, 2009), pp. 17–28. He takes a *via media*: there was a school at Chartres, though its importance may have been overstated.

52. Jeauneau, *Rethinking*, p. 35.

53. Jeauneau, *Rethinking*, p. 38.

He also commented on Porphyry: 'There are two kinds of effect of the divine mind, one which he creates from a subject matter or which is created along with it, another which he makes of himself and contains in himself, requiring no outside aid. The heavens indeed he made in his intellect from the beginning, and to form them there he needed neither matter nor extrinsic form.'[54] The details of their teaching need not detain us: their mere presence assures us that Platonism was alive and well in the West as well as the East.

Cambridge Platonism

The Cambridge Platonists proper were a group of seventeenth-century scholars, generally associated with Emmanuel College, who sought to offer an alternative to the Puritanism regnant in the mid-century English academy. But Platonism was to have a long-reaching effect in Cambridge and elsewhere through the ensuing centuries, and so we will also include in our discussion the Romantically tinged Platonism of Samuel Taylor Coleridge. The early Cambridge Platonists were primarily driven by the need to vindicate reason as a viable means of knowing God. They were not typically putting forward an all-embracing theology of creation as such. While they embraced Proverbs 20:27, 'the spirit of man is the lamp of the LORD', as their scriptural watchword, it is clear that they were influenced in this by Plato's assertion that reason within man provided a direct connection to the Supreme Reason that abides in God.[55] They thus had a far more sanguine view than their Puritan contemporaries as to what one might learn from nature concerning the ways of God. As one of their leading lights, Benjamin Whichcote says:

> The written word of God is not the first or only discovery of the duty of man. It doth gather and repeat and reinforce and charge upon us the scattered principles of God's creation . . . Therefore these things have a double sanction from God. They are the principles of His creation, discoverable and knowable by natural light. They are again declared and included in the terms of the covenant of grace.[56]

Plato, then, was chiefly their guide with respect to epistemology. But broadly Platonic ideas do make their way into the Cambridge group's ruminations

54. From *Metalogicus*, IV, 35, in Ralph McInerny, *A History of Western Philosophy* (2 vols; University of Notre Dame Press, 1963–1970), 2:159.

55. See Frederick J. Powicke, *The Cambridge Platonists: A Study* (Westport, CT: Greenwood, 1970), pp. 21–24.

56. Benjamin Whichcote, in Powicke, *Cambridge Platonists*, pp. 31–32.

on creation. They were happy, for instance, to follow the Eastern church fathers in speaking of the deification of humanity. Whichcote tells his readers, 'Do not stumble at the use of the word', since it finds scriptural warrant in 2 Peter 1:4, and theological grounding in the incarnation of Christ.[57] At least for Whichcote, deification seems to be a way of speaking about our intimate union with Christ, and our moral transformation into godly people who share the divine character. Both concepts are easy enough to justify from Scripture.[58] But Platonism certainly lent a distinct flavouring to their use of the term. As C. A. Patrides notes, the idea of a divine reason within people already lent a certain 'deiformity' to their existence.[59] The Platonic idea of *participation* also offered some sort of conceptual grid for thinking about how the divine and human might coalesce in this way (though the problem of precisely how visible things participated in the ideas had of course bedevilled Platonism from the very beginning).[60]

Henry More sought to provide a 'careful draft of natural theology or metaphysics' in his book *An Antidote against Atheism*.[61] More begins his argument in good Platonist fashion by saying that 'with our own natural light' we can conceive of 'a being absolutely perfect', who is God.[62] More would ask the atheist who denies God 'what idea or notion they frame of that they deny or doubt of'.[63] This argument is stronger than might first appear (it is analogous to asking someone who denies that there is meaning in life where they got the category of 'meaning'), but our chief concern is the argument that in More's mind follows logically upon it:

> But it is manifest that that which is self-subsistent, infinitely good, omniscient and omnipotent is the root and original of all things. For omnipotency signifies a power that can effect anything that implies no contradiction to be effected; and creation implies no contradiction. Therefore this perfect being can create all things. But if it found the matter or other substances existing beforehand of themselves, this omnipotency or power of creation will be in vain, nay indeed a full omnipotency will not be in this absolute omnipotent . . . And according to natural light that which is thus, is to be adored and worshipped of all that

57. C. A. Patrides, *The Cambridge Platonists* (Cambridge: CUP, 1980), pp. 70–71.

58. See the comments of Tod E. Jones, *The Cambridge Platonists: A Brief Introduction* (Lanham, MD: University Press of America, 2005), p. 24.

59. Patrides, *Cambridge Platonists*, pp. 18ff.

60. T. Jones, *Cambridge Platonists*, pp. 24–25.

61. See Gerald R. Cragg, ed., *The Cambridge Platonists* (New York: OUP, 1968), p. 163. We may note that the creative titling of books is not a strong suit of studies in the Cambridge Platonists.

62. Henry More, *An Antidote against Atheism*, chs 1–8, see esp. the text in Cragg, *Cambridge Platonists*, p. 176.

63. More, *Antidote*, 3, in *Cambridge Platonists* (ed. Cragg), p. 168.

> has the knowledge of it, with all humility and thankfulness; and what is this but to be acknowledged to be God?[64]

More's conclusions of course have numerous counterparts in earlier theological reflection; but he does raise the significance of an innate *idea* of God to prominence.

Another demonstrably Neoplatonic teaching in More is his use of the language of emanation to describe God's act of creation.[65] While emanationism could be deployed to account for flaws in the design of the world—the further you get from the shining source of life the more attenuated the beams become—More is doing quite the contrary. While he recognizes the infelicity of saying the world simply is God, the pagan pantheists were not entirely mistaken in their suppositions:

> Hence is the strange opinion of God being all, and that there is nothing but God. But it is not at all strange that all things are the mere energie of God, and do as purely depend on him, as the Sun-beams of the Sunne. So that so farre forth as we may say the body, *lux & lumen* of the Sunne, all put together is the Sunne; so farre at least we may be bold to say that God is all things, and that there is nothing but God.[66]

As an antidote to pantheism, this could be deemed pretty weak medicine. But we are at least a long way from the allegedly necessary denigration of the world that is often thought to follow logically upon Platonism.

The most extended reflection on the structure of creation itself may be found in Ralph Cudworth's modestly titled *The True Intellectual System of the Universe*.[67] Like More, Cudworth's stated goal is to combat the atheism that lurked on the margins of the tumultuous seventeenth-century religious scene, and in so doing he devotes a considerable amount of attention to the nature of the created world. Cudworth draws upon a variety of ancient sources in his construal of the universe, but the resulting mélange can still be broadly construed as 'Platonist'.[68]

64. More, *Antidote*, 7, in *Cambridge Platonists* (ed. Cragg), pp. 176–77.

65. See Daniel C. Fouke, *The Enthusiastical Concerns of Dr Henry More: Religious Meaning and the Psychology of Delusion* (Leiden: Brill, 1997), pp. 29–35.

66. Henry More, *The Complete Poems of Dr. Henry More* (ed. Alexander Grosart; Edinburgh: Edinburgh University Press, 1878), p. 142; discussion in Fouke, *More*, p. 32.

67. References here are to the first American edition, Ralph Cudworth and Thomas Birch, *The True Intellectual System of the Universe* (2 vols; Andover: Gould and Newman, 1837). The most relevant material may also be found in *Cambridge Platonists* (ed. Cragg), pp. 235ff.

68. He makes his debts to Plato evident in *True System*, 1.214, though he affirms that Aristotle (and most other Greek philosophers for that matter) taught the same thing.

Perhaps his most interesting contribution is the idea of a 'plastic nature' employed by God as the means by which he brings his wisdom to bear on the world.[69] Cudworth is fighting on two fronts: on the one hand there are the atheists who would argue that 'every thing comes to pass fortuitously, and happens to be as it is, without any mind or understanding'; on the other, there are those who would have God hand-making everything, down to the least fly or gnat.[70] The former involves a universe driven only by 'mechanical necessity', an increasingly popular option in Cudworth's era. He believes the order and complexity of the world belies such a mechanical view. Christians who adopt it (presumably under the pressure of apparent design flaws or the presence of evil in the world) 'make God to be nothing else in the world, but an idle spectator of the various results of the fortuitous and necessary motions of bodies: and render his wisdom altogether useless and insignificant'. He goes on to elaborate the argument from design, with an assist from Aristotle: denying divine artifice in the world is like a carpenter saying his carving was simply the result of the random movements of hatchets, planes, and chisels.[71]

As for countering the apparently more pious option that God does everything immediately, Cudworth begins with the somewhat weak contention that it might be deemed 'indecorous' of God to attend to every little detail of the universe: the Divine Providence would seem 'operose, solicitous, and distractious'. One detects a certain Aristotelian or Neoplatonic flavouring in his assertion that 'it seems far more august and becoming of the Divine Majesty, that a certain power and virtue, derived from him, and passing through the universe, should move the sun and the moon and be the immediate cause of those lower things done here upon earth'.[72] Cudworth is on much firmer ground when he goes on to argue that God's direct involvement in every detail of the world would jeopardize its proper independence;[73] it 'should be quite superceded or made to signify nothing, God himself doing all things immediately and miraculously'. As we will see below with Berkeley and Edwards, if secondary causation is not allowed, God must well and truly do everything all the time, in which case the word 'create' is drained of all meaning. One might well wonder if there is really a world there at all. Equally potent is his acknowledgement that the emergence of things in the world not only takes time; it is 'sometimes frustrated and disappointed by the indisposition of matter'.[74] The Greek legacy

69. For a succinct account of the plastic nature, see *Cambridge Platonists* (ed. Cragg), pp. 234–35.

70. Cudworth, *True System*, 1.209.

71. Cudworth, *True System*, 1.210.

72. Cudworth, *True System*, 1.212.

73. Colin Gunton stresses this point throughout his book *The Triune Creator*.

74. Cudworth, *True System*, 1.213.

is evident in the idea of the indisposition of matter, but it is hard to dispute the force of his argument: if God is doing everything directly, why does it take time, and why do so many things seem to go wrong along the way?

Cudworth's *via media* is the plastic nature. He describes it as the 'inferior and subordinate instrument' of God which 'doth drudgingly execute that part of his Providence, which consists in the regular and orderly motion of matter'.[75] He relates it to the seminal reason (*logos spermatikos*) of the Stoics, and it bears at least some resemblance to the World Soul of the *Timaeus* and Henri Bergson's later concept of the *élan vital*.[76] It appears to be something midway between a force and a mind, both more subtle and more active than 'laws of nature'. Cudworth himself admits it is a thing 'not without some difficulty in the conception of it'.[77] It is incorporeal (contra the Stoics) and can in no way be conflated with God himself: it is 'but the mere umbrage of intellectuality, a faint and shadowy imitation of mind and understanding'.[78]

Perhaps his best description of it derives again from Aristotle: 'So that the meaning of this philosopher [Aristotle] is, that nature is to be conceived as art, acting not from without and at a distance, but immediately upon the thing itself which is formed by it. And thus we have the first general conception of the plastic nature, that it is art itself, acting immediately on the matter as an inward principle.'[79] The chief difference between the work of the plastic nature and the work of human art is that the latter can only shape matter with 'a great deal of tumult and hurly-burly, noise and clatter', while the former does its work 'easily, cleverly, and silently'.[80] But not perfectly. Cudworth cites Plotinus approvingly that nature is but a poor 'image or imitation of wisdom, the last thing of the soul, which hath the lowest impress of reason shining upon it'.[81] This downgrading of the plastic nature helps him to account for imperfections in the material world, and prevents the unwary from supposing with the Stoics that nature is in fact the supreme God.

We will discuss at the end of the chapter whether Cudworth and his fellow Platonists fully succeed in fusing faith and philosophy. The plastic nature might seem to be a kind of *semideus ex machina* without quite enough divine power or skill to set all things aright. But he certainly recognized the contours of the problems raised by a naïve account of God's work in

75. Cudworth, *True System*, 1.213.

76. *Cambridge Platonists* (ed. Cragg), p. 235. Cudworth describes the plastic nature in terms of 'vital energy', e.g. *True System* 1.228–30.

77. Cudworth, *True System*, 1.219.

78. Cudworth, *True System*, 1.243.

79. Cudworth, *True System*, 1.219.

80. Cudworth, *True System*, 1.220.

81. Cudworth, *True System*, 1.223.

the world—problems that would only grow worse with the advent of comprehensive experimental science and a growing philosophical scepticism. While he is generally forgotten today, he did leave a considerable legacy.

Coleridge and Romantic Platonism

Among those who read *The True Intellectual System* was Samuel Taylor Coleridge, who discovered the book in 1795, the same year he first came to appreciate the depth of Wordsworth's genius.[82] The convergence of these two events is of immense significance for us. For Coleridge, Platonism offered as much as anything a romantic vision of reality, the supposition of a grand world lying beyond what merely met the eye. Coleridge once remarked that 'every man is born an Aristotelian, or a Platonist . . . They are the two classes of men, besides which it is next to impossible to conceive a third.'[83] He had in mind something like the image of the two philosophers in Raphael's *The School of Athens*, where Plato points upwards to the heavens, and Aristotle gestures towards earth. Aristotelian empiricism dominated British academic pursuits in Coleridge's day, but this had sparked a renewed appreciation of Plato and his seventeenth-century followers. As David Newsome notes, 'This was the intellectual context of Romanticism, which was itself the upsurge of the previously-subdued spirit, confident in the claims of the visionary power, the intuitive faculty in man, to unfold the deepest secrets of the universe.'[84] Platonism had in effect become the philosophical justification for an essentially *apocalyptic* vision of the world—remembering that the original sense of *apocalypsis* is 'unveiling' rather than simply 'the end of the world'.

Coleridge's indebtedness to Cudworth is evident in his poem 'The Aeolian Harp':

> And what if all of animated nature
> Be but organic Harps diversely framed,
> That tremble into thought, as o'er them sweeps
> Plastic and vast, one intellectual breeze,
> At once the Soul of each, and God of all?[85]

---

82. John Spencer Hill, *Imagination in Coleridge* (London: Macmillan, 1978), p. 9. Note that Coleridge had also read Eriugena.

83. Quotation in David Newsome, *Two Classes of Men: Platonism and English Romantic Thought* (London: John Murray, 1972), p. 1.

84. Newsome, *Two Classes*, p. 3.

85. See Hill, *Coleridge*, pp. 9–10. Coleridge's 'At once the soul of each, and God of all' appears to toss away the safeguards Cudworth employs against pantheism. But in the ensuing lines he accepts his companion's chastisement and seems to admit these

If the turns of phrase are Cudworth's, however, the sentiment behind them goes much further back in Coleridge's life. Witness his reflection on his childhood:

> I remember, that at eight years old I walked with my father one winter evening from a farmer's house, a mile from Ottery—& he told me the names of the stars—and how Jupiter was a thousand times larger than our world—and that the other twinkling stars were Suns that had worlds rolling round them—& when I came home, he shewed me how they rolled round . . . I heard him with a profound delight & admiration; but without the least mixture of wonder or incredulity. For from my early reading of Faery Tales, & Genii &c &c—my mind had been habituated to the Vast—& I never regarded my senses in any way as the criteria of my belief. I regulated all my creeds by my conceptions not by my sight—even at that age.[86]

One can see how he considered himself born a Platonist. One can also see that the Platonic sense of wonder could accommodate both Faery Tales and the scientific knowledge imparted to him by his father. In Coleridge's own terms, the empirical 'Understanding' of Aristotle was perfectly valid, provided it was seen in light of the genuine Wisdom from above.[87] The natural world was not to be split from the ideal world; the visible was not to be divided from the invisible: 'but those Sonnets appear to me the most exquisite, in which moral Sentiments, Affections, or Feelings, are deduced from, and associated with, the scenery of Nature. Such compositions generate a habit of thought highly favourable to delicacy of character. They create a sweet and indissoluble union between the intellectual and the material world.'[88]

When it comes to the resurrection of the body, Coleridge shows an interesting blend of adherence to the tradition and innovation. He repeatedly affirms the resurrection of Christ and believers as core doctrines of the faith, and clearly means more by this than a wispy affirmation of the 'Easter faith' of the disciples. But his views on the nature of the resurrection body are quite nuanced. We may begin with a brief note with clear dependence on 1 Corinthians 15: 'When the spirit by sanctification is fitted for an incorruptible body, then shall it be raised into a world of incorruption, and a celestial body shall burgeon forth thereto; the germ of which had been

---

are, 'shapings of the unregenerate mind;/Bubbles that glitter as they rise and break/On vain Philosophy's aye-babbling spring.'

86. In Hill, *Coleridge*, p. 5.

87. See Newsome, *Two Classes*, p. 3.

88. In David Jasper, *Coleridge as Poet and Religious Thinker* (Allison Park, PA: Pickwick, 1985), p. 33.

implanted by the redeeming and creative Word in this world.'[89] But elsewhere he qualifies in what respect 'the body' will be raised. He notes, for example, that speaking of 'incorruptible flesh and blood' is like speaking of 'marble flesh and blood':

> In the sense of St. Paul, as of Plato and all other dynamic philosophers, flesh and blood is *ipso facto* corruption, that is, the spirit of life in the mid or balancing state between fixation and reviviscence. *Who shall deliver me from the body of this death?* is a Hebraism for 'this death which the body is'. For matter itself is but *spiritus in coagulo*, and organized matter the coagulum in the act of being restored; it is then repotentiating.[90]

Coleridge may have read a little too much of Plato into 1 Corinthians 15, but he was also wrestling with serious questions concerning the resurrection body. While his knowledge of biology was necessarily imprecise by modern standards, he recognized that the 'atoms' in our bodies are constantly being swapped out over time, and so reasoned that the fundamental continuity of the person must consist in something other than the endurance of an unchanging singular body.[91] He can thus serve as a helpful model of affirming the scriptural witness while actively engaging responsible philosophical and scientific interlocutors.

Jonathan Edwards

'[W]e have also shewn that all existence is mental, that the existence of all exterior things is ideal.'[92] It would be hard to find a more thoroughgoing statement of strict philosophical idealism than this one offered by Jonathan Edwards (1703–58) in 'The Mind'. His thought bears comparison with the founding father of radical immaterialism, Bishop George Berkeley (1685–1753), whose philosophy is perhaps best known from its attempted refutation by a rock-kicking Samuel Johnson. While it is difficult to know how much of Berkeley Edwards had read, we do know that Edwards had

89. In 'Notes on Leighton', *The Complete Works of Samuel Taylor Coleridge* (7 vols; ed. W. G. T. Shedd; New York: Harper, 1854), 5:371.

90. *The Works of Jonathan Edwards* (26 vols; New Haven: Yale University Press, 1997–2009), 5:221. Passages like this drew the wrath of men like T. H. Skinner, who in *Coleridge and the Moral Tendency of His Writings* (New York: Leavitt, Trow, & Co., 1844) explodes, 'And who can hesitate to class the advocate of this doctrine with Sadducees?' (p. 86, discussion on pp. 82ff.)

91. Texts in Skinner, *Coleridge*, p. 82.

92. Jonathan Edwards, 'The Mind' 9, *The Works of Jonathan Edwards* (26 vols; New Haven: Yale University Press, 1997–2009), 6:341.

read the Cambridge Platonists, as witnessed, for instance, by the approving citations of Cudworth's *True Intellectual System* on Plato's cave ('The Mind' [40]) and on the fundamental distinction of the visible and invisible worlds ('Images' [209–10]).[93] Edwards has moreover been characterized as an occasionalist, believing that God is the only real cause in the universe.[94] As Oliver Crisp memorably puts it, the world for Edwards is rather like a film containing an infinite number of cells strung together; God recreates the world with each instant, implementing incremental changes along the way.[95]

Crisp makes a convincing case for Edwards' occasionalism, yet Edwards' underlying belief that only Mind was really real did nothing to diminish his interest in the natural world. The youthful Edwards produced a well-known work on the habits of spiders, and his scientific interests continued throughout his life. He integrated an early version of atomic theory into his philosophy, and seems to have kept up to date with astronomical discoveries: his *Apocalyptic Writings*, for instance, contain some fascinating speculations as to whether the 'New Earth' of Revelation might be some distant planet.[96] This does not mean Edwards fully embraced 'modern science'—as Avihu Zakai has argued at length, Edwards was deeply suspicious of its philosophical roots and denied some of its central findings such as the Copernican view of the universe.[97] But here we find another instance of a thoroughgoing idealist, with some connection to Platonist thought, celebrating the beauty and intricacy of the created order. Since we devote considerable attention to Edwards elsewhere, we will hasten on to the twentieth century.

C. S. Lewis

Lewis, while not a professional theologian, certainly had enough of an effect as an 'amateur' to warrant inclusion in our discussion. After dipping into various philosophical streams early in his life, he eventually settled into a

93. Edwards, 'The Mind' 9, *Works*, 6:359, and Wallace E. Anderson's notes in the same volume, pp. 23–24, on the influence of Henry More on Edwards. See also the detailed discussion in Michael J. McClymond, 'Salvation as Divinization: Edwards, Palamas, and Neoplatonism', in *Jonathan Edwards: Philosophical Theologian* (ed. Paul Helm and Oliver Crisp; Aldershot: Ashgate, 2003), pp. 141–44.

94. This view has been challenged by Sang Hyun Lee, but see the refutations of Oliver Crisp, *Jonathan Edwards on God and Creation* (New York: OUP, 2012), pp. 23–31. Similar views were held by the Islamic Ash'arite group; see Sorabji, *Time*, p. 295.

95. Crisp, *God and Creation*, p. 162.

96. Edwards, 'A Humble Attempt', *Works*, 5:140–41.

97. Avihu Zakai, *Jonathan Edwards's Philosophy of Nature: The Re-enchantment of the World in the Age of Scientific Reasoning* (London: T&T Clark, 2010), p. 117.

Christian Platonism which pervaded both his fantasy stories and his non-fiction addresses.[98] It is noteworthy that his fundamental shift from materialism to idealism appears to have taken place as he undertook research on Henry More, while also rereading Plato's *Phaedrus*.[99]

As with Coleridge, though, Lewis's Platonism was no mere rational deduction. It sprang equally from an overwhelming desire for a better world, a romantic *Sehnsucht* which coloured his works at every turn. Note the trio of quotations that introduces his fictionalized spiritual autobiography, *The Pilgrim's Regress*:

> This every soul seeketh and for the sake of this doth all her actions, having an inkling that it is; but what it is she cannot sufficiently discern, and she knoweth not her way, and concerning this she hath no constant assurance as she hath of other things.—Plato
>
> Whose souls, albeit in a cloudy memory, yet seek back their good, but, like drunk men, know not the road home.—Boethius
>
> Somewhat it seeketh, and what that is directly it knoweth not, yet very intentive desire thereof doth so incite it, that all other known delights and pleasures are laid aside, they give place to the search of this but only suspected desire.—Hooker[100]

It is hard to imagine a more straightforward declaration of Lewis's Platonic sensibilities. It is a Platonism, moreover, of precisely the same form we saw in Coleridge: in Plato they find a philosophical mooring for the sense that there is more out there than meets the eye, that the wonders of the world are a gateway to more and greater wonders beyond.

Two vignettes from Lewis's fiction serve to illustrate the particular shape of his Christian Platonism. The first is the well-known conclusion to the Narnia series. While Lewis was not a devotee of the Greek fathers,[101] his description of the journey in the renewed Narnia 'further up and further

---

98. The most thorough account of Lewis's philosophical journey may be found in Adam Barkman, *C. S. Lewis and Philosophy as a Way of Life* (Allentown, PA: Zossima, 2009), esp. pp. 21–65. Barkman (p. 5) describes the admittedly eclectic Lewis as 'a proponent of Neoplatonic Christianity, a philosophy that attempts to synchronize, as well as it can, the best of Plato, Aristotle, the Stoics and pagan religion with Christianity'. See more briefly Mary Carman Rose, 'The Christian Platonism of C. S. Lewis, J. R. R. Tolkien, and Charles Williams', in *Neoplatonism and Christian Thought* (ed. Dominic O'Meara; Albany: SUNY, 1982), pp. 203–12.

99. Barkman, *Lewis*, pp. 40–41.

100. C. S. Lewis, *The Pilgrim's Regress; An Allegorical Apology for Christianity, Reason, and Romanticism* (Grand Rapids: Eerdmans, 1959), preface.

101. Barkman, *Lewis*, p. 196.

in' bears a strong resemblance to the dynamic eschatology of Origen and Gregory, with its continual advancement of the soul in the love of God. Just in case the reader has failed to appreciate the Platonic underpinnings of Lewis's epic, he comes out and declares it through Lord Digory:

> When Aslan said you could never go back to Narnia, he meant the Narnia you were thinking of. But that was not the real Narnia. That had a beginning and an end. It was only a shadow or copy of the real Narnia, which has always been here and always will be here; just as our own world, England and all, is only a shadow or copy of something in Aslan's real world.[102]

Digory then mutters under his breath, 'It's all in Plato, all in Plato: bless me, what *do* they teach them at these schools?' Lewis appears to part company with the Origenists, however, in describing the physicality of the 'real' Narnia. He gropes for words just as Eriugena did, but rather than running from material images, Lewis as it were runs further into them: 'The new [Narnia] was a deeper country; every rock and flower and blade of grass looked as if it meant more. I can't describe it any better than that: if you ever get there, you will know what I mean.'[103]

Lewis makes a similar point in his biting satire *The Great Divorce*. A busload of reprobates are permitted to make a tour of heaven, but find the experience more than they can bear:

> At first, of course, my attention was caught by my fellow-passengers, who were still grouped about in the neighbourhood of the omnibus, though beginning, some of them, to walk forward into the landscape with hesitating steps. I gasped when I saw them. Now that they were in the light, they were transparent—fully transparent when they stood between me and it, smudgy and imperfectly opaque when they stood in the shadow of some tree. They were in fact ghosts: man-shaped stains on the brightness of that air. One could attend to them or ignore them at will as you do with the dirt on a window pane. I noticed that the grass did not bend under their feet: even the dew drops were not disturbed.
>
> Then some re-adjustment of the mind or some focussing of my eyes took place, and I saw the whole phenomenon the other way round. The men were as they always had been; as all the men I had known had been perhaps. It was the light, the grass, the trees that were different; made of some different substance, so much solider than things in our country that men were ghosts by comparison.[104]

---

102. C. S. Lewis, *The Last Battle* (New York: Macmillan, 1956), pp. 169–70.

103. Lewis, *The Last Battle*, p. 171.

104. C. S. Lewis, *The Great Divorce* (New York: Macmillan Company, 1946), pp. 27–28.

This is a not only a long way from the putatively 'Platonic' idea that the soul is imprisoned in the body. It is in fact just the opposite: the ghosts are imprisoned in their insubstantiality. One might protest and say that Lewis is only telling a story and that he 'really' means something along the lines of Eriugena and the purely 'spiritual' body. If there is a convergence of thought here between Lewis and Eriugena, however, we might say that Lewis has found a more effective way to capture the reality to which Eriugena was gesturing. The fact that this happens through an imaginative narrative is itself of immense theological significance. If the nature of the resurrection body really is beyond our current understanding, gesturing towards it in a self-consciously imaginative way makes perfect sense.

Assessment

We began this chapter by noting the often-repeated charge that Platonism poses an inherent threat to a robust theology of creation. In light of our admittedly brief survey, we are in a position to draw some tentative conclusions. We might first note that the influence of Platonism in its various permutations has been remarkably consistent over the centuries. It is woven into the fabric of the theology of the Eastern Church, and it has likewise threaded its way, albeit more subtly, through the West as well. Our study could be considerably lengthened if we looked at Platonic influence on thinkers like Thomas Aquinas, an Aristotelian who nonetheless was profoundly affected by the Platonic tradition.[105] If nothing else, this indicates that 'idealism' broadly conceived cannot be tossed aside out of hand.

If one begins from the premise that a theology of creation ought to remain strictly within the imagery and concerns of biblical revelation, then any rapprochement with Plato will be excluded as a matter of principle. Much popular Protestant theology has operated within just such a

105. See e.g. Gilles Emery's examination of the exitus–reditus structure in Thomas's thought in 'Trinity and Creation', in *The Theology of Thomas Aquinas* (ed. Rik van Nieuwenhove and Joseph Wawrykow; Notre Dame: University of Notre Dame Press, 2005), pp. 58–76. Thomas is squarely in the tradition of the Christian Platonists when he writes, 'Just as the procession of persons is the reason of the production of creatures by the first principle, so too this same procession is the reason for the return of creatures to their end; since, just as we have been created by the Son and the Holy Spirit, so too it is by them that we are united to our ultimate end.' Aquinas, *1 Sent.* D.14 q.2 art. 2, in Emery, 'Trinity and Creation', p. 67. Cf. David B. Burrell, *Freedom and Creation in Three Traditions* (Notre Dame: University of Notre Dame Press, 1993), pp. 115–17, noting Aquinas, *ST* 1.15.1: 'As then the world was not made by chance, but by God acting by His intellect, as will appear later there must exist in the divine mind a form to the likeness of which the world was made. And in this the notion of an idea consists.'

framework—at least with respect to creation. When it comes to matters such as justification, of course, Protestant divines have plunged into philosophical waters with an abandon to match any of the medievals. We need only cite the formative role in Protestant scholasticism of Aristotelian 'formal' and 'material' principles to see that the church consistently works with the philosophical tools that lie to hand on matters of pressing concern. If it be granted that the theology of creation is one such pressing concern, Plato and his kin deserve at least a respectful hearing.

The first question to address is whether the Bible can accommodate the basic 'Platonic' framework of an ideal realm that somehow informs or provides the template for the visible world. In its mildest form, this seems unobjectionable: God surely has some *idea* of what he is doing in the world. As Augustine says, 'For neither are there many wisdoms, but one, in which are untold and infinite treasures of things intellectual, wherein are all invisible and unchangeable reasons of things visible and changeable which were created by it. For God made nothing unwittingly; not even a human workman can be said to do so.'[106] The very word 'create' carries with it a sense of planning or purpose, whatever the process might be by which that purpose is realized. The Bible does not go into detail as to the ontology of God's plans, or the precise mechanism by which things on earth are connected with the celestial ideas, but it hardly seems beyond the pale of orthodoxy to speculate as to how it all might play itself out.

Moreover, if there is nothing strictly Platonic in the Scriptures, there is material we might deem Platon*ish*, and its presence might further validate some of the idealism we meet with in the tradition. We need not follow Philo and Augustine in trying to divine the creation of the intelligible realm in Genesis 1; this is hardly a natural reading of the text. But the basic contrast of an enduring, invisible realm and a perishable, visible one is a recognizable part of the landscape of the New Testament. The book of Hebrews provides the most extended treatment of the contrast. While the focus is on the distinction between the transitory nature of the temple cult and the abiding nature of Christ's heavenly sacrifice, this is rooted in a broader divergence between the present 'shakeable' age and the 'unshakeable' age to come (Heb. 12:25–29). The same point is made through the example of Abraham, who was content to live as a pilgrim in Canaan, since he was looking forward to the 'city with foundations, whose architect and builder is God' (11:10 NIV). The author of Hebrews gives no hint that this age to come is a purely 'noetic' one; but neither does he posit a seamless continuity between the now-world and the new-world.

106. Augustine, *Civ.* 10. Cf. Augustine, *Div. quaest. LXXXIII* 46: Since it is clear God has created all things, 'who would dare to say that God has created all things without a rational plan?'

Paul's correspondence with the Corinthians provided some particularly seminal ideas for later Christian Platonists. Paul himself speaks of an eternal, unseen realm in 2 Corinthians:

> So we do not lose heart. Though our outer nature is wasting away, our inner nature is being renewed every day. For this slight momentary affliction is preparing for us an eternal weight of glory beyond all comparison, because we look not to the things that are seen but to the things that are unseen; for the things that are seen are transient, but the things that are unseen are eternal. For we know that if the earthly tent we live in is destroyed, we have a building from God, a house not made with hands, eternal in the heavens. Here indeed we groan, and long to put on our heavenly dwelling, so that by putting it on we may not be found naked. For while we are still in this tent, we sigh with anxiety; not that we would be unclothed, but that we would be further clothed, so that what is mortal may be swallowed up by life. He who has prepared us for this very thing is God, who has given us the Spirit as a guarantee (2 Cor. 4:16–5:5).

It is not as if Paul has suddenly abandoned his affirmation of the resurrection in 1 Corinthians 15 and decided that the body as such is a prison, after all. But as in Hebrews, so in 2 Corinthians the world in its present state is fragile; the enduring realm is presently unseen.

The first letter to the Corinthians, and particularly chapter 15, had an even more decisive effect on later theology. The Neoplatonic exitus–reditus scheme had at least surface similarities to the cosmic drama as depicted by Paul in 1 Corinthians 8 and 15 (cf. Phil. 2:6–11): God creates the world through Christ; Christ enters the world to bring it under God's rule; and ultimately Christ gives the subdued cosmos back to God, at which point God is said to be 'all in all'. Eriugena's language of water drops and streams is not the happiest, but he admits he is trying to make sense of the apparent equation of God and the world in Scripture and tradition. His frequent demurrals underscore that he does not want to simply collapse God and creation.

There is at least some congruity, then, between the basic shape of a broadly Platonist or idealist outlook and some portions of Scripture. One might still argue that idealism disrupts the overall rhythms of the biblical witness, particularly in Platonism's putative denigration of the natural world. One need only point to Eriugena's attenuated version of the resurrection, or popular piety's 'the point in life is to die and go to heaven' to see how such thinking can play itself out. Idealism of any stripe encourages (at the very least) a formal subordination of matter to Spirit or Mind or Form. In his more Neoplatonical moments, someone like Augustine can refer to matter as 'close to nothing'. The ascetic rigours of monastic living were no doubt encouraged by a dualistic view of body and mind, and this lifestyle would in turn reinforce the dualistic view. The ideal realm is frequently, and unhelpfully, described as 'more real' than the sensible world.[107]

But formal subordination does not necessitate denigration in a strongly negative sense. Time and again we see avowed Platonists like Eriugena or Coleridge or Lewis express a deep appreciation for the beauty of the natural world. A consummate idealist like Edwards could spend countless hours meditating on stars and spiders. Christian Platonism has often been marked by a sacramental view of nature, in which created things make visible, albeit imperfectly, the invisible glories of the divine Ideas. Even Eriugena attempts to argue that his spiritualized eschaton somehow captures and ennobles matter rather than doing away with it.

It is precisely in the eschaton that the tension between Platonism and the Bible is most keenly felt. Coleridge and Eriugena raise interesting questions about the nature of the resurrection body, and by extension the nature of the new creation as a whole, but they do not necessarily provide much in the way of answers. The Neoplatonic tendency to see the world absorbed back into God seems to threaten the very coherence of a new creation. It is all well and good to speak of the barriers between God and humanity being broken down, but does this permit the ongoing existence of anything besides God? Has Augustine made a coherent Christian point when he avers that in heaven we will 'know all totally and simultaneously without any succession of time'[108]—or has he replaced the dynamic biblical vision of the future for static concepts derived from Greek philosophy?

The questions are worth asking. An eschatology of return coupled with Platonist idealism does run the risk of leaving the world spinning its wheels unto eternity. The New Jerusalem in Revelation, for instance, is not a timeless archetype to which the saints return, but the historically conditioned city that descends from heaven to earth to fulfil God's vision for the creation project. But it is curious that Christian Platonists, for all their flaws, have made so many contributions to a life-affirming theology. The arch-Platonist Origen appears to have given rise to the attenuated view of the resurrection body that dogged his successors like Eriugena. But it was also Origen who inspired the idea of a continual progress in our understanding of God in the eternal state. We might say Origen did this in spite of his Platonism rather than because of it, but the fact remains that he and Gregory provide a vivid view of eschatological life that is far more compelling than the common Protestant notion that the new creation is simply a church service that lasts forever. 'Platonism' as understood by Coleridge and Lewis represents the Romantic desire for a world greater than the one we experience, one happily

107. See e.g. Edwards, *Miscellany* 42, cited in Zakai, *Nature*, p. 22.
108. Augustine, *Conf.* 12.13.

removed from the dissolution that marks the present cosmos. Lewis's friend J. R. R. Tolkien, to take but one example, is constantly evoking the world beyond our Middle Earth, and his fictional creation account in the Silmarillion is quite consonant with Christian Platonism. But he was also—or for that very reason—as staunch a defender of 'nature' as anyone. For these thinkers, the current world order is merely not a symbol in the thinnest sense, an arbitrary sign pointing towards something else. Rather it is a sacrament giving a genuine foretaste of greater glories to come.

7

Easily, Cleverly, Silently: The Process of Creation

How does God create the world? There are at least two ways of approaching the question. On the one hand, one can gain information about how the world unfolds and label that as God's creative act. A scientifically minded Christian might rely more heavily on theory and observation of the natural world, while a theologian would couple that with insights from Scripture and tradition. But in both cases one is looking at the exterior processes and confessing that God has done this. But there is also the *interior* question as to what precisely God is doing to make things what they are. How does he come into contact with the cosmos to shape it according to his designs? What level of independence (if any) does the world have?

Although these issues are very much intertwined, for the sake of our discussion we will begin with the theological account of world formation, and then turn to the scientific account. At that point we will attempt to see how these different approaches might coinhere, and address the even more difficult question of how God brings about the unfolding of the world.

Process: The Theological Account

The Bible and process

Genesis 1 is naturally the focal point for much of the discussion on the process by which God created the world, and we will examine the tradition of interpretation in a moment. But it is worth remembering that this is not the only account of creation in the Scriptures. There is of course the complementary story in Genesis 2, though this focuses much more on the creation of Adam and Eve than on the surrounding world. A text like Psalm 104, however, is a detailed account of the fashioning of the world, and one that depicts the process from a perspective that is very different from that of Genesis 1. Not only is the six-day scheme absent; the transition from original creation to *creatio continua* is barely perceptible. In the beginning of the poem, the heavens are stretched out, the earth is established, and the smothering abyss is cast off the mountains—primordial stage-setting in line with the opening verses of Genesis. But the subdued waters seem to flow straight to present-day creatures:

> Thou makest springs gush forth in the valleys;
>   they flow between the hills,
> they give drink to every beast of the field;
>   the wild asses quench their thirst.
> By them the birds of the air have their habitation;
>   they sing among the branches.
> From thy lofty abode thou waterest the mountains;
>   the earth is satisfied with the fruit of thy work.
> Thou dost cause the grass to grow for the cattle,
>   and plants for man to cultivate,
> that he may bring forth food from the earth,
>   and wine to gladden the heart of man,
> oil to make his face shine,
>   and bread to strengthen man's heart (vv. 10–15).

A similar lack of concern for temporal strictures can be found in Psalm 74:

> Yet God my King is from of old,
>   working salvation in the midst of the earth.
> Thou didst divide the sea by thy might;
>   thou didst break the heads of the dragons on the waters.
> Thou didst crush the heads of Leviathan,
>   thou didst give him as food for the creatures of the wilderness.
> Thou didst cleave open springs and brooks;
>   thou didst dry up ever-flowing streams.
> Thine is the day, thine also the night;
>   thou hast established the luminaries and the sun.
> Thou hast fixed all the bounds of the earth;
>   thou hast made summer and winter (vv. 12–17).

As we have noted earlier, the boundaries are so blurred that it is hard to tell whether the crushing of Leviathan is a militarized image of God subduing the abyss (with a nod towards Marduk and Tiamat), or whether it is an evocation of the exodus remixed with imagery from the primal creation.[1]

None of this means that the authors of the psalms would have necessarily disavowed that God made the world in six days. It does indicate that a

1. See Jon Douglas Levenson, *Creation and the Persistence of Evil: The Jewish Drama of Divine Omnipotence* (Princeton: Princeton University Press, 1988), pp. 7–10.

creedal affirmation of the six days was not their first order of business when reflecting on God's acts of creation. They instead emphasized the beauty of the world, the goodness of God evident in his provision of life for all creatures, and the intricate interweaving of creation and salvation—precisely the sorts of things which will receive attention in later meditations upon Genesis 1.

Genesis 1

We will eschew here a detailed analysis of Genesis 1 and its history of interpretation, since in effect the discussion of Genesis permeates everything written about creation. We have already touched directly upon aspects of the text in our discussions of Christology, time and eternity, and creation *ex nihilo*, and we will devote particular attention to the creation of humanity in the following chapter. We are concerned here more with the general tenor of theological approaches to Genesis, particularly as they relate to the process of God's creative activity.

We may briefly note contemporary interpretations which attempt to read the text in its ancient setting. Points of contact with Ancient Near Eastern texts like the *Enuma Elish* have been duly noted, though most would agree that Genesis 1 features at best muted echoes of the combat motif in the creation myths of surrounding cultures. Depending on one's theological orientation, such parallels might signal either an attempt to make sense of Israel's religious experience in light of widely accepted ancient conventions of world formation, or a polemic against the false accounts of creation, written with contextual sensitivity to ensure maximum impact. Like other provisions in Torah, it would serve as a barrier against the pagan ways of the nations.

With respect to the structure and message of the text, some recent scholars have noted the parallelism between the creation of three 'kingdoms' on days one through three (light and darkness; sea and sky; dry land), and the creation of their respective 'kings' or inhabitants on the ensuing three days (sun and moon, which are explicitly said to 'rule' the day and night; birds and fish; land animals and humans).[2] Such a poetic reading eliminates the need to read a precise process in the narrative, and helps clear up problems like the appearance of a light source on day one, long before the creation of the sun.[3] Some traditionalist readers have reached a *modus vivendi* with

2. See among many Meredith Kline, 'Space and Time in the Genesis Cosmogony', *PSCF* 48 (1996): pp. 2–15.

3. This difficulty was noted from the very earliest days of the church; see e.g. Augustine, *Gen.Litt.* 1.12.

modern geological notions of time by suggesting a 'day–age' theory whereby the days of Genesis could constitute vast ages.[4]

All parties can find something to support their interpretation in the history of interpretation. Perhaps the majority of pre-modern theologians started with the assumption that the six days meant six days, and that the subsequent genealogies indicated the world had been created a few thousand years ago. The Bible was the authoritative text for understanding the world, and in the absence of any firm scientific evidence to the contrary, Genesis could be taken at face value.

But this is hardly the whole story. To begin with, plenty of ancient scholars eschewed the 'literal' interpretation of the text. We have already seen that Philo and Augustine move in this direction (despite the title of the latter's work *The Literal Interpretation of Genesis*). For Augustine, it made no philosophical sense to imagine that God had to string out his creative endeavours over a period of time. The world had been made not in time, but with time, and in his view it must have sprung into existence all at once. This is surely true of the divine ideas, but it seems to have held for the visible creation as well.[5]

As we have seen, for Platonist interpreters the first step in the process of creation was the formation of the Ideas of things in the divine mind. It is not surprising in light of this that great weight was placed in the tradition on the creation of angels, who were taken to be purely intelligible beings, and in this respect thus closest to the divine ideas. The making of angels is not even mentioned in the six-days narrative (it does appear in Psalm 104), though Augustine and others equated the creation of 'heaven' in the beginning with the creation of angels.[6] The importance of the angels lay rather in filling up the 'Great Chain of Being', as A. J. Lovejoy has termed it. While Lovejoy has drawn his share of criticism, he makes a convincing case that theologians through the Middle Ages were strongly influenced by a sense drawn from Plato and his followers that the world ought to be *filled up* with things by way of reflecting the divine perfection.[7] This

4. See the examples adduced by Davis Young in Howard J. van Till et al., *Portraits of Creation: Biblical and Scientific Perspectives on the World's Formation* (Grand Rapids: Eerdmans, 1990), pp. 58–59.

5. Étienne Gilson, *The Christian Philosophy of Saint Augustine* (trans. L. E. M. Lynch; New York: Random House, 1960), p. 197.

6. Gilson, *Philosophy of Augustine*, pp. 197–98. See also the equation of heaven and the angels in the standard textbook of medieval theology, Peter Lombard's *Sent.* 2.

7. Arthur O. Lovejoy, *The Great Chain of Being: A Study of the History of an Idea* (Cambridge: Harvard University Press, 1936), ch. 3. The biblical language of fullness no doubt also contributed to this line of thinking; see e.g. Col. 1:19, 25; 2:9–10; Eph. 1:23; 4:10, 13.

involved not only variations in size, but also in types of things: the angels sat atop the ontological ladder of created things, with humans mediating between the intelligible realm and the visible one of animals and sticks and stones.

Why, then, the six days? Tertullian was happy to affirm that the gradual unfolding of things was all a part of God's good plan:

> God, indeed, consummated all His works in a due order; at first He paled them out, as it were, in their unformed elements, and then He arranged them in their finished beauty. For He did not all at once inundate light with the splendour of the sun, nor all at once temper darkness with the moon's assuaging ray. The heaven He did not all at once bedeck with constellations and stars, nor did He at once fill the seas with their teeming monsters. The earth itself He did not endow with its varied fruitfulness all at once; but at first He bestowed upon it being, and then He filled it, that it might not be made in vain.[8]

For Augustine, the delineation was as much about previewing the history of the world as it was looking back to a sequential creation:

> I think we should consider more carefully why this rest is attributed to the seventh day. For throughout the whole text of the divine Scriptures I see that six work ages are, as it were, distinguished from one another by their limits so that in the seventh age rest is hoped for. These same six ages bear a likeness to the six days in which God made those things which Scripture reports that he made.[9]

Whatever the flaws of Augustine's interpretation might be, he was in good company. From Irenaeus to (at least) Jonathan Edwards, theologians took the six days as a template for the future: six thousand years of history followed by the millennium, a Sabbath rest for the first creation. Basil notes at the beginning of his *Hexaemeron*: 'The dogmas of the end, and of the renewing of the world, are announced beforehand in these short words put at the head of the inspired history. In the beginning God made. That which was begun in time is condemned to come to an end in time. If there has been a beginning do not doubt of the end.'[10] It is a tribute to the vitality of the tradition that Edwards would still be inclined to adopt a modified version of it in the 1700s: 'As the world was six days in the making, so I believe that the kingdom of God, that it will be six days in making before 'tis finished. That is, things will be overturning six days in order to it; and the seventh day there shall be rest, putting a thousand years for a day, as the apostle

8. Tertullian, *Herm*. 29.
9. Augustine, *Gen. Man*. 1.23.
10. Basil, *Hex*. 1.3.

Peter does.'[11] (We note that Edwards' millennium is a spiritual reality rather than a literal earthly reign of Christ.)

The eschatological reading of Genesis seems at first blush a source of embarrassment to the church: once the meter on the fatally flawed six-thousand-year scheme runs out, we meet with a succession of clumsy re-workings involving seemingly arbitrary assignations of significance to a host of random events and personages (usually popes) in Western European history. But underneath the ungainly surface, there are sound exegetical and theological instincts at work here. Israel clearly saw its weekly seven-day cycle as a derivative of the primal creation. Just as the workweek was meant to culminate in rest and celebration, so history was meant to usher in an eschatological Sabbath. This is evident throughout the New Testament. As we saw in chapter 2, the Gospel of John is rife with creation imagery, such that the work of Jesus (note the proliferation of words with the *erga-* root in the gospel) reaches to the Sabbath, with the resurrection marking the dawn of the new creation. Jesus declares 'It is finished' in 19:30, and the very next verse twice notes that the following day was the Sabbath.

The book of Hebrews is even clearer on the matter. The epistle's central thrust is that 'there remains a sabbath-rest (*sabbatismos*) for the people of God' (4:9), and that entering this rest requires faithfulness to the Messiah who has secured it for his people. This *sabbatismos* almost certainly refers to the rest in the eschatological Jerusalem that awaits believers at the end of the age, hence the book's repeated exhortations to remains steadfast during the present time of testing.[12]

Among modern theologians, Wolfhart Pannenberg has captured the essential dynamics of the eschatological interpretation of Genesis in sophisticated theological fashion. Pannenberg's central idea is that created things are only seen in their fullness when they reach their eschatological destiny. This helps him make sense of at least one aspect of the ascription of creation to Christ: since he brings things to fulfilment in the end, he may properly be seen as their originator in the beginning. He writes:

> On the basis of the eschatologically oriented Israelite understanding of truth, according to which the essence of a thing has not always existed—even though hiddenly—but is decided only by what becomes of it, the predestination of all things toward Jesus, their eschatological summation through Jesus, is identical with their creation through Jesus . . . Christ's mediation of creation is not to

---

11. Jonathan Edwards, 'Notes on the Apocalypse' 16, *The Works of Jonathan Edwards* (26 vols; New Haven: Yale University Press, 1997–2009), 5:129.

12. There is a slim chance that the rest is a present-day 'spiritual reality', but even this would be an eschatological rest patterned on Genesis 1: note 1:2, 'in these last days he has spoken to us in the Son'.

> be thought of primarily in terms of the temporal beginning of the world. It is rather to be understood in terms of the whole of the world process that receives its unity and meaning in the light of its end that has appeared in advance in the history of Jesus.[13]

Barth, too, is able to find theological significance in the Genesis 1 text despite the radically altered scientific landscape. He famously describes Genesis as 'saga' in an attempt to find a term somewhere between 'myth' and 'history'. His concern here was not merely to take a few furtive steps back from the onrushing tide of science, but rather to do justice to the Genesis account itself. At root, he is seeking to affirm the genuine creative work of God while asking the very relevant question of how you can have a proper 'history' of events pre-dating any human witness.[14] At times he veers towards an almost allegorical reading of the text. This is particularly striking in the case of Barth's handling of 'darkness' and the *nihil*. Barth argues that the divisions of Genesis 1—most notably the division of light and darkness—constitute a rejection of chaos and an affirmation of life.[15] As for eschatology, this is woven into the fabric of creation: again, the covenant is the interior basis of creation, and creation is the external basis of the covenant. The separation of light from darkness in the beginning represents God's choice of life over death, and he commits himself to bring life to its fullness, whatever obstacles might appear to stand in his way.

One major question remains with respect to creation 'in the beginning'. Granted that many Christians have accommodated the insights of modern science in their view of world formation, does it even make sense for the church to speak of creation as a primal act of God? Should we rather re-engineer the doctrine with *creatio continua* as its new centrepiece? This would certainly fit with developmental trajectories that dominate thinking in geology and biology. It would also help align theological discourse with the idea of reality as a space-time continuum, rather than a receptacle into which God places various items.[16] Widening the timescale of what counts as

---

13. Wolfhart Pannenberg, *Jesus, God and Man* (Philadelphia: Westminster Press, 1968), p. 391. Cf. his comment on p. 169, 'What they are is decided by what they will become.'

14. Karl Barth, *Church Dogmatics* (4 vols; Edinburgh: T&T Clark, 1956–75), *CD* III/1, pp. 76–91. Similar considerations, though from a different set of exegetical assumptions, seem to have shaped Meredith Kline's description of Gen. 1 as an 'apocalypse of Elohim', in *Images of the Spirit* (Eugene, OR: Wipf & Stock, 1999), p. 26.

15. See Matthew Rose, *Ethics in Barth: God, Metaphysics and Morals* (Farnham: Ashgate, 2010), pp. 177–80. Rose notes (p. 178), 'The puzzling thing about nothingness is that it exists only on account of God's having said No to it.'

16. See esp. Alan Torrance, '*Creatio Ex Nihilo* and the Spatio-Temporal Dimensions, with Special Reference to Jurgen Moltmann and D. C. Williams', in *The Doctrine of Creation* (ed. Colin Gunton; T&T Clark, 1991), pp. 83–103.

'creation' might give new life to the church fathers' eschatological reading of the six days. It would also provide an apologetic for apparent design flaws: if God's creative work is an ongoing reality, it cannot be judged until the final word is issued.

There is no question that *creatio continua* needs to be an integral part of the doctrine of creation. Indeed, as we will see in our next section, the idea that the Father is 'always working' has been a feature of theological tradition from the beginning. It may even be the case that the relative weights of fixity versus process need to be recalculated; this has already happened in fairly literal terms as most theologians have moved beyond the six-thousand-year-old earth and the literal six-day creation scheme. The positing of a Big Bang does not obviate the problem, since one can say that not much in particular is created at that point—particularly since the Big Bang does not necessitate the introduction of a cosmic seed which will inevitably grow into the universe as we know it.

Despite all this, the language of creation in the beginning is still essential. To begin with, the world *as the stage for human history* has largely been set. Some might object that this is too anthropocentric a view of things. But what other point of view makes sense for human beings to hold? We can claim to have a theocentric view of things, but the thought that God would vouchsafe humanity such a vantage point already supposes an exalted view of man and thus is functionally anthropocentric—we are seeing things from God's perspective, but it is still our eyes that do the seeing. The same might be said for an ecologically friendly geocentric view of things—and here there is the added problem of how precisely one would take the 'view' of a planet. On any account of origins, humans came into a world that was ready for them.

God, then, has given humans this world in its present form as their living space. Thus it is meaningful in this sense to speak of the world as created. Taking a broader lens, it is equally true that from the beginning he created it to be *this sort of a world*, and no other. There is an interesting debate to be had as to whether we ought to speak of 'natural laws' or 'habits of God'. But there is an undeniable consistency of rhythm to things in the world. It is this principle that allows science to proceed in the first place: if the world were subject to continually changing operating principles, we could not speak meaningfully about what happened five minutes ago, let alone what happened five billion years ago. An ancient resident of Pompeii might understandably see Aetna as an emblem of the irruption of chaos; but the volcanologist studies it in the hope of finding a rationale for why it erupts when it does. People may not be able to predict how events will transpire in the natural world, but they do move forward in a discernibly orderly fashion; their proclivity to do so bespeaks creation.

Finally, a denial of creation in the beginning vitiates the notion of Sabbath, and thus unmoors the Christian hope from its anchor. If God has never really accomplished anything by way of world formation, a question mark hangs over his promise to 'make all things new'. But God has made this cosmos, and thus the biblical writers can look backwards towards the mighty work of creation to draw encouragement for the mighty work of recreation yet to come.

We might use a humble metaphor to drive home the relationship of primal creation and what follows. When a baby is born, we can rightly say that the work of gestation is complete, and a new human being has entered the world; proud parents might even declare the infant 'perfect'.[17] But even the 'perfect' baby has a necessary developmental trajectory—it is well and truly there, but it also has somewhere to go. In the same way, this world as we have it is indeed good, but this does not prevent it from moving forward.

Continuous creation

The term 'continuous creation' is a useful one, though like anything it is subject to misunderstanding. For the reasons stated above, we do not want to completely displace creation in the beginning with continuous creation. This is the danger in occasionalism, such as we see at times in Edwards: if God is the only real cause, then we are left with him conjuring the world into existence at every moment. At that point the word 'creation' is drained of all meaning. More helpful is David Burrell's reading of Aquinas: God is always 'creating' in the sense that he is always 'bestowing existing' on things. This is distinguished from conservation only in that conservation involves things which are already on the scene.[18] Burrell distinguishes this from occasionalism by denying a 'univocal notion of *acting*'. Most critically, God's acting is not to be understood as a change.[19] As Aquinas himself says (*ST* 1.104.1): 'The preservation of things by God is a continuation of that action whereby He gives existence, which action is without either motion or time; so also the preservation of light in the air is by the continual influence of the sun.'

Creatio continua easily mingles with the doctrines of providence and preservation, and much of what we might include in continuous creation

17. Recall from chapter 1 the words ascribed to Moses' mother in Exod. 2:2, 'And she saw that he was good, he.'

18. David B. Burrell, *Freedom and Creation in Three Traditions* (Notre Dame: University of Notre Dame Press, 1993), pp. 68–73.

19. Burrell, *Three Traditions*, p. 69.

has been subsumed in theological discourse under providence.[20] But *creatio continua* remains a useful term in its own right. 'Providence' is particularly helpful as a label for God's overseeing of events in the already created world, with the story of Joseph providing the parade example. As such, it does not consist in the production of novel items, but rather refers to the mysterious way in which God directs existing realities for the benefit of his people. 'Preservation' likewise works best as a term for the maintenance of things that are already there: the world is not completely independent of God, but at the deepest level hangs upon his word for its ongoing existence.[21] *Creatio continua* may be used to speak precisely to the irruption of new things into the world by the hand of God. The phrase works particularly well for miraculous works of healing or deliverance which point to the direct working of God's hand, but it can also serve to describe the creation of new realities within the existing processes of the cosmos: from the birth of a baby boy (Exod. 2:2) to the gestation of stars in stellar nurseries.

We have seen that the Bible seems to imply something like 'contiuous creation', even if it does not use that precise term. This might take the form of the serene flow from primal to present-day waters in Psalm 104, or the agonistic vision of the ongoing struggle against chaos some have seen in Psalm 74.[22] Especially telling is Psalm 104:30: 'When thou sendest forth thy Spirit, they are created [*bara'*, as in Gen. 1]; and thou renewest the face of the ground.' The mighty works of Jesus may be seen as irruptions of new creation into a hopelessly broken world, but they may equally be seen as restorative works within the present creation. The healing miracles in particular speak to God's ongoing concern for what he has made. This comes out with particular force in John's gospel, which not coincidentally features one of the most direct statements of *creatio continua*: 'My Father is working still, and I am working' (John 5:17). In the prologue, John seems to deliberately blur the lines between primal creation and God's continual work in the world. The Word is with God in the beginning, and all things came into being through him; but is the 'life' that is 'in him' reduced to events in the beginning? Does his 'light' shine only on the first day? The latter question receives a definitive answer in the healing of the man born blind in John 9. Not only does Jesus bring light to the man's eyes. He does it, as we have seen, by employing the Adamic dust of the earth to complete what was left undone at the man's birth. The light continues to shine in the darkness and to bring order out of chaos.

---

20. Note e.g. the scholastic slogan *conservatio creatio continua est*.

21. See Aquinas; Burrell wants to see all as creation, *Three Traditions*.

22. See esp. Levenson, *Creation*, pp. 17–20.

Whatever terms we employ, speaking of God's ongoing involvement with the creation requires great care. We have noted the dangers of occasionalism, which threatens the very notion of 'creation': if God is always creating, is he ever really creating; and if things are continually being created, are they ever really *there*? At one level, there must be some space, some breathing room, between God and creation for the creation to exist at all. Otherwise, we might say, he would suffocate it by his sheer omnipotence. But the church has equally tried to resist flying to the other extreme, where God sets the world in motion in the beginning and then leaves it to its own devices. The failure to resist this temptation is of course most notably evident in deism, with its Watchmaker God.

In and of itself, a mechanical image for the creation could be serviceable. Peter Lombard had used the phrase 'the Machine of the World' long before Newton came on the scene: in three days 'the machine of all this world [*huius mundi machina*] was arranged and its parts organized . . . the four elements of the world were differentiated and arranged in their places. In the following three days those elements were adorned.'[23] As a metaphor, the idea of the world-machine could address one aspect of creation: just as we set up various devices that aid us in our labour, so God set up a well-organized world which hums along nicely to serve his purposes. It might even reinforce what Colin Gunton calls the world's *Selbständigkeit* or 'proper independence'—the world as a created entity is free to be itself without God conjuring it into existence every moment. Genesis 1 already recognized secondary causality of some sort in the reference to the creation of plants which would self-propagate: 'And God said, "Let the earth put forth vegetation, plants yielding seed, and fruit trees bearing fruit in which is their seed, each according to its kind, upon the earth." And it was so' (Gen. 1:11). Basil helpfully compares God's work in this regard to human work in his *Hexaemeron*:

> Among arts, some have in view production, some practice, others theory. The object of the last is the exercise of thought, that of the second, the motion of the body. Should it cease, all stops; nothing more is to be seen. Thus dancing and music have nothing behind; they have no object but themselves. In creative arts on the contrary the work lasts after the operation. Such is architecture—such are the arts which work in wood and brass and weaving, all those indeed which, even when the artisan has disappeared, serve to show an industrious intelligence and to cause the architect, the worker in brass or the weaver, to be admired on account of his work. Thus, then, to show that the world is a work of art displayed for the beholding of all people; to make them know Him who created it, Moses does not use another word. In the beginning, he says God created. He does not say God worked, God formed, but God created (1.7).

23. *Sent.* 2.14.9, trans. in Robert Bartlett, *The Natural and the Supernatural in the Middle Ages* (Cambridge: CUP, 2008), p. 38.

But the machine metaphor is liable to get out of control. For the Deists, Newtonian mechanics served to lock God out of his own house. Once the machine is set up by the Master Designer, what need is there for him to tinker with it further? His laws are perfect, his craftsmanship unimpeachable, and so the cosmos abides as an essentially self-sustaining entity. *Creatio continua* ceases to be a meaningful term, and in its extreme form, the Machine takes over what had formerly been subsumed under God's providence. Miracles, let alone a 'new heavens and new earth', could be excluded on principle. Gotthold Lessing could throw around the terms 'creation' and 'providence' to describe the world's inner processes, but as Barth acerbically notes, 'It is hard to say what difference this is supposed to make, and perhaps only Lessing's Masonic wisdom prevented his frankly confessing that it makes no difference at all.'[24]

In the end, no single term or model of divine action may adequately capture what we have subsumed under continuous creation. God is intimately involved with the creation, sustaining things in their inmost being, and calling forth new life. It is equally true that he gives the world the space to be itself. While he is well aware of the basic facts of life, the psalmist can still confess: 'For thou didst form my inward parts, thou didst knit me together in my mother's womb' (Ps. 139:13). The affirmation of God's creative activity in the world thus sits comfortably alongside the recognition of genuine 'secondary' causes—'secondary' in the sense that they remain under God's sovereign hand, not that God pushes them around as if he were simply one more link in the causal chain. William Cowper's familiar words remain as good a summary as any: 'God moves in a mysterious way/ His wonders to perform'.

De-creation

In his comments on the plagues of the book of Revelation, Jacques Ellul introduces the immensely helpful term 'de-creation' to the theological lexicon:

> In these verses we find ourselves both in the presence of a recollection of the 'plagues of Egypt', which all the commentators have noticed . . . and also, which has been rarely seen, a sort of 'de-creation', a putting in question by going back, of the works of the third day (the vegetation and the waters), of the fourth day (the lights), of the fifth day (the fish).[25]

24. Quoted in Leo Scheffczyk, *Creation and Providence* (trans. Richard Strachan; New York: Herder & Herder, 1970), p. 204.

25. Jacques Ellul, *Apocalypse: The Book of Revelation* (trans. G. W. Schreiner; New York: Seabury, 1977), p. 74.

Ellul's comments, we will see, are relevant not only to the Apocalypse but to much of the rest of the Scripture as well.[26]

While God's acts of de-creative judgement are understandably missing from many treatments of creation, there is much to commend their inclusion in the doctrine. To begin with, an awareness of de-creation assists in making sense of the tumultuous transition from primal creation to new creation. It is tempting to portray the creation project as a march from glory to glory—the world is declared very good in the beginning, and it just gets better from there. This ignores the readily observable fact that things tend to lapse back into a state of chaos, as well as the scriptural witness that ascribes many of these lapses to the will of God. In many such instances, the connection with creation is made explicit, lest we imagine that God has lost sight of the fact that the things he is tearing apart are his own handiwork.

This de-creation motif stands out in two of the seminal narratives of the Hebrew bible. The story of Noah ends in recreative glory, with Noah and his children set free on the dry land to go forth and multiply like Adam and Eve of old. But the recreation only happens because of the prior de-creation. The waters that had been separated to create space for terrestrial life now collapse back into chaos: 'In the six hundredth year of Noah's life, in the second month, on the seventeenth day of the month, on that day all the springs of the great deep burst forth, and the windows of the heavens were opened' (Gen. 7:11). The de-creative nature of divine judgement is equally apparent in the story of the exodus. God disorders Egypt's world in the plague sequences, and in the climactic moment of deliverance the waters of the sea rush back to engulf Pharaoh and his army.

The threat of a return to chaos was not confined to Israel's distant past. The Edenic splendour of the promised land was subject to the incursion of the wild world beyond should Israel fail to keep its end of the covenant. The Day of the Lord 'will be darkness, not light', Amos declared (5:18 NIV). Of all the covenant curses that threatened the nation, the most grievous was exile, an exile that surely corresponds to the expulsion of Adam and Eve from the garden. The connection of God's judgement with primordial emptiness is made clearest in Jeremiah. With Babylon poised to invade the land, the prophet laments:

> I looked on the earth, and lo, it was waste and void; and to the heavens, and they had no light. I looked on the mountains, and lo, they were quaking, and all the hills moved to and fro. I looked, and lo, there was no man, and all

26. For de-creation in the Old Testament, see esp. Gregory Mobley, *The Return of the Chaos Monsters—and Other Backstories of the Bible* (Grand Rapids: Eerdmans, 2012), pp. 16–33.

> the birds of the air had fled. I looked, and lo, the fruitful land was a desert, and all its cities were laid in ruins before the LORD, before his fierce anger (Jer. 4:23–26).

We find something analogous in the curses of Leviticus 26:14–39. In an inversion of the command to Adam and Eve in Genesis 1:26–28, Israel's dominion over the land will be overturned: 'and your strength shall be spent in vain, for your land shall not yield its increase, and the trees of the land shall not yield their fruit . . . And I will let loose the wild beasts among you, which shall rob you of your children, and destroy your cattle, and make you few in number, so that your ways shall become desolate' (26:20, 22). Of special interest is the note on the Sabbaths of the land in verses 34–35: 'Then the land shall enjoy its sabbaths as long as it lies desolate, while you are in your enemies' land; then the land shall rest, and enjoy its sabbaths. As long as it lies desolate it shall have rest, the rest which it had not in your sabbaths when you dwelt upon it.' The text is clearly taking its point of departure from the creation account, now expanded to include Sabbath years in addition to the weekly day of rest (Lev. 25:1–17). We might see this as simply retributive judgement along the lines of an eye for an eye: 'if you do not want to keep the Sabbath, I will keep the Sabbath for you.' But one could also construe it as a divine work of judgement which will issue in Sabbath rest for the land. However one takes it, this text was foundational for later Jewish eschatological schema.[27]

The book of Job, finally, offers a searing account of personal de-creation:

> After this Job opened his mouth and cursed the day of his birth. And Job said: 'Let the day perish wherein I was born, and the night which said, "A man-child is conceived." Let that day be darkness! May God above not seek it, nor light shine upon it. Let gloom and deep darkness claim it. Let clouds dwell upon it; let the blackness of the day terrify it. That night—let thick darkness seize it! let it not rejoice among the days of the year, let it not come into the number of the months. Yea, let that night be barren; let no joyful cry be heard in it. Let those curse it who curse the day, who are skilled to rouse up Levi'athan. Let the stars of its dawn be dark; let it hope for light, but have none, nor see the eyelids of the morning; because it did not shut the doors of my mother's womb, nor hide trouble from my eyes.'[28]

---

27. See James M. Scott, *On Earth as in Heaven: The Restoration of Sacred Time and Sacred Space in the Book of Jubilees* (Leiden: Brill, 2005), pp. 90–103. Note too that the eschatological framework of Dan. 7 is predicated on a similar inversion of the creation account: the Son of Man (Israel) labours under the dominion of the beasts (the surrounding nations). The promised deliverance consists in the restoration of right order, as the Son of Man regains his proper dominion.

28. Job 3:1–10; thanks to Daniel Brown for alerting me to this passage.

The New Testament continues in the same vein.[29] Revelation provides the most elaborate theological treatment of the theme. God is praised as the Creator of all in the foundational vision of chapter 4, and again in chapter 14, but the book is better known for its three sevenfold sequences of judgement upon the world. The Egypt plagues provide much of the theological capital for the scheme, and Joshua's destruction of Jericho surely informs the seven trumpet blasts of chapters 8–11. But in light of Ellul's insight, it is hard to miss the parallels with the creation week. In each sequence of the seals, trumpets, and bowls, we have six depictions of catastrophe, followed by an interlude in which certain people are 'sealed' against divine wrath, with a definitive act of judgement coming in the seventh item. We thus have what might be termed 'de-creation weeks' followed by a Sabbath of consummate judgement. Things come to a climax in 20:11, where 'heaven and earth flee away' from the one seated on the throne. John stages the scene carefully: final judgement is rendered in the no-place between the disappearance of the present world order in 20:11 and the appearance of 'a new heaven and a new earth' in 21:1.

This is only the most extended example of a persistent New Testament theme. Jesus' apocalyptic discourse (Mark 13 and parallels) is an obvious place to begin, with its falling stars and darkened sun. But this is only the logical extension of Jesus' systematic disassembly of core elements of Israel's corporate life: family ties, traditional ways of observing Torah, and even the temple itself must be reoriented around Jesus' proclamation of the kingdom of God in their midst. In a culture where cosmic order and social order were of a piece, Jesus' call to a radical change in religious observance aligns well with a dissolution of the universe itself. The crucifixion, with the accompanying end-times phenomena of darkness and earthquakes, marks the acme (or the nadir, depending on how one looks at it) of the de-creative enterprise.[30] The re-visioning of Torah forms a central thread of Paul's letters, while cosmic dissolution shows up in places like Romans 8 and 2 Peter 3.[31]

Gregory Nazienzen saw the relevance of such biblical texts when his own community suffered under plague, drought, and hail. Note particularly the last line of this passage from his *Oration on Hail*:

---

29. I have a detailed account of this in 'Paradise by the Desolation Trail', in *As Long as the Earth Endures* (ed. Jonathan Moo and Robin Routledge; Downers Grove, IL: IVP, 2013).

30. Note esp. Matt. 27:51–54, with its eschatological earthquake and proto-resurrection.

31. For a detailed discussion of these texts, and their place in a theology of creation, see Jonathan Moo, 'New Testament Hope and a Christian Environmental Ethos', in *As Long as the Earth Endures* (ed. Moo and Routledge), pp. 146–68.

> Terrible is an unfruitful season, and the loss of the crops. It could not be otherwise, when men are already rejoicing in their hopes, and counting on their all but harvested stores. Terrible again is an unseasonable harvest, when the farmers labour with heavy hearts, sitting as it were beside the grave of their crops, which the gentle rain nourished, but the wild storm has rooted up, whereof the mower fills not his hand, neither he that binds up the sheaves his bosom, nor have they obtained the blessing which passers-by bestow upon the farmers. Wretched indeed is the sight of the ground devastated, cleared, and shorn of its ornaments, over which the blessed Joel wails in his most tragic picture of the desolation of the land, and the scourge of famine; while another prophet wails, as he contrasts with its former beauty its final disorder, and thus discourses on the anger of the Lord when He smites the land: before him is the garden of Eden, behind Him a desolate wilderness (*Oration on Hail* 6).[32]

Medieval churchmen likewise looked on the plague-battered world through apocalyptic lenses: Paul the Deacon wrote of the Ligurian plague of the 560s: 'pastoral places had been turned into a desert, and human habitations had become places of refuge for wild beasts.'[33] The Annals of Xanten for AD 873 report: 'Later, in the middle of the month of August, the ancient plague of the Egyptians once again appeared through the land from the east, namely countless swarms of locusts, like bees leaving the hive.'[34] Gregory the Great juxtaposed the recent destruction a hurricane had wreaked on trees, house, and churches, with the looming judgement of all the world:

> We must reflect that to bring these things about our unseen Judge caused the movement of a very slight breeze; he called a storm out of a single cloud and overthrew the earth, he struck the foundation of many buildings, causing them to fall. What will that Judge do when he comes in person, when his anger is burning to punish sinners, if we cannot bear him when he strikes us with an insignificant cloud? What flesh will withstand the presence of his anger, if he moved the wind and overthrew the earth, stirred up the air, and destroyed so many buildings?[35]

It should be evident from the examples of above that the linking of creation and judgement is not merely a wistful bit of symmetry embedded in Scripture: the rise and fall of the Israelite Empire. De-creation is rather the

---

32. New Advent translation.

33. See Sarah Foot, 'Plenty, Portents, and Plagues', in *God's Bounty? The Churches and the Natural World* (ed. Peter Clarke and Tony Claydon; Woodbridge: Boydell, 2010), p. 37.

34. Foot, 'Plenty, Portents, and Plagues', p. 32.

35. Gregory the Great, 'Homilies on the Gospels' 1.3; cf. Foot, 'Plenty, Portents, and Plagues', p. 40.

necessary preparation for recreation. The shape of the relationship may be parsed in several ways.

From the standpoint of humanity, the dissolution of the cosmos serves to underscore the absolute worth of the infinite Creator. There is an inveterate human tendency to imagine the world as a self-contained, self-sufficient entity subject to our control. De-creation dissolves this idolatrous dream. Irenaeus' comments on the resurrection body hold true for the dissolution of the cosmos as a whole. Why are we permitted to die? Irenaeus answers:

> in order that we may never become puffed up, as if we had life from ourselves, and exalted against God, our minds becoming ungrateful; but learning by experience that we possess eternal duration from the excelling power of this Being, not from our own nature, we may neither undervalue that glory which surrounds God as He is, nor be ignorant of our own nature, but that we may know what God can effect, and what benefits man receives, and thus never wander from the true comprehension of things as they are, that is, both with regard to God and with regard to man. And might it not be the case, perhaps, as I have already observed, that for this purpose God permitted our resolution into the common dust of mortality, that we, being instructed by every mode, may be accurate in all things for the future, being ignorant neither of God nor of ourselves?[36]

De-creation can also be seen as an inherent part of the progress of God's creation project. God created the world good, but it still had a road to travel: the command to 'fill the earth and subdue it' comes before the fall. Just as the child must in certain respects give way to the adult it will become, so the world in its present state must be removed to make room for the perfected world.

This is of course only one piece of the puzzle. The transition to adulthood, after all, occurs without the catastrophic dismantling of the child in question. One could counter that at the cellular level such destruction and recreation is in fact happening, but from a theological standpoint it is necessary to see that de-creation is triggered by the estrangement of God and humanity. The world is not only in need of progress; it is in need of purgation. The 'little apocalypse' of Isaiah captures this neatly:

> The earth mourns and withers, the world languishes and withers; the heavens languish together with the earth. The earth lies polluted under its inhabitants; for they have transgressed the laws, violated the statutes, broken the everlasting covenant. Therefore a curse devours the earth, and its inhabitants suffer for their guilt; therefore the inhabitants of the earth are scorched, and few men are left (Isa. 24:4–6).

---

36. Irenaeus, *Haer*. 5.2.

The ritual defilement requires a radical cleansing. The dissolution of the old order is not simply a primitive, punitive measure, the irrational venting of divine wrath on hapless matter. It is instead the breaking of a vessel that has become unfit for divine service—but with a view towards its reformation as the new heavens and new earth (Isa. 65:17). De-creation creates a space for recreation: 'For behold, darkness shall cover the earth, and thick darkness the peoples; but the LORD will arise upon you, and his glory will be seen upon you' (Isa. 60:2).

'Ritual defilement' may seem out of place in a secular age, until we consider the modern horror at *pollution*, a word rife with religious associations. Green politicians may stress the practical consequences of ecological destruction, but much of the emotional energy in modern environmentalism stems from a revulsion at the *miasma* of spilt oil or tasteless shopping malls in the sacred space of nature. Since the apocalyptic visions in Scripture do not demand a particular mechanism by which God visits destruction on the world, it is possible that humanity's pollution of the earth is one of the means by which God's mysterious work of de-creation proceeds. If this is the case, some of the strangest and seemingly most foreign elements in the Bible may prove most useful in gaining a hearing for Christian theology in the wider world.

The theological importance of de-creation is seen nowhere so clearly as in the crucifixion of Jesus. We have noted the cosmological phenomena attending the event. Isaac Watts captured the irony of the moment well:

> Well might the sun in darkness hide
> And shut his glories in,
> When Christ, the mighty Maker died,
> For man the creature's sin.[37]

Like Watts, the New Testament writers lay the most weight on the atoning nature of Christ's death. Paul's teaching on our death in Christ (e.g. Rom. 5) shows how the de-creation of the cross paradoxically brings liberation for the world.

But the fact that it is 'the mighty Maker' who dies invites further theological reflection. In our investigation of Maximus, we noted the vitality of his notion of the relationship between the *logos* and the *logoi*. The *logoi* are in some ways an outflow or reflection of the *logos*, radiating out from him like spokes from a wheel. But each one also has its unique path to take towards the perfection of its nature: from being to well-being to eternal being.

37. Isaac Watts, 'Alas! And Did My Saviour Bleed', in *Hymns and Spiritual Songs* (London: J. Humphreys, for John Lawrence, 1707), book 2, no. 9.

But if the *logos* itself were to suffer, what of the *logoi*? To paraphrase Yeats, if the centre cannot hold, how can things fail to fall apart?

At this point we may be entering not simply the deep waters of theology, but a genuinely fathomless abyss. The utmost caution is in order. On the one hand, we have seen that the suffering of Christ somehow triggers a cataclysm in the world. Given that it is the Son of God who stands at the centre of this storm, it would seem strange to imagine that 'God' is watching all of this at a safe remove, especially when we reckon with the character of the scriptural God as depicted by Moltmann:

> But through the presence of his own being, God participates in the destiny of his own creation. Through the Spirit he suffers with the sufferings of his creatures. In his Spirit he experiences their annihilations. In his Spirit he sighs with the enslaved creation for redemption and liberty. What is true of the Shekinah which dwells in Israel and wanders with Israel into exile, is in its own way true also of the Shekinah of the Creator in his creation. Through his Spirit the Creator is himself involved in his creation. The Spirit is capable of suffering. He can be 'quenched' or 'grieved' (1 Thess. 5.19; Eph. 4.30). For he is the power of the love from which creation has issued and through which it is sustained.[38]

Gregory Nazienzen presses the paradoxical blend of de-creation and recreation at the cross even further:

> Many indeed are the miracles of that time: God crucified; the sun darkened and again rekindled; for it was fitting that the creatures should suffer with their Creator; the veil rent; the Blood and Water shed from His Side; the one as from a man, the other as above man; the rocks rent for the Rock's sake; the dead raised for a pledge of the final Resurrection of all men; the Signs at the Sepulchre and after the Sepulchre, which none can worthily celebrate; and yet none of these equal to the Miracle of my salvation. A few drops of Blood recreate the whole world, and become to all men what rennet is to milk, drawing us together and compressing us into unity.[39]

At the same time, theologians have understandably been reluctant to say that the eternal *logos* 'died': if this had been the case (assuming this *could even be the case under any circumstances*), would we not see the collapse of the entire cosmos, as opposed to some admittedly spectacular but still localized phenomena in the environs of Jerusalem?

There is no certain answer here, but the safest route to explaining the de-creative nature of the cross may be that of seeing Christ crucified as the

38. Jürgen Moltmann, *God in Creation: A New Theology of Creation and the Spirit of God* (Minneapolis: Fortress, 1993), pp. 96–97.

39. Gregory Nazienzen, *Or. Bas.* 45.29.

embodiment of true humanity. Since according to Genesis the fate of creation in some sense rests in the hands of its human vice-regents, the death of Christ would signal the effective demise of the older world order, which is symbolized by the earthquake and the darkening of the heavenly bodies. To deploy the language of Barth, God has pronounced the definitive 'No' to this old world order in the person of Christ who has been made sin for us, but only so that he might say 'Yes' to resurrection and recreation. At one level, the world returns to *nihil* so that God might speak anew the word of creation: 'Behold, I make all things new' (Rev. 21:5).

New creation

The term 'new creation' is used in the first instance of the transformation of believers in Christ in the present. Second Corinthians 5:17 reads literally, 'so that if anyone is in Christ, new creation; the old things have passed away, the new things have come'; the personal approach of most translations—'he or she is a new creation'—is a perfectly acceptable interpretation. Paul also uses the phrase in Galatians 6:15: 'For neither circumcision counts for anything, nor uncircumcision, but a new creation.' Clear allusions to the creation narrative are likewise a feature of Colossians 3:10: 'put on the new nature, which is being renewed in knowledge after the image of its creator'; and 2 Corinthians 4:6: 'For it is the God who said, "Let light shine out of darkness," who has shone in our hearts to give the light of the knowledge of the glory of God in the face of Christ.' John refers to the creation narrative, and the light motif in particular, throughout his corpus, e.g. 1 John 2:8: 'Yet I am writing you a new commandment, which is true in him and in you, because the darkness is passing away and the true light is already shining.'

Even in these passages, however, the transformation of individuals is seen in light of the transformation of the ages, and the inner changes presage the changing out of the whole old world order. Romans 8:18–25 provides one of the most dramatic juxtapositions of personal and cosmic renewal:

> I consider that the sufferings of this present time are not worth comparing with the glory that is to be revealed to us. For the creation waits with eager longing for the revealing of the sons of God; for the creation was subjected to futility, not of its own will but by the will of him who subjected it in hope; because the creation itself will be set free from its bondage to decay and obtain the glorious liberty of the children of God. We know that the whole creation has been groaning in travail together until now; and not only the creation, but we ourselves, who have the first fruits of the Spirit, groan inwardly as we wait for adoption as sons, the redemption of our bodies. For in this hope we were

> saved. Now hope that is seen is not hope. For who hopes for what he sees? But if we hope for what we do not see, we wait for it with patience.

Revelation likewise frames the experiences of the seven churches (chs 2–3) with the dissolution and restitution of the cosmos (chs 6–22).

Theologians through the centuries have struggled with two related issues with respect to the new creation: the *materiality* of the new creation, and the *continuity* between the old creation and the new. The New Testament emphasis on present-day spiritual transformation, and its critique of the obsolescing present world order, could sometimes diminish the importance of physical entities. That this sat well with aspects of Greek thought made the temptation to see the eschaton in immaterial terms all the stronger. Yet our prior examination of Christian Platonism has shown that even the most ardent idealists paused in the face of bodily resurrection. Paul had specified that the resurrection body was 'spiritual' in 1 Corinthians 15, but this probably meant an *enhanced* materiality able to bear the Spirit of God and the glories of the new creation: a purely 'spiritual' (= immaterial) afterlife would almost certainly have not taxed the imaginations of the Corinthians the way bodily resurrection did. Paul's lengthy defence of resurrection necessitates some type of corporeality.

It is, to be sure, a corporeality that transcends the frail flesh and blood of the present age. Paul was duly cautious about spelling out the physics of the matter, but he encouraged the Corinthians to think about the different and wondrous bodies God provides for things in the present as a means of opening their minds to the possibilities that awaited them in the future. Even Eriugena, whose view of the resurrection comes close to the shadows of immateriality, felt obliged to protest that our bodies will not be done away with, but be caught up in a greater glory. How much more the many theologians who confessed the resurrection of the body in more conventional terms, and thus committed themselves (whether they were always conscious of it or not) to some sort of material environment in which these resurrected bodies could dwell.

The question of *continuity* necessarily follows that of materiality. Granted some sort of future material existence for the world, is this the same world renewed, or is it a completely new heaven and earth? The simple answer is that there are aspects of both continuity and discontinuity. The event of God's coming is so staggering that it defies straightforward description. At times it must be spoken of as a radically new incursion of God's purposes into reality, and at other times it must be spoken of as an enhancement of the existing world order. We may repeat here our earlier remarks about the New Jerusalem. In Revelation 20, discontinuity is stressed as heaven and earth flee away from the one seated on the throne, and in 21:1 we are told 'the first heaven and the first earth had passed away'. The situation in 2 Peter 3:10 is a close analogue: 'But the day of the Lord will come like a thief, and then the heavens will pass away with a loud noise, and the elements will be dissolved with fire, and the earth and the works that are upon it will be burned up.' At other times, particularly in the Prophets, the eschaton is seen in close continuity with the present age: the new age will be marked by agricultural abundance (Amos 9:13–14) and peace in the land (Isa. 11:1–9). The fact that Isaiah speaks in terms of extraordinarily long life, rather than endless life, in the 'new heavens and a new earth' (Isa. 65:17, 20) underscores the assumption of connectedness with what has gone before.

As with materiality, the resurrection of Jesus and believers in their turn allows us to grapple with the problem of continuity in the most fruitful way possible. The body of the resurrected Christ is clearly distinct from his earthly body in key respects, imperishability being chief among them (the apparent ability to walk through walls is a less crucial but nonetheless remarkable one, see John 20:26). Yet the continuity of Jesus' body is equally stressed: the disciples must know that *this Jesus* has suffered and this Jesus has risen. The endurance of his scars demonstrates that he is who he was, and thus establishes him as the one who is still in solidarity with humanity. Paul makes a similar point in 1 Corinthians. We have stressed the dramatic newness of life in the 'spiritual body' of the resurrection, a body that can be distinguished from corruptible 'flesh and blood'. But Paul is equally concerned to stress the connection of the now and the new in 1 Corinthians 6. Why should the Corinthians refrain from consorting with prostitutes? Because what they do in the present body is meaningfully related to life in the resurrection: 'The body is not meant for immorality, but for the Lord, and the Lord for the body. And God raised the Lord and will also raise us up by his power' (1 Cor. 6:13–14).

It is fitting to conclude our brief musings on the theological account of *process* with the possibility of eternal *progress* in the new creation. The prospect of an eschatological Sabbath was a great comfort to weary saints beset by woes on every side. And perhaps it is a function of modern complacency that we should sometimes wonder if there is anything beyond the beauty of the beatific vision. Nonetheless, once the question arises, it must be addressed. One approach to a more dynamic view of the eschaton is to recover the earthiness of the Old Testament prophetic vision. In the history of the church, this earthy prophetic hope has regularly been housed in the millennium: the goodness of life on this earth will be vindicated in the 1,000-year reign of Christ, after which we will enter into the consummate joys of the beatific vision. This is an ancient tradition, and worthy of respect, but one wonders why the blessedness of earthly life must be restricted to an interim reign to be superseded by something else.[40] While some aspects of the Old Testament witness do require an 'upgrading'—for instance, the long life of Isaiah 65 should be seen as pointing towards genuinely eternal life—there is nothing in the New Testament which forbids us embracing embodied life in the new creation. The precise nature of this life must elude us in the present, but we are regularly invited by Scripture to think of it in terms of the blessings of the present writ large.

Irenaeus provides some very interesting food for thought in this regard. He is well known for his defence of the materiality of life 'in the kingdom' (his term for the millennium) in the face of 'gnostic' denigration of the world.[41] He writes of the eschaton:

> For since there are real men, so must there also be a real establishment, that they vanish not away among non-existent things, but progress among those which have an actual existence. For neither is the substance nor the essence of the creation annihilated (for faithful and true is He who has established it), but 'the *fashion* of the world passeth away'; that is, those things among which transgression has occurred, since man has grown old in them. And therefore this [present] fashion has been formed temporary, God foreknowing all things; as I have pointed out in the preceding book, and have also shown, as far as was possible, the cause of the creation of this world of temporal things. But when this [present] fashion [of things] passes away, and man has been renewed, and flourishes in an incorruptible state, so as to preclude the possibility of becoming old, [then] there shall be the new heaven and the new earth, in which the new man shall remain [continually], always holding fresh converse with God (5.36.1).

In addition to Irenaeus' affirmation of the physical reality of the future world, the word 'progress' (*proficere*) catches the eye. What Irenaeus means by progress, however, involves a somewhat curious scheme depicting various levels of closeness to God in the eschaton:

> [They say, moreover], that there is this distinction between the habitation of those who produce an hundred-fold, and that of those who produce sixty-fold, and that of those who produce thirty-fold: for the first will be taken up into the heavens, the second will dwell in paradise, the last will inhabit the city; and that it was on this account the Lord declared, 'In My Father's house are

40. See Richard Bauckham, 'Eschatology in The Coming of God', in *God Will Be All in All: The Eschatology of Jürgen Moltmann* (ed. Richard Bauckham; Edinburgh: T&T Clark, 1999), pp. 1–34.

41. As Christopher R. Smith notes, Irenaeus has no clear line of demarcation between the millennium and the 'eternal state': 'in his theology there is an essential continuity between the restored paradise and the subsequent new creation.' Christopher R. Smith, 'Chiliasm and Recapitulation in the Theology of Ireneus', *VC* 48 (1994): p. 317.

> many mansions.' For all things belong to God, who supplies all with a suitable dwelling-place; even as His Word says, that a share is allotted to all by the Father, according as each person is or shall be worthy. And this is the couch on which the guests shall recline, having been invited to the wedding. The presbyters, the disciples of the apostles, affirm that this is the gradation and arrangement of those who are saved, and that they advance through steps of this nature; also that they ascend through the Spirit to the Son, and through the Son to the Father, and that in due time the Son will yield up His work to the Father, even as it is said by the apostle, 'For He must reign till He hath put all enemies under His feet. The last enemy that shall be destroyed is death' (5.36.2).

Irenaeus is avowedly drawing on tradition and Scripture here, and endeavouring to make sense of Jesus' statements about differing rewards in the afterlife. But, as compelling as so much of his eschatological vision may be, he does seem rather to fall between two stools here: the scheme lacks the elegance of the highly spiritual beatific vision, while it tends to diminish the significance of the earthly New Jerusalem as the low-rent district of the new heavens and new earth. This is especially problematic if the phrase 'that this is the gradation and arrangement of those who are saved, and that they advance through steps of this nature' indicates some type of advance through the different levels.[42] This would seem to leave the earthly city bereft of inhabitants.

Gregory may have been giving a philosophical turn to the tradition represented by Irenaeus when he writes of the continual progress of the soul, which we have cited earlier: 'You see how boundless is the path for those rising up to God, yet how it is that what the soul has comprehended is the beginning of something beyond her?'[43] As so often, the New England Reformed theologian Jonathan Edwards says something remarkably close to his patristic counterparts:

> Let the most perfect union with God be represented by something at an infinite height above us; and the eternally increasing union of the saints with God, by something that is ascending constantly towards that infinite height, moving upwards with a given velocity; and that is to continue thus to move to all eternity. God who views the whole of this eternally increasing height views it as an infinite height. And if he has respect to it, and makes it his end, as in the whole of it, he has respect to it as an infinite height, though the time will never come when it can be said it has already arrived at this infinite height.[44]

42. The Latin for the last phrase reads *et per huius modi gradus proficere*, which links to the 'progress' of the prior paragraph.

43. Gregory of Nyssa, *Cant.* 11, in Morwenna Ludlow, *Universal Salvation: Eschatology in the Thought of Gregory of Nyssa and Karl Rahner* (Oxford: OUP, 2000), p. 63.

44. Edwards, 'Concerning the End', *Works*, 8:534.

Whether we take for our watchword the prophetic vision of a new earth, or the more philosophical speculations on the infinity of God, we should rest assured that the eschaton is more than assured rest. Whatever its exact shape may be, our life in God will be one of unending joy and endless progress in the knowledge of his infinite glory.

Process: The Scientific Account

Up to this point, we have considered the process of creation from the theological angle. But since God is affirmed as the Creator of *this* world, the doctrine has always had to reckon with observations and theories about how this world actually seems to work. While many recitations of history assume that the problem of 'faith and science' emerges only during the Enlightenment, this discussion in fact goes back to the early days of the church. There is no question that modern science raised the dialogue to another level, but whether the science is Old or New, similar concerns prevail throughout the course of church history. As Barth sagely notes, faith has always been content to operate within the territory of the learning of its day, but not to be detained at its borders.[45]

Old science

Ancient theologians were perfectly willing to engage with what we can broadly term 'science'. It is decidedly unfair to judge these thinkers in light of later scientific developments, as if they ought to have intuitively grasped matters like the age of the earth or the workings of DNA. We might as well expect them to have developed a vaccine against polio. The question is whether they read Genesis in a completely self-contained way, or whether they were open to observations and speculation about the world around them as a means of informing their view of the text. The evidence is that they did. David Lindberg and Ronald Numbers put it plainly: 'The often-repeated notion that Christian thinkers attempted to obtain their world-view from the Bible alone is a ludicrous distortion of the facts.'[46]

As is true of all ancient thinkers, their speculations only occasionally hit the target of reality. Basil provides a wealth of zoological information in his

45. Barth, *CD* III/2, p. 9.

46. David Lindberg and Ronald Numbers, *God and Nature: Historical Essays on the Encounter between Christianity and Science* (Berkeley: University of California Press, 1986), p. 10.

Hexaemeron (most of it drawn from classical sources like Aristotle), with evident delight in the visceral details of living creatures. He notes of fish:

> With us the lung, that porous and spongy portion of the inward parts which receives air by the dilatation of the chest, disperses and cools interior warmth; in fish the motion of the gills, which open and shut by turns to take in and to eject the water, takes the place of respiration. Fish have a peculiar lot, a special nature, a nourishment of their own, a life apart.[47]

Less inspiring of trust are assertions that tortoises eat marjoram as an antidote to snake venom, or that hedgehogs have two openings to their holes, so that they can close up one when the north wind is blowing, and close up the other when the wind is from the south (*Hexaemeron* 9.3). One might argue that a too trusting reliance on tortoise and hedgehog lore is the very antithesis of the scientific spirit, and there is no denying that there is a qualitative difference between an experiment-based, peer-reviewed article in a modern scientific journal and Basil's sermonic musings. But they remain evidence of a mind keenly interested in the world around him.

We find a similar interest throughout the tradition, with varying results. Cosmas Indicopleustes ('India voyager'; sixth century AD) was a great traveller for the ancient world, and he provides charming and reasonably accurate accounts of Indian flora and fauna in book 12 of his *Christian Topography*. Unfortunately, his speculations about the wider cosmic scene are derived from a reading strategy towards Scripture and tradition that combines a penchant for literalism with an enthusiasm for liberal extrapolation. Isaiah 49:22, for instance, proves surprisingly informative in his hands with respect to the shape of the cosmos:

> The Deity accordingly having founded the earth, which is oblong, upon its own stability, bound together the extremities of the heaven with the extremities of the earth, making the nether extremities of the heaven rest upon the four extremities of the earth, while on high he formed it into a most lofty vault overspanning the length of the earth. Along the breadth again of the earth he built a wall from the nethermost extremities of the heaven upwards to the summit, and having enclosed the place, made a house, as one might call it, of enormous size, like an oblong vaulted vapour-bath. For, saith the Prophet Isaiah (xlix, 22): '*He who established heaven as a vault.*'[48]

Augustine's *Literal Commentary on Genesis* is full of observations from the natural world. At one point he even says that 'it is almost like a scientist

47. Basil, *Hex*. 7.1.

48. Book 2 of *Christian Topography* (trans. J. W. McCrindle; London: The Hakluyt Society, 1897).

(*scienter tamquam*) that the Spirit of God, who was assisting the writer, says flying things were produced from the waters'.[49] Augustine defends the fact that fish have memory by his personal observations at the pool in Bulla: people have thrown food to them in the past, and so whenever people show up, the fish gather for more.[50] Even Augustine's discussion of 'dragons' (which would have appeared in his texts of Pss. 74:14 and 104:26) shows a certain scientific caution: 'As for dragons, which lack feet, they are said to take their rest in caves, and to soar up into the air. While these are not too easy to come across, this kind of animated creature is for all that definitely mentioned not only in our literature, but also in that of the Gentiles.'[51]

New science

As the centuries rolled by, of course, humanity's knowledge increased, and dragons had to flee even their remote caves to the realms of fantasy. Matters come to a head with the so-called 'scientific revolution' and the subsequent re-visioning of natural history. The story is well known. Venerable ideas of the structure of the cosmos were undermined by the discoveries of Galileo and Copernicus. The notion of a six-thousand-year-old earth was already running out of time in the medieval era, but eighteenth-century advances in geology began to push the theory to the margins of belief even within the church. Lastly, Charles Darwin and his theory of evolution seemed to threaten the very notion that humanity was specially created in the image of God.

The story is so well known, in fact, that it runs the risk of becoming a fable: science, while resisted by the backwards-looking church, makes its inevitable march forwards in the bright Today with the prospect of a brighter Tomorrow. Thankfully, an ever-growing body of literature on faith and science has brought much-needed shading to this simplistic portrait.[52] There is no denying that plenty of professing Christians permitted their ideological convictions to override the evidence of scientific investigation. It is equally true that many of these scientists on the cutting edge of science

49. Augustine, *Gen. Litt.* 3.7, 9. One might render *scienter tamquam* more woodenly as 'as if knowingly', but the translation offered fits the context well. The 'science' in question here concerns antiquated notions of the combination of the various elements in flying things; but the point is that Augustine is commending Scripture for understanding what counted as science in his day.

50. Augustine, *Gen. Litt.* 3.8.12.

51. Augustine, *Gen. Litt.* 3.9.13, p. 223, with notes on the biblical background.

52. In addition to Lindberg and Numbers, see e.g. Alister McGrath, *The Foundations of Dialogue in Science and Religion* (Oxford: Blackwell, 1998).

were themselves professing Christians, and that plenty of people within the church embraced the new discoveries in varying measures.

We may isolate at least two streams which fed into the advance of science. The first is the compounding effect of learning and technology that had begun with the very advent of civilization. Even the primeval history of Genesis notes technological advancement: the sons of Cain (ominously) make stringed instruments and produce implements of iron and bronze (Gen. 4:21–22).[53] Ideology may have stunted or advanced learning at various times, but it is just as likely that the ongoing process of trial and error simply needed a given amount of time before it could issue in the explosion of innovation that began in the eighteenth century. Since the incremental gain in technological mastery did not in and of itself precipitate a theological crisis, we may turn to the other stream, which will require significantly more discussion.

The second stream is a shift in the assumptions underlying how the world works and how one should go about investigating it. Scientists like Kepler, Galileo, and Copernicus wished to rely on observation and experiment to explain the natural world, rather than on tradition or scriptural texts. While observation was already playing some role in theological discourse on creation, this was nevertheless a disruption to the tradition which clearly rankled many theologians, as witnessed by Galileo's trials and the rejection of Copernicanism by as keen a thinker as Jonathan Edwards. But Galileo and his kin could make a very credible case from within the faith that the Bible was never meant to offer lessons in practical astronomy. Perfectly orthodox theologians had argued from the beginning that phrases like 'the hand of God' were never meant to be taken literally, so why could the same principle not be extended to expressions like 'the four corners of the earth'?

Such a seismic shift in perspective might indeed open the door for a reappraisal of religion, but we must recognize that the radical disavowal of God as Creator goes well beyond a penchant for practical science. Even the pragmatic decision to treat the world *as if* it were a closed system is far different from a philosophical assertion that the world *must be* a closed system with no ongoing involvement from the 'outside'. No doubt many thinkers,

53. In the Enoch literature, the dawn of technology is even more troubling: it is the evil angels who teach the practical arts to human beings, particularly the arts of weaponry and cosmetic adornment: 'And Azazel taught men to make swords, and knives, and shields, and breastplates, and made known to them the metals of the earth and the art of working them, and bracelets, and ornaments, and the use of antimony, and the beautifying of the eyelids, and all kinds of costly stones, and all colouring tinctures. And there arose much godlessness, and they committed fornication, and they were led astray, and became corrupt in all their ways' (*1 En.* 8:1–3).

particularly during the so-called Enlightenment, held the latter view. It is even possible that the wider adoption of such a view materially contributed to the growth of scientific endeavour, as more people felt emboldened to explore the world for its own sake. But it is hardly a necessary precondition for science as such. Even a radical idealist like Edwards could observe and analyse the natural world; how much more bona fide scientists and Christians like James Clerk Maxwell or Michael Faraday. The precise nature of divine action in the world was recognized as a complicated business long before Hume or Kant came on the scene.

In fact, we might argue that the scientific revolution succeeded not merely because Galileo and Kepler and all were better scientists than their scholastic predecessors, but because they were better theologians—at least with respect to the problem of faith and science. Kepler recognized that Scripture does not intend to give lessons in astronomy, and that it 'speaks in accordance with human perception when the truth of things is at odds with the senses'.[54] Far from corrupting people's faith, the disciplined study of the heavenly spheres should lead people to extol God all the more:

> I hope that, with me, he [the reader of *Astronomica Nova*] will praise and celebrate the Creator's wisdom and greatness, which I unfold for him in the more perspicacious explanation of the world's form, the investigation of causes, and the detection of errors of vision. Let him not only extol the Creator's divine beneficence in His concern for the well-being of all livings things, expressed in the firmness and stability of the earth, but also acknowledge His wisdom expressed in its motion, at once so well and so admirable.[55]

Francis Bacon (1561–1626) provides a sterling defence of the 'New Philosophy' in his *New Organon* (*Org.*). The purpose of this work was to put in place a new framework for scientific investigation, one that would bring discipline to the field and gather up scattered observations into a coherent whole. It is a remarkably forward-thinking piece in that regard, and it illustrates vividly the pragmatic approach to nature that formed the bulwark of the New Philosophy. But its interest for us lies in the ground-clearing apologetic that opens the work. 'Ground-clearing' might be too timid: it is more of a scorched-earth policy that seeks to raze the entire scientific–philosophical tradition. Bacon's rod is unsparing: Plato, Aristotle, and the medieval

---

54. Quote in Avihu Zakai, *Jonathan Edwards's Philosophy of Nature: The Reenchantment of the World in the Age of Scientific Reasoning* (London: T&T Clark, 2010), pp. 70–71. Cf. Galileo's comments that his opponents tried to refute him 'with passages taken from places in the Bible which they had failed to understand properly, and which were ill suited to their purpose.' In Zakai, *Nature*, p. 77.

55. In Zakai, *Nature*, p. 71.

scholastics are all lambasted for a devotion to theory over experiment. The neatness of their syllogisms is completely undermined by their faulty premises, which were based on little or no actual observation. There was no hope in building science on the shoddy foundations of the past: 'those foolish and apish images of worlds which the fancies of men have created in philosophical systems must be utterly scattered to the winds' (*Org*. 124).

Bacon does not hide from the religious dimensions of the question. Indeed, he takes an almost prophetic stance against what he deems bad theology. He realizes that there are those who 'attempt to found a system of natural philosophy on the first chapter of Genesis, on the book of Job, and other parts of the sacred writings'; but this is to 'seek the dead among the living' (*Org*. 65). As Galileo and Kepler also argued, the Bible was never meant to be a science textbook. On the positive side, because God had in fact created the world, investigating its actual workings represented the surest path to truth: 'Be it known then how vast a difference there is (as I said above) between the idols of the human mind and the ideas of the divine. The former are nothing more than arbitrary abstractions; the latter are the Creator's own stamp upon creation, impressed and defined in matter by true and exquisite lines. Truth, therefore, and utility are here the very same things' (*Org*. 124). Discoveries 'are as it were new creations, and imitations of God's works' (*Org*. 129). Far from being forbidden by God's word, they are arguably the fulfilment of the prophecy of Daniel that with the advancing ages 'many shall go to and fro, and knowledge shall increase' (*Org*. 93).

In one remarkable paragraph, Bacon summarizes the fears that keep theologians from embracing science. Four centuries later, it has lost none of its bite:

> Lastly, you will find that by the simpleness of certain divines, access to any philosophy, however pure, is well-nigh closed. Some are weakly afraid lest a deeper search into nature should transgress the permitted limits of sober-mindedness, wrongfully wresting and transferring what is said in Holy Writ against those who pry into sacred mysteries, to the hidden things of nature, which are barred by no prohibition. Others with more subtlety surmise and reflect that if second causes are unknown everything can more readily be referred to the divine hand and rod, a point in which they think religion greatly concerned—which is in fact nothing else but to seek to gratify God with a lie. Others fear from past example that movements and changes in philosophy will end in assaults on religion. And others again appear apprehensive that in the investigation of nature something may be found to subvert or at least shake the authority of religion, especially with the unlearned. But these two last fears seem to me to savor utterly of carnal wisdom; as if men in the recesses and secret thought of their hearts doubted and distrusted the strength of religion and the empire of faith over the sense, and therefore feared that the

> investigation of truth in nature might be dangerous to them. But if the matter be truly considered, natural philosophy is, after the word of God, at once the surest medicine against superstition and the most approved nourishment for faith, and therefore she is rightly given to religion as her most faithful handmaid, since the one displays the will of God, the other his power. For he did not err who said, 'Ye err in that ye know not the Scriptures and the power of God,' thus coupling and blending in an indissoluble bond information concerning his will and meditation concerning his power. Meanwhile it is not surprising if the growth of natural philosophy is checked when religion, the thing which has most power over men's minds, has by the simpleness and incautious zeal of certain persons been drawn to take part against her (*Org.* 89).

In the event, of course, the 'movements and changes in philosophy' did 'end in assaults of religion'. But this cannot be laid at the door of Bacon, whose *theological* reasoning here is unimpeachable.

What is crucial to our investigation is the extent to which the rise of modern science reshaped the doctrine of creation. Certainly the new discoveries in astronomy, geology, and biology required a significant remodelling of the doctrine. The six-thousand-year-old earth was stripped from all but the most fundamentalist theologies, while the geocentric cosmos was removed even from these. Evolution was a harder sell, since it impinged so directly on the nature of humanity. Even here, however, many Christians were willing to embrace a broadly evolutionary scheme, particularly if they could opt out with a special creation of Adam and Eve.[56] All of these were treasured elements of the theological tradition, and their adherents were unwilling to give them up without a fight. In this sense we might be justified in speaking of them as part of a 'theological crisis' in the sixteenth century and beyond. At the same time, one could counter that these changes were only superficial adjustments. Augustine and other church fathers had opened the door to non-literal readings of the creation narrative, which made dating the beginning a decidedly secondary concern. They also recognized that the Scriptures regularly used technically inaccurate turns of phrase in order to communicate their message plainly to ordinary people. If God did not literally have a 'hand', the question of how he set about organizing the cosmos was likewise an open-ended one.

Even the more substantial changes to the doctrines were not wholly novel issues. As we have seen, the 'disenchantment of the world' attributed to the New Philosophy of the scientific revolution has variously been laid at the door of the voluntarists of the medieval era, or even Augustine.[57] No

56. See David Livingstone, *Darwin's Forgotten Defenders: The Encounter between Evangelical Theology and Evolutionary Thought* (Grand Rapids: Eerdmans, 1987).

57. See Zakai, *Nature*, pp. 51–85.

doubt the new discoveries gave encouragement to those who wished to see nature drained of its magic.[58] But people continued (and continue) to wonder at the world, and the disappearance of faith some longed for has yet to (de-)materialize.

C. S. Lewis demonstrates the resiliency of the idea of cosmic enchantment in the face of scientific advance. The medieval vision of the cosmos was a perpetual inspiration to him. Michael Ward has even argued that the ancient conception of the seven planets lies at the heart of Lewis's classic Narnia series.[59] Lewis had an antiquarian bent, but his affection for the medieval system of astronomy was grounded as much in a keen awareness of the philosophical issues at stake as it was in nostalgia for a bygone aesthetic. He was a keen amateur astronomer who knew his way around the sky, and he could hardly pretend that the old Ptolemaic system of the cosmos matched the facts.[60] At the same time, the vision of the universe set forth in places like Dante's *Divine Comedy* held such an attraction for him that he was convinced there must be something to it: 'the character of the planets, as conceived by medieval astrology, seem to me to have a permanent value as spiritual symbols—to provide a *Phänomenologie des Geistes* which is specially worthwhile in our own generation'.[61]

Lewis would not have regarded this belief as mere mystical raving. As he wrote in *The Abolition of Man*: 'it is not the greatest modern scientists who feel most sure that the object, stripped of its qualitative properties and reduced to mere quantity, is wholly real. Little scientists, and little unscientific followers of science, may think so. The great minds know very well that the object, so treated, is an artificial abstraction, that something of its reality has been lost.'[62] He captured the same truth in imaginative guise in *The Voyage of the Dawn Treader*. When the children encounter Ramandu, a 'retired star', the rehabilitated but still rather prosaic Eustace remarks, 'In our world . . . a star is a huge ball of flaming gas.' Ramandu replies, 'Even in your world, my son, that is not what a star is but only what it is made of.'[63]

When it comes to the disenchantment of the world, then, Lewis's experience encourages us to ask the question: disenchanted *for whom*? The Ptolemaic system may have seemed to Lewis a more congenial home for the divine presence than the Copernican one, but he was still able to experience

58. Cf. Zakai's extended discussion of the metaphysical poet John Donne and his reaction to the New Philosophy, in *Nature*, pp. 86–124.

59. Michael Ward, *Planet Narnia: The Seven Heavens in the Imagination of C. S. Lewis* (Oxford: OUP, 2008).

60. Ward, *Planet Narnia*, pp. 247–49.

61. Ward, *Planet Narnia*, p. 43.

62. For quotation and discussion, see Ward, *Planet Narnia*, p. 248.

63. C. S. Lewis, *Voyage of the Dawn Treader* (New York: Macmillan, 1967), p. 175.

God in the world despite his modern scientific knowledge. There is no need even to think that the Ptolemaic version of things serves better as an image of spiritual reality. One can imagine the author of Job happily embracing modern astronomy as a confirmation of his vision of the vanishing smallness of humanity when set against a world that owns only God as its Lord:

> Can you bind the chains of the Pleiades,
> or loose the cords of Orion?
> Can you lead forth the Mazzaroth in their season,
> or can you guide the Bear with its children?
> Do you know the ordinances of the heavens?
> Can you establish their rule on the earth? (Job 38:31–33)

The world itself goes along on its course; the disenchantment is an existential experience of given human beings, and its sources must be sought in the heart and not just the head.

The New Philosophy also pressed the question of how God was at work in the world with particular force. It is not merely that Darwinism introduced a mechanism that accounted for the evident flaws that popped up in nature (and particularly in people)—theologians were well aware of these apparent design problems and managed them in a variety of ways. If one believed, for example, that the estrangement of God and humanity had led to catastrophic consequences for the creation, the precise means by which these disruptions arose in the world was not of central concern. The problem of human death was even more obvious, and had correspondingly received even more theological attention. Darwin himself was troubled by the apparent wastefulness involved in the evolutionary process, though this might strike us as a curiously moralistic note in an otherwise objective scholarly inquiry. In any case, the savagery of the animal world was hardly *terra incognita* before Darwin's voyage to the Galapagos. The fact that death is introduced along with the curse in Genesis 3 might seem to be an Achilles' heel for the biblical account, but this could be accounted for in various ways. One might say, for instance, that the current *experience* of human death as existential crisis does signal a deep rupture between God and humanity, and that the intent of the Genesis text is to address this aspect of dying. The prospect of eschatological restoration could also be deployed against the apparently hopeless mechanics of natural selection: if the body is a seed presaging greater fruit to come, its current dissolution (whatever its physical origins might be) would be adequately compensated for by its future glory.

The renewed emphasis on immanence in the wake of Darwin's writings can also be seen in a positive light. William Paley's *Principles of Moral and Political Philosophy* and *Natural Theology* were immensely popular textbooks in the nineteenth century, and they epitomized the vision of the Watchmaker God fine-tuning the universe for the benefit of human beings.[64] Even in their ascendency, however, thoughtful critics were pointing out their deficiencies. Coleridge was particularly irritated by Paley, who 'substitutes the Lockian and Newtonian—From God we *had* our Being—for the Pauline—*In* whom we move and live and *have* our Being. The moderns take the *ho theos* [Greek in original quote] as a hypothetical Watchmaker and degrade the *to theion* into a piece of Clock-Work—they live without God in the world.'[65] Coleridge unsurprisingly chooses a Pauline formulation (itself probably taken from a Greek poetic source) closest to his own Platonist leanings, but this does not invalidate his critique. A God purported to work only on the outside of things in the beginning might be subject to the critiques levelled in Richard Dawkins' *The Blind Watchmaker*. Coleridge—writing before Darwin's floruit, and self-consciously drawing on long Christian tradition—emphasizes God at work on the inside of things, and in so doing proposes a model of divine action that is at once more reflective of the biblical outlook than Paley's, and more supple in meeting the challenges posed by contemporary science.

It might appear as if the idea of randomness is the exception to our contention that theological change in the wake of the New Philosophy was evolutionary rather than revolutionary. In place of a well-ordered artistic creation, Darwinism proffers random genetic variation coupled with natural selection. As with all the issues we are discussing here, there was a genuine need to rethink how the doctrine of creation was to be articulated in light of Darwin's new vision. But the tradition still had the resources to cope with it. Genesis 1:11 states that God made 'plants yielding seed . . . each according to its kind', thus acknowledging the reality of secondary causation. Subsequent genetic variation can fit comfortably enough alongside this text. While Paul was hardly writing a horticultural treatise to the Romans, it is perhaps worth noting that he has no problem introducing selective breeding and plant hybridization into his discussion as part of the created order overseen by God (Rom. 11:17–24, cf. Rom. 1:20).

We must also consider what is implied in the word 'randomness'. 'Randomness' helps us to label phenomena which people are unable to predict or for which they are unable to account. The theological flaw lies in assuming that what we experience as randomness must necessarily count as randomness for God as well. Once these two ideas are decoupled, it is perfectly

64. R. J. Berry, 'Does Disputing Darwinism Discourage Creation Care?', in *As Long as the Earth Endures* (ed. Moo and Routledge), pp. 217–38. We may observe in passing that Darwin had read Paley.

65. Coleridge, *Collected Letter* 4:768, quoted in Alan Gregory, *Coleridge and the Conservative Imagination* (Macon, GA: Mercer University Press, 2003), p. 204.

reasonable to speak meaningfully of randomness in events from the human perspective, without concluding that God has thereby been caught off guard or that he remains unable to fathom what is going on the world. Nor is such a move a desperate novelty conjured up in the face of the repeated battering of theology by science. The best theologians never claimed to know precisely what God was up to: 'For my thoughts are not your thoughts, neither are your ways my ways, says the LORD. For as the heavens are higher than the earth, so are my ways higher than your ways and my thoughts than your thoughts' (Isa. 55:8–9). The church can in turn ask for the origin of our perception of and appreciation for order in a world allegedly governed by 'mere' chance. Genuine order can exist alongside (apparent) randomness.

All of the above necessitated a reworking of the doctrine from within. The lasting external challenge to the doctrine was the apparent support it provided for an atheistic denial of creation. Richard Dawkins has averred that while atheists existed before Darwin, Darwinism allowed people to become 'intellectually fulfilled atheists'.[66] But this only provides another instance of confounding scientific deductions with philosophical assertions. The idea that the cosmos was a self-contained and self-sustaining whole—that it *just was*—had been around at least since the ancient Greeks. Epicurus shows how even the gods could be accommodated within what is by Christian standards a functionally atheistic world-view. Plato rejected this understanding of the world not because Greek philosophers like Empedocles lacked a sufficient basis of evidence for their proto-evolutionary theories, but because he believed their theories lacked the ability to make full sense of the human experience of the world, particularly its intelligibility. Modern thinkers like Lewis have made an analogous point: if the reason by which we deduce the causes of the universe amounts to the random concatenation of atoms in the void, what is the basis for our trust in it?[67] Dawkins' claim is a metaphysical one: based on the posited process by which life emerged on earth, he deduces that God cannot have been the final cause. This is a non sequitur. He and his fellow atheistical evolutionists are propounding an essentially religious belief as if it were demonstrable scientific fact, which accounts for the curiously religious flavour of much evolutionary rhetoric.[68]

66. Richard Dawkins, *The Blind Watchmaker* (New York: Norton, 1986), pp. 6–7.

67. C. S. Lewis, *Mere Christianity* (London: HarperCollins, 2001), p. 26. See also Alvin Plantinga, *Where the Conflict Really Lies: Science, Religion, and Naturalism* (New York: OUP, 2011). Plantinga's basic point is that evolutionary theory as such poses no threat to Christian belief; the difference lies with those who assume that evolution must be devoid of divine influence.

68. See above all Mary Midgley, *Evolution as a Religion: Strange Hopes and Stranger Fears* (London: Routledge, rev. edn., 2006), which it should be noted is not written from an explicitly religious point of view.

The philosophical critique of naturalism is only one pillar supporting the ongoing relevance of Christian views on creation in the light of modern advances in science. The literary and artistic legacy of the church is an equally powerful apologetic witness. Lewis was not drawn to the *Divine Comedy* by a mere zeal for antiquity. Dante's poem is a masterpiece which has lost little if any of its force today; and that force is due as much as anything to its majestic architecture rooted in medieval cosmology. The same may be said in an even more literal sense for the great cathedrals of the Middle Ages, which embody a vision of the harmonious cosmos.[69]

Artefacts like the *Divine Comedy* or the cathedral at Chartres do not of course guarantee the literal viability of medieval cosmology as a scientific system. But their beauty should remind us that there was something about the way the ancients construed reality that is of enduring value: the sense of cosmic coherence and divine presence in the world was not 'disproven' by the scientific revolution. Science itself is often driven by a sense of wonder at the world, and an appreciation for the beautiful order revealed in its workings. The involved zoological parables of the *Physiologos* might have lost their currency in the present day, but this hardly means the world has lost its meaning.

What of new creation? Here the intrepid theologian may venture where the scientist (qua scientist) cannot tread. Science by virtue of its discipline can only extrapolate from the data to hand. This often takes the shape of grim reminders that our middle-aged sun will sooner or later burn out, taking whatever might be left of life on earth with it. *Sic transit gloria mundi.* But optimists will occasionally pop up with 'near-term' predictions of a glorious humanity enhanced through the evolutionary process. People sometimes imagine the process will be sped up by technology, making the eventual pay-off seem less distant. The question of how this all benefits you the reader may be dismissed as irrelevant, though in some schemes the prospect of storing one's biological information is held out as a means to something resembling eternal life.

The Christian, who believes that God has already acted in an unpredictable way in raising Jesus from the dead, need not be confined to what may be extrapolated from current data—or, one might say, he or she is free to include the resurrection of Christ as the indispensable datum for future projections. A Christian is equally free to embrace predictive science as a heuristic tool, since God may be counted on to preserve the current world order with its processes until he sees fit. But those predictions will be held loosely compared to the conviction that God will bring his creation project to its goal in the resurrection of the saints and the renewal of the world.

69. See Émile Mâle, *The Gothic Image: Religious Art in France of the Thirteenth Century* (New York: Harper, 1958).

How?

Thus far we have looked at various ways the church has thought about the creation in light of Scripture and observations from the world. Left unanswered is the question of precisely how this happens—what are the mechanisms by which one goes from cause to effect, from God to the world? Is there some discernible point of connection between the two? We are not asking about the material process which gives rise to a given entity, as important as that question is. We are asking the theological question: given the conviction that God has created the world, may we speak further as to *how* he creates it?

We have seen some preliminary answers in previous chapters. Since the earliest days of the church, creation has been affirmed as a Trinitarian act: the Father creates through the Son or by the Spirit. But no orthodox Trinitarian would reduce the Son or the Spirit to a mere instrument in the hand of God. If, for instance, we want to say that the Spirit vivifies animals (Ps. 104:30), we cannot imagine this is a detachable 'part' of God that goes off, does some work, and then returns to God. 'All the works of the Trinity *ad extra* are indivisible.' The Spirit's work *is* God's work. The declaration that God creates through the Son or the Spirit brings us no closer to an understanding of the mechanics of his involvement in the world.

An analogous move has been made by distinguishing God and his powers or energies. While this is commonly associated with Gregory Palamas (fourteenth century AD), the basic structure of thought goes back to Philo and becomes disseminated in Christianity by thinkers like Gregory of Nyssa.[70] Cudworth's idea of the 'plastic nature' might fit here as well: the world is shaped by some impersonal force derived from God but unable to fully subjugate the world to God's purposes. Christian Platonists insert another logical step in the process with the introduction of the divine Ideas. In its crudest form this is likened to the establishing of a template or a blueprint which is then used in the creation of the world. Plato himself was also interested in mathematical proportions (a theme he derived from the Pythagoreans) and Augustine was happy to follow in his train.[71] Thus when

---

70. See Lewis Ayres, 'On Not Three People: The Fundamental Themes of Gregory of Nyssa's Trinitarian Theology as Seen in To Ablabius: On Not Three Gods', in *Re-thinking Gregory of Nyssa* (ed. Sarah Coakley; Malden, MA: Blackwell, 2003), pp. 15–44.

71. The rabbis appear to have been thinking along similar lines when they spoke of creation through the letters of the divine name (cf. *Genesis Rabbah* 12.10). On the one hand this harkens back to creation through the Word—especially if one relates the 'Let it be!' of Genesis to the name YHWH, which as we have seen can be understood as 'the One who is'. But letters also served as numbers in Hebrew, hence creation-through-letters/numbers may have been an attempt at a rabbinic rapprochement with Platonic accounts of creation.

Descartes and Newton speak of mathematics as key to the world, they are developing an ancient theme.[72]

These are all valuable observations on the processes we observe in the world, but they fall short of a full explanation of *how* God works. If one of our central theological assertions is correct, however, this is exactly what we should expect: God as Creator is both absolutely distinct from the world he has created, and intimately involved in the world he has created. The latter assures us that we can affirm *that* God has worked; the former cautions us that we will never have an exhaustive account of *how* he has worked.

If we wish to put forward one 'mechanism' by which God works, however, we might draw upon Aristotle and use the notion of *desire*. Desire, he writes in the *Metaphysics*, is what permits the Prime Mover to move all things without itself being moved: 'there is something which moves without being moved, being eternal, substance, and actuality. And the object of desire and the object of thought move in this way; they move without being moved . . . The final cause, then, produces motion as being loved, but all other things move by being moved.'[73] One need not accept the Philosopher's entire metaphysical vision to think he has lighted upon a very happy turn of phrase here. Certainly human beings are shaped by desire for good and ill, yet one would be hard pressed to say that desire *forces* people to do things. Nor does desire function only when two entities are in proximate physical contact—absence proverbially makes the heart grow fonder, and even the non-Romantic may feel their deepest desires lie not only out of reach, but somewhere beyond even their ability to conceive.

Desire instead exists as a relational reality, flaming up in the conjunction of the inner wishes of the desirer and the object of desire. But while the desire of the soul for God constitutes the clearest application of Aristotle's model, it can also help us speak of God's action with respect to all created entities. He not only upholds them in their being at a basic level; he also implants in them a 'yearning' to become what they ought to be.

---

72. The same may be said for John Polkinghorne's fascinating suggestion that the presence of *information* in natural systems may give us an inkling of the Spirit's work in creation. See John Polkinghorne, 'The Hidden Work of the Spirit in Creation', in *The Spirit in Creation and New Creation* (ed. Michael Welker; Grand Rapids: Eerdmans, 2012), pp. 3–10.

73. Aristotle, *Met.* 7.

8

The Role of Humanity

Theology is done by humans, and so it is understandable that accounts of the story of humanity tend to crowd out discussion of other aspects of creation.[1] Our own discussion has necessarily made much of God's interaction with human beings. Theological treatises and scholarly analyses of Genesis 1:26–28 abound, not to mention endless volumes devoted to the subsequent history of men and women east of Eden. Especially in the New Testament, imagery from the creation account is regularly deployed with reference to the church: believers are a 'new creation' (2 Cor. 5:17) and 'have put on the new nature, which is being renewed in knowledge after the image of its creator' (Col. 3:10). The trend continues in most of the theological tradition. Thus, for example, when Maximus speaks of the *logos* and the *logoi*, it is sometimes difficult to tell whether he is speaking of things in general, or people in particular. Since our purpose is to discuss creation as a whole, what follows will be a very brief overview of humanity's role in the creation project.

Genesis 1:26–28

We may begin with a glimpse at the creation of humanity in Genesis. The words of Genesis 1:26–28 are familiar, but worth repeating:

> Then God said, 'Let us make man in our image, after our likeness; and let them have dominion over the fish of the sea, and over the birds of the air, and over the cattle, and over all the earth, and over every creeping thing that creeps upon the earth.' So God created man in his own image, in the image of God he created him; male and female he created them. And God blessed them, and God said to them, 'Be fruitful and multiply, and fill the earth and subdue it; and have dominion over the fish of the sea and over the birds of the air and over every living thing that moves upon the earth.'

1. Note Barth's comments on the centrality of humanity to the theology of creation in the introduction to Karl Barth, *Church Dogmatics* (4 vols; Edinburgh: T&T Clark, 1956–75), III/2.

We will confine our comments at this point to one distinctive aspect of the Ancient Near Eastern background which is sometimes obscured in the theological tradition: the original sense of what it meant to be created in the 'image and likeness of God'. While later theologians were to make much of the supposed distinction between 'image' and 'likeness', it is likely that these are roughly synonymous terms referring to the representative status of human beings as those who belong to God's family, and who serve as his vice-regents on earth.[2] Such a *kinship* and *kingship* reading of the text is supported by the literary context of Genesis. The theme of dominion is evident in verse 28, while the theme of kinship is clear in the parallel text in Genesis 5:1–3:

> This is the book of the generations of Adam. When God created man, he made him in the likeness of God. Male and female he created them, and he blessed them and named them Man when they were created. When Adam had lived a hundred and thirty years, he became the father of a son in his own likeness, after his image, and named him Seth.

While the remainder of the Old Testament makes virtually no reference to the specifics of the creation of Adam and Eve,[3] there are numerous references to the creation of humanity in the New Testament. The most salient for our purposes are those instances where the creation of the new humanity in Christ is likened to the creation of Adam and Eve in the beginning. Colossians, which has proved fruitful already for many aspects of creation theology, is useful here as well. Paul begins the letter with two references to Genesis 1:28. He speaks of both the gospel and the Colossians as 'bearing fruit and growing' (1:6, 10); while this differs slightly from the Septuagint's rendering of Genesis 1:28, it is a perfectly acceptable rendering of the Hebrew *pru wrbu*. There is another allusion to the creation narrative in 3:9–10, where the believers are told that they have 'put off the old man with its practices, and put on the new man who is being renewed according to the image of the one who created him' (my translation). In this case the phrase 'according to the image' (*kat' eikona*) is lifted verbatim from Genesis 1:26.

2. On the lexicography of 'image' (*demuth*) and likeness (*tselem*) in light of ANE archaeology, see Alan R. Millard and Pierre Bordreuil, 'A Statue from Syria with Assyrian and Aramaic inscriptions', *BA* 45 (1982): pp. 135–41, and W. R. Garr, '"Image" and "Likeness" in the Inscription from Tell Fakhariyeh', *IEJ* 50 (2000): pp. 227–34, p. 228 nn. 8–11. For the broader significance of the terms, see Catherine McDowell, *The 'Image of God' in the Garden of Eden: The Creation of Humankind in Genesis 2:5–3:24 in Light of the* mis pi pit pi *and* wpt-r *Rituals of Ancient Mesopotamia and Egypt* (Winona Lake, IN: Eisenbrauns, 2015).

3. We have one debatable reference in Hos. 6:7, which could be rendered, 'As at Adam, they have broken the covenant' (NIV) or 'they like men have transgressed the covenant' (KJV) or 'like Adam they transgressed the covenant' (ESV).

Arguably the most interesting allusion to the creation narrative comes in the description of Christ in Colossians 1:15–16: 'the image of the invisible God, the first-born of all creation; for in him all things were created'. The association of image and creation is clear enough: the real problem has been identifying the source of the 'image' language. The most popular choice in modern scholarship has been to identify the image with the creative divine wisdom of Proverbs 8. Wisdom is described as the 'image' (*eikōn*) of God's goodness in Wisdom 7:26, though in Colossians itself Christ is said to possess God's wisdom, rather than to simply be God's wisdom (Col. 2:3). A background in Wisdom traditions cannot be excluded—we have seen that the general identification of Christ and Wisdom was a widespread feature of patristic theology.[4]

It seems more likely, however, that Colossians 1:15 constitutes an interpretation of the phrase 'according to our image' in Genesis 1:26. Christian Stettler has pointed out the relevance for Colossians of Ezekiel 1, where the prophet sees the 'likeness of man' on the throne, the centrepiece of his vision of 'the appearance of the likeness of the glory of the LORD'.[5] While the LXX uses *homoiōma* rather than *eikōn* for 'image' here, the Hebrew *demuth* still takes us back to Genesis 1:26. Humanity, then, is created on the pattern of the archetypal image of God, who is Christ himself. This fits with 2 Corinthians 4:4, where Paul speaks of the 'light of the gospel of the glory of Christ, who is the image of God', as well as Hebrews 1:3, where the Son is described as 'the effulgence of [God's] glory and the exact representation of his being' (my translation).

Irenaeus affirms this identification of Christ as the archetypal image: 'For He made man the image of God; and the image of God is the Son, after whose image man was made'.[6] He develops the motif further by sometimes distinguishing between 'image' and 'likeness': the former refers to the basic bodily and intellectual capacities of human beings, while the latter refers to a genuine reflection of God's nature that is a gift of the Spirit. He writes, 'But if the Spirit be wanting to the soul, he who is such is indeed of an animal nature, and being left carnal, shall be an imperfect being, possessing indeed the image [of God] in his formation, but not receiving the similitude through the

4. See e.g. Origen, *Princ.*, 2.1.

5. See Christian Stettler, *Der Colosserhymnus* (Tübingen: Mohr Siebeck, 2000), pp. 111–14. Calvin accepts the association of Christ and Ezekiel's 'likeness of a man' in his commentary on Ezek. 1:26: 'But, with reference to this passage, it ought to suffice us, that the Prophet saw God only in the person of Christ, because what is said of the likeness of a man cannot be transferred to either the Father or the Spirit: for neither the Father nor the Spirit was ever manifested in flesh, but God was manifested to us in flesh when Christ appeared, in whom resides the fullness of the Divinity.'

6. Irenaeus, *Demonstration of the Gospel* 22; for a crisp summary of image and likeness in Irenaeus, see Eric Osborn, *Irenaeus of Lyons* (Cambridge: CUP, 2001), pp. 211–12.

Spirit; and thus is this being imperfect.'[7] As a strict lexicographical analysis of Genesis 1, this may leave something to be desired. But it is a clever way of managing the paradox that human beings, particularly in their broken state, are a curious mix of fitful God-likeness and appalling God-unlikeness.[8]

In keeping with his doctrine of recapitulation, the language of image and likeness also had an eschatological dimension for Irenaeus. He argues that the free will of human beings stems from their creation in the image of God: 'But because man is possessed of free will from the beginning, and God is possessed of free will, in whose likeness man was created, advice is always given to him to keep fast the good, which thing is done by means of obedience to God.'[9] Irenaeus' opponents might wish that God had created automata which 'are drawn by necessity and compulsion to what is good, in which things there is one mind and one usage, working mechanically in one groove (*inflexibiles et sine judicio),* who are incapable of being anything else except just what they had been created' (*Haer*. 4.37.6); but this is not the divine plan. The capacity for choosing the good is an aspect of the divine image in humanity; but it is equally true that the proper use of this capacity is what brings about the full flowering of the image and likeness (and note that in this section of the *Against Heresies* Irenaeus makes no hard and fast distinction between image and likeness):

> God thus determining all things beforehand for the bringing of man to perfection, for his edification, and for the revelation of His dispensations, that goodness may both be made apparent, and righteousness perfected, and that the Church may be fashioned after the image of His Son, and that man may finally be brought to maturity at some future time, becoming ripe through such privileges to see and comprehend God (*Haer*. 4.37.7).

For Irenaeus, it is not simply that the eschatological restoration of the image in Christ is *like* the first creation. It is in certain respects the *completion* of the first creation, as the following passage makes clear:

> For thou dost not make God, but God thee. If, then, thou art God's workmanship, await the hand of thy Maker which creates everything in due time; in due time as far as thou art concerned, whose creation is being carried out. Offer to Him thy heart in a soft and tractable state, and preserve the form in which the Creator has fashioned thee, having moisture in thyself, lest, by becoming hardened, thou lose the impressions of His fingers. But by preserving the

---

7. Irenaeus, *Haer*. 5.6.1.

8. Thus, e.g., Jesus can refer to some of his opponents as children of the devil (John 8:44), while James can forbid cursing fellow men and women because they are 'made in the likeness of God' (3:9).

9. Irenaeus, *Haer*. 4.37.4.

framework thou shalt ascend to that which is perfect, for the moist clay which is in thee is hidden [there] by the workmanship of God (*Haer.* 4.39.2).[10]

Adam, who are you?

Debates about the historicity of Adam have heightened in the wake of studies in the human genome that suggest the implausibility of humanity's descent from a primal couple. But the peculiarity of Adam's nature was noted far back in the tradition, and was arguably woven into the fabric of Genesis itself. With his generic name 'Man' (*'adam*), and the undertones of 'earth' (*'adamah*), Adam clearly functions as a representative figure. Of equal interest are the evident ties between Adam's story and Israel's story. If Adam at one level represents all of humanity, at another level his creation and fall is the literary prelude to Israel's conquest of and expulsion from the Land. This is especially true if the curious fact of his transport to Eden from the outside is taken as an analogue to Israel's story. The geographical oddities of paradise, meanwhile, contribute to the 'mythological' sense of the narrative. In some early Jewish traditions (e.g. *Sib. Or.* 3:24), Adam's name was said to be composed of the letters of the four directions of the world, signifying that he summed up the whole world in himself. Even stranger tales were told of the giant Adam: 'I saw there a man very great in height and fearful in breadth, incomparable in aspect embracing a woman, who likewise approximated to the aspect and shape of the man' (*Apoc. Ab.* 23:5–6).[11]

The story of Adam's progeny unfolds in the sadly familiar world east of Eden, but even here one meets perplexities. Where, for instance, did Cain's wife come from? Early Jewish interpreters recognized the problem, and there was an inevitable desire to fill in the blanks. *Jubilees* 4:1, 9 asserted that Cain's wife, named Awan, was also his sister, a tradition echoed by some rabbis (e.g. *Pirqe R. El.* 21). In Pseudo-Philo, she is not said to be his sister, and she is given the name Themech, while Josephus mentions sisters of Cain and Abel but does not say whether Cain took one of them to wife (*Ant.* 1.52); some rabbis, meanwhile, affirmed the tradition that his wife was his sister (*Pirqe R. El.* 21).[12]

10. Augustine, too, regards Christ as the primal image according to whom the rest of humanity was created: 'insofar as the likeness of God to which man was made can be taken to be that very Word of God, that is to say, the only-begotten Son; not of course that man himself is that same image and likeness, equal to the Father.' *Gen. Imp.* 61, in *On Genesis* (trans. Edmund Hill; Hyde Park: New City, 2002), p. 150.

11. See Andrei Orlov, *Heavenly Priesthood in the Apocalypse of Abraham* (Cambridge: CUP, 2013), pp. 37–38.

12. On all this, see John Byron, *Cain and Abel in Text and Tradition: Jewish and Christian Interpretations of the First Sibling Rivalry* (Leiden: Brill, 2011), pp. 24–27.

The notion that humankind in general, and not just the first man, somehow encapsulated the world in itself was an ancient one in Greek thought.[13] The details of how humanity mirrored the cosmos could vary, but central to the notion was humanity's unique union of flesh and spirit. Philo speaks explicitly of man as a 'small cosmos' (*brachys kosmos*) and the world as a 'large man' (*megas anthrōpos*) in *Heres* 155.[14] We have just noted the tradition concerning Adam's name and the points of the compass. The idea of man as microcosm proved popular in Christian circles as well. Although Gregory of Nyssa rejected the idea in *De Hom. Opif.* 16 (he thinks connecting man merely to the visible world reduces him to the level of a gnat or a mouse), he embraces the core conception of man as a union of the sensible and noetic realms.[15] Calvin notes in his Genesis commentary that humanity 'is deservedly called by the ancients, microcosmos, "a world in miniature" '.[16]

Maximus develops the microcosm theme in connection with his theory of the *logoi*. In *Ambiguum* 41, he argues that humankind was meant to unite all things in itself, but instead has become subject to the world around it with its divisions. Christ remedies this through his redemptive work:

> Through himself he has, in accordance with nature, united the fragments of the universal nature of all, manifesting the universal *logoi* that have come forth for the particulars, by which the union of the divided naturally comes about, and thus he fulfills the great purpose of God the Father *to recapitulate everything both in heaven and earth in himself* (Eph. 1:10) *in whom everything has been created* (Col. 1:10).[17]

---

13. See e.g. the discussion in W. K. C. Guthrie, *A History of Greek Philosophy* (6 vols; Cambridge: CUP, 1967–81), 2:471–73.

14. See the discussion in Peder Borgen, *Philo of Alexandria, An Exegete for His Time* (Leiden: Brill, 1997), pp. 218–23.

15. As noted by Paul M. Blowers, *Drama of the Divine Economy: Creator and Creation in Early Christian Theology and Piety* (Oxford: OUP, 2012), p. 357. He also points out that Nemesius of Emesa embraced the idea in *De Nat. Hom.* 1. Cf. the comments of Louis Dupré on Nicholas of Cusa: 'As the human person "contracts" God in himself, so does all other creation contract the person's spiritual universality. Human nature includes everything within itself and attains all things by the power of its sense, intellect, and will.' Louis K. Dupré, *Passage to Modernity: An Essay in the Hermeneutics of Nature and Culture* (New Haven: Yale University Press, 1993), p. 97.

16. On Gen. 1:26; see Peter Wyatt, *Jesus Christ and Creation in the Theology of John Calvin* (Allison Park, PA: Pickwick, 1996), p. 72.

17. Eriugena takes things in a very similar direction, as Moran notes: 'Developing Augustinian and Greek Christian anthropology—as expressed by the Cappadocian Fathers (especially Gregory of Nyssa) and by Maximus Confessor—Eriugena gives the human being a crucial role in the mirroring and extension of the divine creative process.' Dermot Moran, 'Nature, Man, and God in the Philosophy of John Scottus Eriugena', in *The Irish Mind: Exploring Intellectual Traditions* (ed. R. Kearney; Dublin: Wolfhound, 1985), p. 97.

Peter Lombard, meanwhile, drew lessons about divine love from the union of flesh and spirit. Why have rational creatures united with flesh? He answers:

> that in the foundation of man a new example would be shown of the blessed union, which is between God and spirit, in which He is loved *with one's whole heart* and is seen *face to face*. For the creature would think, that it could not be united to its Creator in so great a proximity, to love and cognize Him with (its) whole mind, unless it saw a spirit, which is the most excellent creature, united to such a very low one, that is to the flesh, which is of the earth, in such great love, that it could not be constrained to this, to will to relinquish it, just as the Apostle showed, saying: *We do not want to be despoiled in body, but to be clothed over*; through which it is shown, that the created spirit is united to the uncreated Spirit by an ineffable love (*Sent.* 2.1.6).

Louis Dupré sums up the ancient ideal of humanity as microcosmos thus: 'Partaking in all parts of the cosmos the person bears a unique responsibility for maintaining and furthering its order. He impresses his own form upon nature and, through this form-giving activity, he conveys to the universe a unity it would otherwise lack.'[18]

Summary of Adam

If the name of Adam was meant to signify the four directions of the compass, the story of his creation pulls the tradition in at least two directions. He is decidedly 'of the earth, earthy': he is created from the dust of the ground, and (at least after the expulsion from the garden) he walks the known earth and has named progeny. He is thus tied into the biological history of the planet and is susceptible to investigation at that level. At the same time, Adam is according to Genesis uniquely created in the image of God and filled with God's breath. He comes directly from the hand of God; his original homeland is a geographical curiosity; his name evokes a representative figure rather than a random individual man; and his early history unmistakably evokes the story of Israel that follows. He is thus in some sense cartographically and ontologically untraceable.

There are various ways to manage the dilemma. One is to push the modern scientific view to the side altogether and take Genesis more or less literally: God hand-makes Adam and Eve a few thousand years ago, they eat the fruit, and humanity begins its sad journey away from God. The

18. Dupré, *Passage to Modernity*, p. 97.

obvious problem with this is running afoul of presumably good-faith efforts to trace back humanity's family tree through scientific means. The less obvious problem is that one focuses so much on the literalistically conceived history of Adam that the theological thrust of the story is lost.

On the opposite extreme, one can hand the wheel to science and let it steer the course as it will. In place of the homey biblical account of a handmade humanity, we would be left with a murky trail back to a smallish cluster of genetically recognizable humans, and back further still to proto-hominids and ultimately to the proverbial primordial ooze. The fact that we might be traced back to such ooze is in and of itself not of great theological significance: the 'dust' of Genesis is making the same essential point, only in drier terms. The real problem with a purely naturalistic account of human origins is how to make sense of us as sense-making creatures. Even those who cry out that the world is meaningless are working with a category of 'meaning'—whence did this arise? To put it another way, Christians affirm as a properly basic belief (to use Alvin Plantinga's term) that we are created in the image of God: given this fact, does it seem plausible that we simply *evolved* into such a position? If not, is the idea of a 'special creation' of humanity really so ludicrous after all?

If these boundaries on the question be admitted, we are still left with a range of options whose relative utility can be mooted by the church. Those who wish to hew as closely as possible to Genesis while preserving the broad outline of contemporary biology may wish to see God specially 'humanizing' Adam and Eve at what government officials might term 'an undisclosed location'. Such a reading will provide a smooth transition to the contrast of Adam and Christ deployed by Paul in his letters. On the other hand, it would also leave some significant genetic loose ends. One might take the Adam narrative (with a nod towards the allegorical exegetical tradition) as a symbolic gesture towards a general humanization by God of the first genetically recognizable humans. This could be seen as a dramatic incursion of God into human history or (with more difficulty) an immanent but divinely guided process somehow arising within the ebb and flow of biological evolution. Paul's Adam would then become a cipher for the situation of estrangement from God in which we simply find ourselves to be.

Creation and Creativity

Whatever the precise meaning of the 'image' language might be, it is clear that humanity plays a critical role in the furthering of God's creation project: while the language of 'co-creation' might be too strong, J. R. R. Tolkien's 'sub-creation' captures the same truth in humbler terms.[19] Portrayals of primal paradise often overlook the dynamism inherent in God's command, 'Be fruitful and multiply, and fill the earth and subdue it'. While Genesis 1 does present a serene unfolding of God's creation by his word, the completion of the creative vision involves a struggle against residual wildness.

The strong phrase 'subdue the earth' is echoed in the language of the conquest narratives (note the use of the same Hebrew verb in e.g. Num. 32:22; Josh. 18:1) and suggests that even before the invocation of the curse the world would offer some kind of resistance to humanity's putative efforts at order. The language has met with criticism in modern times, since it suggests an inescapably violent and oppressive relationship between humanity and nature. It is true that the word has militaristic connotations in the Hebrew bible. It is possible, and even likely, that the connection is deliberate: Adam's story foreshadows that of Israel in important ways (the exile motif being the most prominent), and it may be that Adam's need to push back against a recalcitrant world is meant to parallel Israel's need to struggle against their hostile neighbours. In neither case will order come cheaply.

That humanity's relation to the earth involves a degree of battling would hardly surprise Ancient Near Eastern readers of the text. It is one thing to admire the beauty of a lion from afar and call for its preservation; it is another if said lion is carrying off your livestock or your children. That being said, the broader picture of the earlier chapters of Genesis hardly endorses an all-out war of humanity against the rest of creation. Adam's naming of the animals implies a friendly dominion in the hands of one who is equally created from the dust of the earth. (Vegetarians have long pointed out that both humans and animals are in the beginning given only plant life for food, and thus argue that flesh-eating is a result of the fall.) All things, including humanity, are under God and exist to serve his purposes. Thus while the word 'subdue' itself can only with difficulty be rendered as something like 'steward', the broader theological currents of Genesis do endorse the idea of friendly dominion or stewardship.

The practice of the Sabbath wove the ongoing movement of the creation project into the fabric of Israel's workweek. The connection is evident in Exodus 20:8–11:

> Remember the sabbath day, to keep it holy. Six days you shall labor, and do all your work; but the seventh day is a sabbath to the LORD your God; in it you shall not do any work, you, or your son, or your daughter, your manservant, or your maidservant, or your cattle, or the sojourner who is within your gates;

---

19. J. R. R Tolkien, 'On Fairy Stories', in *The Tolkien Reader* (New York: Ballantine, 1986). While Tolkien is writing specifically about the production of fictional works, the term remains a useful one for all positive human endeavours.

> for in six days the LORD made heaven and earth, the sea, and all that is in them, and rested the seventh day; therefore the LORD blessed the sabbath day and hallowed it.

While part of the rationale for the Sabbath is to remember that all things come from God, the mirroring of the creation week suggests that humanity contributes to the effoliation of the creation through its weekly labour. In Deuteronomy 5:15, meanwhile, the Sabbath is grounded in God's acts of deliverance: 'You shall remember that you were a servant in the land of Egypt, and the LORD your God brought you out thence with a mighty hand and an outstretched arm; therefore the LORD your God commanded you to keep the sabbath day.' The connection between creation and redemption is familiar by now; we need only add that the Israelite who liberates his household (including his animals) from work on the Sabbath furthers the liberating, recreative plan of God himself.

Ordinary human labour is an integral part of the 'continuous creation' of the world. Psalm 104 is routinely regarded as the Scripture's supreme paean to the beauties of nature, but note how work fits seamlessly into the psalmist's portrait:

> The young lions roar for their prey,
> seeking their food from God.
> When the sun rises, they get them away
> and lie down in their dens.
> Man goes forth to his work
> and to his labor until the evening (Ps. 104:21–23).[20]

Theodoret of Cyrus is one of many theologians who sees in human creative labour an expression of what it means to be in the image of God: 'In imitation of the Creator, man also creates houses, walls, cities, harbors, ships, dockyards, chariots, and countless other things, including likenesses of heaven, representations of the sun, moon, and stars, and images of people and brute beasts. Nonetheless, the difference in creating is infinite.'[21] Eriugena takes an even more expansive view of human creation, arguing that reason is itself a kind of art.[22]

20. Meat-lovers may note that the supposed vegetarian scruples of the Garden have here given way to a divine approbation of carnivores and their ways.

21. Theodoret of Cyrus, *The Questions on the Octateuch*, vol. 1, Gk. text rev. John Petruccione (trans. Robert C. Hill; Washington, DC: Catholic University of America Press, 2007), p. 53.

22. John J. O'Meara, *Eriugena* (Oxford: Clarendon, 1988), p. 100; Myra L. Uhlfelder and Jean Potter, *Periphyseon: On the Division of Nature* (Indianapolis: Bobbs-Merrill, 1976), pp. 119–20.

The curse on Adam, of course, strikes directly at his labour, such that what might have been a delightful cultivation of the earth often becomes drudgery. We need not restrict ourselves to the canon to make the point: Virgil's words in the *Georgics, labor omnia vicit* ('toil conquers all'), have been taken as a clarion call to the glories of hard work, but in context they are part of a nuanced account of work that functions almost as a poetic commentary on Genesis 1–3. While labour may improve the soul, and beautify the earth, it is just as much a grim necessity in the face of a flinty world: 'Therefore, unless your hoe is ever ready to assail the weeds, your voice to terrify the birds, your knife to check the shade over the darkened land, and your prayers to invoke the rain, in vain, poor man, you will gaze on your neighbour's large store of grain, and you will be shaking oaks in the woods to assuage your hunger.'[23] As we will see below in our discussion of Babylon, once people get the upper hand over nature, things can get even worse.

Especially relevant for our purposes are the so-called 'creative arts', wherein humans self-consciously mirror the divine work of creation. In his landmark essay, 'On Fairy Stories', Tolkien was particularly concerned to vindicate his endeavours in creating fantasy literature. He does so with great theological finesse. Creativity in general stems from our creation in the image of God: 'Fantasy remains a human right: we make in our measure and in our derivative mode, because we are made: and not only made, but made in the image and likeness of a Maker.'[24] But an artist like Tolkien is attempting not only to enrich the created world, but to produce a fully realized secondary world:

> What really happens is that the story-maker proves a successful 'sub-creator'. He makes a Secondary World which your mind can enter. Inside it, what he relates is 'true': it accords with the laws of that world. You therefore believe it, while you are, as it were, inside. The moment disbelief arises, the spell is broken; the magic, or rather art, has failed. You are then out in the Primary World again, looking at the little abortive Secondary World from outside.[25]

Tolkien is well aware of the perils attendant upon making a secondary world in this fashion, though he deems them no greater than the perils of fabricating false gods in the realms of politics and economics. Sub-creation is worth the risk, because it helps people return to the primary world with a fresh perspective. More than that, good fairy stories can lead the reader towards God's own story of creation and recreation:

23. Virgil, *Georg.* 1.155–59.
24. Tolkien, 'On Fairy Stories', p. 75.
25. Tolkien, 'On Fairy Stories', p. 60.

> I would venture to say that approaching the Christian Story from this direction, it has long been my feeling (a joyous feeling) that God redeemed the corrupt making-creatures, men, in a way fitting to this aspect, as to others, of their strange nature. The Gospels contain a fairy-story, or a story of a larger kind which embraces all the essence of fairy-stories. They contain many marvels—peculiarly artistic, beautiful, and moving: 'mythical' in their perfect, self-contained significance; and among the marvels is the greatest and most complete conceivable eucatastrophe. But this story has entered History and the primary world; the desire and aspiration of sub-creation has been raised to the fulfillment of Creation. The Birth of Christ is the eucatastrophe of Man's history. The Resurrection is the eucatastrophe of the story of the Incarnation. This story begins and ends in joy. It has pre-eminently the 'inner consistency of reality.' There is no tale ever told that men would rather find was true, and none which so many sceptical men have accepted as true on its own merits. For the Art of it has the supremely convincing tone of Primary Art, that is, of Creation. To reject it leads either to sadness or to wrath.[26]

Bulgakov writes in very similar terms. He puts 'the gift of aesthetic appreciation' as one of three 'gifts' granted to humankind created in God's image.[27] But humanity is not simply to appreciate what God has made: 'Because he has been created in the image of God he is called to create.'[28] This is obviously not done *ex nihilo*: artists not only work with materials given in creation; they are also giving expression to a beauty which is given with the world, and which stems from the eternal and ineffable beauty of God himself. Bulgakov's Platonist leanings are evident in his discussion of the central purpose of art: 'Art sees not the outward, but the inward aspect of the object; it looks for the primordial idea of the object, an idea which is sometimes but slightly and dimly discernible through the outward covering.'[29]

In keeping with the dynamic conception of the *logoi* in Maximus, however, the artist is not simply re-imagining the original idea along slightly more abstracted lines. Genuine art is a kind of prophetic act, a declaration of the essence of a thing which will be fully realized in the eschaton: 'Things are transfigured and made luminous by beauty; they become the revelation of their own abstract meaning. And this revelation through beauty of the things of the earth is the work of art. The world, as it has been given to us, has remained as it were covered by an outward shell through which art

---

26. Tolkien, 'On Fairy Stories', pp. 88–89.

27. Sergei Bulgakov, 'Religion and Art', in *The Church of God: An Anglo-Russian Symposium, Fellowship of St Alban and St Sergius* (ed. E. Mascall; London: SPCK, 1934), pp. 175–91, p. 177; the other two are 'a will directed to the good' and 'reason and wisdom'.

28. Bulgakov, 'Religion and Art', p. 177.

29. Bulgakov, 'Religion and Art', p. 179.

penetrates, as if foreseeing the coming transfiguration of the world.'[30] The image of *transfiguration* is carefully chosen: just as the Mount of Transfiguration revealed both the essence of Jesus and his coming glory, so art reaches out to the roots of things in God's wisdom, and in so doing gives us a glimpse of their eternal destiny in the presence of God.

Finally, humanity is to mirror God in the world through ethical excellence. Israel was called to live in obedience to God's commandments as a witness to the glory of God for the surrounding nations:

> Keep them and do them; for that will be your wisdom and your understanding in the sight of the peoples, who, when they hear all these statutes, will say, 'Surely this great nation is a wise and understanding people'. For what great nation is there that has a god so near to it as the LORD our God is to us, whenever we call upon him? And what great nation is there, that has statutes and ordinances so righteous as all this law which I set before you this day? (Deut. 4:6–8)

Jesus makes the same point in his comment in the Sermon on the Mount about believers being a 'city on a hill'. What is most striking is that Jesus' commands hearken back to the original design of creation. To take the most obvious example, Jesus asserts that Moses permitted divorce as a concession to the hard-heartedness of the people. The messianic community is to be marked out by its adherence to God's primal purposes (Matt. 19:3–9):

> And Pharisees came up to him and tested him by asking, 'Is it lawful to divorce one's wife for any cause?' He answered, 'Have you not read that he who made them from the beginning made them male and female, and said, "For this reason a man shall leave his father and mother and be joined to his wife, and the two shall become one flesh"? So they are no longer two but one flesh. What therefore God has joined together, let not man put asunder.' They said to him, 'Why then did Moses command one to give a certificate of divorce, and to put her away?' He said to them, 'For your hardness of heart Moses allowed you to divorce your wives, but from the beginning it was not so. And I say to you: whoever divorces his wife, except for unchastity, and marries another, commits adultery.'

The advent of the eschaton in the ministry of Jesus opens up the possibility for God's people to fulfil his creative design for humanity.

30. Bulgakov, 'Religion and Art', pp. 177–78. See the discussion in Brian Horne, 'Divine and Human Creativity', in *The Doctrine of Creation: Essays in Dogmatics, History and Philosophy* (ed. Colin E. Gunton; London: T&T Clark, 2004), p. 175.

The Curse

In the event, the promised happy dominion over the earth vanishes almost as the words leave God's lips. Adam and Eve's assertion of radical autonomy brings with it only estrangement: cast out from the presence of God, they will wander on the hostile earth until at last it swallows them up again. As with the creation, so the curse raises fresh questions in our scientific age. We will address here only two of the most pressing ones: did death not exist in the world prior to the putative act of disobedience? How far does the curse affect the created order?

The question of human death should not be restricted to merely biological concerns. Physical death is explicable enough from an evolutionary perspective, as we have noted, but it typically presents people with an existential crisis: we do not want to die, and we are terrified at the prospect of non-existence. In many cases we invoke the adjective 'tragic' as a protest at the sheer wrongness of certain deaths. Even if we dismiss other people's death at a ripe old age as 'natural', this is small comfort as we contemplate our own demise. Whatever physical processes might have led to our frail and transient lives, we live them under a certain shadow that goes beyond an instinct for survival. We have fallen from where we know we ought to be.

With respect to the fall and the created order as a whole, it should be noted that Genesis only speaks explicitly of the ground yielding thorns and thistles as an obstacle to human dominion. The initial commission to Adam and Eve presupposes that the world is still in need of some taming. What changes is again the human *experience* of the world. While we cannot rule out God instituting a fundamental change in the fabric of the world at the fall, it is equally likely that the human experience of estrangement from God is what engenders the futility of life. We might, for instance, with only a moderate exercise of imagination think of a world in which Spirit-inspired humans deftly tamed everything from microbes to mosquitoes and directed them towards a harmonious earthly order.

Babylon: The Corpse of Beauty

Sin and the de-creation it triggers are only one aspect of humanity's negative effects on the creation project. The blasphemous pretensions of *counterfeit creation* are equally pertinent. From Babel in Genesis to Babylon in Revelation, the Scriptures detail the propensity of human beings to use their creative powers to create an anti-cosmos, a world divorced from God. The similarity in names is no accident: the tower builders at primeval Babel are clearly the prototype for Israel's quintessential imperial foe and the destroyer of its temple, Babylon. Babylon in turn becomes the model for the Roman Empire of John's day. It encompasses the same essential territory as the comparable New Testament term 'the world'. While the latter emphasizes the pervasive nature of corruption in society, it has had the unfortunate effect of colouring the church's view of creation in general.

The idolatry that sits at the heart of the Babylonian enterprise constitutes the supreme misuse of humanity's creative powers. The adjective 'handmade' in the OT generally refers to idols crafted by humankind, and Babylon is above all characterized in Scripture as the sinkhole of idolatry.[31] Isaiah's prophecy of Babylon's looming judgement mocks the city's so-called gods: 'Bel bows down, Nebo stoops, their idols are on beasts and cattle; these things you carry are loaded as burdens on weary beasts. They stoop, they bow down together, they cannot save the burden, but themselves go into captivity' (Isa. 46:1–2). Such deities are the fabrications of human hands, and they will wither under God's consuming fire.

Yet in seeking to establish the City of Man, people are not acting as absolutely independent agents. The latter portion of Revelation (chs 12–22) is in essence a confrontation between the Holy Trinity and the blasphemous Satanic trinity of the Dragon, the Beast, and the False Prophet.[32] From chapter 17 on, the focus becomes the two cities belonging to their respective lords: Babylon and the New Jerusalem. Compare 17:1 and 21:9:

> Then one of the seven angels who had the seven bowls came and said to me, 'Come, I will show you the judgment of the great harlot who is seated upon many waters' (17:1).

> Then came one of the seven angels who had the seven bowls full of the seven last plagues, and spoke to me, saying, 'Come, I will show you the Bride, the wife of the Lamb' (21:9).

Both women are bedecked with gold and pearls, both exercise wide dominion and draw the nations to themselves—but one is a dragon's lair of ill-gotten gain, doomed for destruction, while the other is the enduring home for the glory of the one true God.

Bulgakov, after viewing an exhibit of Picasso's paintings in Paris, acknowledged the technical skill of the artist, but felt that his work was a fundamental distortion of the purpose of art, indeed a demonic counterfeit: 'he gives us not beauty, but its corpse'.[33] One may differ with Bulgakov's

31. For 'handmade' idols, see e.g. Lev. 26:1; Isa. 2:18; 10:11.

32. Richard Bauckham, *The Climax of Prophecy: Studies on the Book of Revelation* (London: T&T Clark, 2007), p. 32.

33. Sergei Bulgakov, 'The Corpse of Beauty', in *A Bulgakov Anthology* (trans. Natalie Duddington and James Pain; London: Westminster, 1976), pp. 67–72.

assessment of Picasso, but as a summary depiction of Babylon's evils his words are without peer. Babylon, as much as the church at Sardis, 'has a name that it is alive', but it is dead. It has established a simulacrum of the worldwide rule held out to Adam, it has fabricated a city to vie with the heavenly Jerusalem, it has raised its towers to the sky—but its foundations are in sand, and its radiance is illusory: it is not beauty, but its corpse.

The cipher Babylon has had a rich history in the church, though its roots in Revelation have lent its deployment something of a fanatical flavour: 'Babylon' is often the first rhetorical shot in the battle against real or perceived imperial threats, whether political or ecclesiastical. The papacy has been a particular target since the Reformation, as witnessed by Luther's seminal 'Babylonian Captivity of the Church', or Edwards' detailed comparison of the Church of Rome and Babylon in his 'Notes on the Apocalypse'. In modern times, Babylon is perhaps best known for its use in reggae music, where it represents variously the Roman Catholic Church, the Jamaican police and government, or oppressive European powers past and present.[34] While its association with the idiosyncrasies of Rastafarian teaching may limit its applicability in the broader church, reggae's creative deployment of Babylon remains a significant appropriation of the apocalyptic tradition.

Babylon should not be restricted to the fringes of modern theological discourse. If anything, its utility has only increased in the increasingly self-contained, self-referential, and totalizing technological matrix of Western society. At the existential level, Louis Dupré speaks of modernity's 'indigent self', a deracinated wanderer in an uncaring cosmos, a 'pure project . . . severed from those sources that once provided its content'.[35] The assumption of radical autonomy comports well with the self-sufficient arrogance of Babylon: 'I am; and there is no one besides me. I shall not sit as a widow or know the loss of children' (Isa. 47:8). Increasing technological mastery has permitted the autonomous self to reshape reality to fit its own desires. This can involve the creation of virtual realities by which one withdraws from the world as it has been given to us, or the manipulation of the given world to suit human fancies. Both are exposed as fantasies by the prophetic critique: the former are tantamount to the futile 'magic spells and sorceries' by which Babylon fought to stave off divine judgement (Isa. 48:12), while the latter mirror Babylon's achievements in culture and commerce, which prove as ephemeral as the 'gods' that underwrote them (Ezek. 27; cf. Rev. 18). Ellul, the great critic of the technological society, sums it up well:

34. See e.g. Stephen A. King, *Reggae, Rastafari, and the Rhetoric of Social Control* (Jackson, MS: University Press of Mississippi, 2007), p. 56.

35. Dupré, *Passage to Modernity*, p. 119.

> She [Babylon] is the very home of civilization and when the great city vanishes, there is no more civilization, a world disappears. She is the one struck in war, and she is the first to be struck in the war between the Lord and the powers of the world. A city greater than a simple city—the finishing of a work that can in no wise be finished, which man starts over indefinitely with ever the same purpose and the same access. Babylon, Venice, Paris, New York—they are all the same city, only one Babel always reappearing, a city from the beginning mortally wounded: 'and they left off building the city.'[36]

Resurrection and Theosis

The future belongs not to the Promethean project of the City of Man, but to the recreative purposes of God Almighty. Foremost among these purposes is the resurrection of the body. Few aspects of Christian tradition are as essential to the doctrine of creation as this one. In addition to the unique view of human destiny wrapped up in bodily resurrection, the teaching has served as a doctrinal anchor for the fate of the wider world. Platonism, we have seen, has made some positive contributions to the Christian understanding of creation. But it did open the door to a purely 'spiritualized' understanding of reality far distant from the biblical portrayal. One suspects that bodily resurrection kept many a theologian from walking through that door (or at least slowed them down, depending on how one assesses figures like Eriugena and Coleridge). A risen body in an immaterial world does not make much sense, and so one either goes to great pains to demonstrate the utter transcendence of the new spiritual body, or more commonly, one accepts (however grudgingly) the reality of bodily resurrection with all that entails for the materiality of the future state.

In certain respects, however, the resurrection of the dead was more theologically problematic than the restoration of the world as a whole. It is all very well to picture the world at large going about its course with renewed harmony: the raising of an individual brings the question so close to home that questions rise up, as they did in the earliest churches: 'How will the dead be raised? With what sort of body will they come?' (1 Cor. 15:35, my translation). Such questions may have arisen from a common-sense scepticism about the dead rising; or from a superstitious fear of a zombie apocalypse of merely resuscitated corpses; or from a philosophically sophisticated critique of material existence as such. In any event, Paul and his theological heirs devoted a considerable amount of attention to answering the queries.

36. Jacques Ellul, *The Meaning of the City* (trans. Dennis Pardee; Grand Rapids: Eerdmans, 1970), p. 21.

Paul's own answer begins with a strong affirmation of the bodily resurrection of Christ and its centrality to the gospel (1 Cor. 15:1–11). If Christ is affirmed as risen, it follows that resurrection in general cannot be ruled out of court (vv. 12–19). Paul goes on to show how the raising of Christ and the saints is a central part of God's purpose to reclaim the entire creation for his own glory (vv. 20–28). After a brief and puzzling mention of 'baptism for the dead', he follows with an extended discussion concerning the nature of the resurrection body (vv. 35–49). Paul's fundamental point is that the resurrection body will be far superior to our present body, just as a flower exceeds a seed in glory. This is rooted in God's power, which can grant different bodies to different things as he pleases. He describes the body as 'spiritual', which as we have seen led to a good deal of Platonically tinged exegesis by the likes of Eriugena. Certainly Paul means to contrast the corrupted body inherited from Adam with the immortal body given by Christ: but taking the new body as essentially immaterial ill suits the context of 1 Corinthians. Paul has already established a strong continuity between the now-body and the new-body in 1 Corinthians 6:12–20. If he was thinking along Eriugena's lines, it is hard to see why he goes to the trouble of writing chapter 15 in the first place: surely a brief affirmation that he was not really talking about bodies in any conventional sense would have been sufficient to quell the Corinthians' concerns.

As it stands, Paul does provide a theologically refined defence of bodily resurrection that undercuts all manner of objections to the doctrine: bodies are a good gift of God, and thus one need not shy away from their materiality; the new body will not be subject to the limitations governing the present one, so one need not worry about disfigured risen corpses stumbling their way through eternity; and God's creative power is such that no amount of decay or dispersion can prevent him from raising his people to eternal embodied life.[37]

Paul's arguments in 1 Corinthian 15 formed the bedrock of later theologians' defence of the resurrection, even as they formed a seedbed for speculation about the precise nature of the resurrection body. Irenaeus provides as robust an affirmation of the reality of cosmic renewal as anyone, and it is no surprise to see him affirm the resurrection of the body in terms drawn directly from 1 Corinthians 15 (*Haer.* 5.2). Later patristic writers devoted considerable attention to the practicalities of resurrection, often with great sophistication. Paul had provided a basic rationale for a glorified risen body,

37. Cf. T. F. Torrance: 'In creation and the affirmation of creation, in recreation and the finalizing of creation, the resurrection is the establishing of the creature in a reality that does not crumble away into the dust or degenerate into nothingness or slip into the oblivion of the past.' T. F. Torrance, *Space, Time and Resurrection* (Edinburgh: T&T Clark, 1998), p. 79.

but he had not offered up much in the way of detail as to how this worked. (Recall Gregory's contention that the soul would recognize the components of its body by a kind of impressed memory.)

Augustine's understanding of the resurrection has spurred much discussion from ancient and modern thinkers.[38] Contemporary scholars see a progression in his thought from an earlier, more Platonic and spiritualized view of the resurrection, to a later view that emphasized more the bona fide flesh-and-blood-ness of the resurrection body.[39] Since Paul himself oscillates between aspects of continuity and discontinuity within the pages of 1 Corinthians itself (never mind his statements in 2 Cor. 4–5), we may wonder whether this is a fundamental shift in view on Augustine's part, or whether like Paul he is simply exploring differing poles of a complex reality. For the sake of simplicity, we may focus on his extended discussion of the resurrection in *City of God* 22. Augustine addresses a catalogue of questions concerning the resurrection here, some familiar (how can the decayed body be reassembled?), some novel (who gets the flesh of a man consumed by someone forced to resort to cannibalism?).[40] He deploys the idea of seminal reasons to address the questions of whether infants stay small in the resurrection: 'In this seminal principle of every substance, there seems to be, as it were, the beginning of everything which does not yet exist, or rather does not appear, but which in process of time will come into being, or rather into sight. In this, therefore, the child who is to be tall or short is already tall or short' (22.14). As for deformities of various sorts, he argues that just as the human workman can remake a jar to suit his purposes, so God will remake the person to bring them to the state of beauty he desires (22.19). This body will be 'spiritual' in the sense that it will be subject to the spirit (22.21).

No doubt many within and without the church continued to wonder about the resurrection down the centuries, but the need for an apologetic to defend the doctrine diminished until the advent of the modern age. Even here it is debatable whether the fundamental contours of the defence really needed to change. Paul and Augustine knew the doctrine was incredible on its face; indeed, for Augustine the fact that so many had nonetheless come to believe it was itself something of a miracle (*Civ.* 22.5). Paul grounded his statements on the resurrection on the power and wisdom of God displayed in the present creation, not on a now-outmoded system of physics. The

38. For a helpful summary of Augustine's views and contemporary discussion, see Caroline Walker Bynum, *The Resurrection of the Body in Western Christianity: 200–1336* (New York: Columbia University Press, 1995), pp. 94–104.

39. Bynum, *Resurrection*, p. 95 n. 132.

40. The first question receives the traditional response that nothing is too difficult for God; for the latter, Augustine deems the flesh of the eaten to be 'on loan' to the eater, such that it will return to the party of the first part.

fathers at times indulged in a bit more detailed rendering of the mechanics of resurrection, but even a proposal like Gregory's 'soul-impression' maintains some interest as speculative theology. Modern sceptics did not pose a new and unimagined threat to the doctrine of resurrection.

If anything, advances in scientific thinking provided fresh ways of imagining what resurrection might entail. Augustine's seminal reasons bear at least some resemblance to DNA, such that there is biological warrant for thinking of the adult existing *in potentia* in infancy. If we posit some connection between the workings of the now-world and the new-world, we could envision the restructuring of the person around a restored DNA code, without worrying about how the constituent elements of the former person might be gathered from the dispersed elements. Of course this still presupposes divine intervention in the form of the retrieval and perfection of the DNA; but as Irenaeus points out, divine intervention is rather the point of the resurrection.

The church, then, has consistently confessed the resurrection of the body. Does human destiny also include *becoming* God? The doctrine of *theosis* or deification has had a mixed reception within Christianity. It has formed a central thread in the Orthodox Church from the earliest days, while Western Christians have been much more reticent to use the term.

The direct biblical antecedents for the language of deification are few. Among early patristic commentators, John 10:34—'I said, you are gods'—occasioned the most discussion, though later it was joined with the more obvious proof text in 2 Peter 1:4, 'that . . . you may . . . become partakers of the divine nature.' Neither text demands to be read as referring to deification in the strongest sense. John 10 is a quotation from Psalm 82, which many modern commentators take to be a reference to angelic beings. The context of 2 Peter 1:4, meanwhile, suggests that 'partakers of the divine nature' refers to the believer's growth in divine love and holiness. The most theologically potent text was arguably 1 Corinthians 15:28 NIV, 'God may be all in all', which played such a formative role in the thinking of Maximus and Eriugena.[41] Whether the Bible puts forth the *substance* of deification under other names naturally depends on what one considers that substance to be. Thus one might be inclined to take the multitudinous references to believers being 'in Christ' as gestures towards theosis: this is often described as a 'mystical union' that will be consummated in the new creation.[42]

41. Cf. *Sir.* 43:27: 'Though we speak much we cannot reach the end, and the sum of our words is: "He is the all."'

42. Grant Macaskill has a detailed argument against reading the texts in this manner, and instead taking them as references to covenant union. See Macaskill, *Union with Christ in the New Testament* (Oxford: OUP, 2013).

Irenaeus provided the basic rhythm for the patristic teaching on theosis in statements like these:

> The Word of God, our Lord Jesus Christ, who did, through His transcendent love, become what we are, that He might bring us to be even what He is Himself (*Haer.*, preface to book 5).
>
> For it was for this end that the Word of God was made man, and He who was the Son of God became the Son of man, that man, having been taken into the Word, and receiving the adoption, might become the son of God (*Haer.* 3.19.1).
>
> For we cast blame upon Him, because we have not been made gods from the beginning, but at first merely men, then at length gods; although God has adopted this course out of His pure benevolence, that no one may impute to Him invidiousness or grudgingness. He declares, 'I have said, Ye are gods; and ye are all sons of the Highest.' But since we could not sustain the power of divinity, He adds, 'But ye shall die like men,' setting forth both truths—the kindness of His free gift, and our weakness, and also that we were possessed of power over ourselves (*Haer.* 4.38.4).

Irenaeus artfully balances the fundamental distinction between the Creator God and humanity, and the union of God and humanity created in his image. Thus while human beings will never be uncreated as God is, they may reflect the divine immortality through their ongoing life in him:

> For from the very fact of these things having been created, [it follows] that they are not uncreated; but by their continuing in being throughout a long course of ages, they shall receive a faculty of the Uncreated, through the gratuitous bestowal of eternal existence upon them by God. And thus in all things God has the pre-eminence, who alone is uncreated, the first of all things, and the primary cause of the existence of all, while all other things remain under God's subjection. But being in subjection to God is continuance in immortality, and immortality is the glory of the uncreated One. By this arrangement, therefore, and these harmonies, and a sequence of this nature, man, a created and organized being, is rendered after the image and likeness of the uncreated God (*Haer.* 4.38.3).

Athanasius put Irenaeus' theme in its most enduring form in his *De Incarnatione* (54:347): 'For He was made man that we might be made God (*theopoiēthōmen*); and He manifested Himself by a body that we might receive the idea of the unseen Father; and He endured the insolence of men that we might inherit immortality.' Augustine said much the same thing (*Trin.* 4.2): 'By joining therefore to us the likeness of His humanity, He took away the unlikeness of our unrighteousness; and by being made partaker of our mortality, He made us partakers of His divinity.' The early tradition reaches its apex in Maximus, who sees theosis as the climax of God's plan not only for humanity, but for the cosmos as a whole.[43]

Those outside the Orthodox tradition may wonder why the language of 'becoming a god' needed to be employed at all in light of its slim biblical profile. While Psalm 82, John 10 and 2 Peter 1 may seem to be isolated texts, they do (arguably) associate human beings with deity, and this warrants some explanation—particularly in a culture where the words 'god' and 'gods' had a far broader purview than in an English-language setting profoundly shaped by monotheistic assumptions. Since the gods in Greek religion were by definition 'the immortal ones', even the fundamental Christian ascription of *endless* life to people could be seen as a de facto assertion of their divinity. The christological controversies of the early centuries of the church also demanded careful attention to the intersection of divinity and humanity in Christ and believers.

In any case, the language of deification was to become a central feature of theology in the East, while maintaining a presence in the West in thinkers like Eriugena and the Cambridge Platonists. Norman Russell has isolated several distinctions within the doctrine among the fathers.[44] The first is a *nominal* one in which humans are titled 'gods' as a sign of honour. This would have particular resonance in the Hellenistic milieu, as noted above. The *analogous* use affirmed that human beings could be called 'gods' in a relative sense: Philo famously exegeted Exodus 7:1 ('I will make you God to Pharaoh', my translation) as an indication that Moses in his wisdom would rule over the foolish king as God rules the world.[45] The *ethical* sense, wherein Christians acquire an increasing likeness to God in their behaviour, can easily be supported from a range of scriptures. Things become somewhat more complex when theosis is seen as a *realistic* union with the deity, often described in terms of *participation*. This last term, which is drawn directly from Platonism, speaks of the believer sharing in a relationship

43. See e.g. Torstein Tollefsen, *The Christocentric Cosmology of St Maximus the Confessor* (Oxford: OUP, 2012), p. 66; on Maximus and theosis, see also Elena Vishnevskaya, 'Divinization as Perichoretic Embrace in Maximus the Confessor', in *Partakers of the Divine Nature* (ed. Michael Christensen and Jeffrey Wittung; Grand Rapids: Baker, 2008), pp. 132–45; and Vishnevskaya, 'Divinization and Spiritual Progress in Maximus the Confessor', in *Theosis: Deification in Christian Theology* (2 vols; ed. Stephen Finlan and Vladimir Kharlamov; Eugene, OR: Pickwick, 2006), 1:134–45.

44. See Russell, *The Doctrine of Deification in the Greek Patristic Tradition* (Oxford: OUP, 2004). Russell's fourfold explanation forms the template for much of his book, but he provides a helpful summary on pp. 1–3.

45. See e.g. *Mut.* 128; discussion in John Lierman, *The New Testament Moses: Christian Perceptions of Moses and Israel in the Setting of Jewish Religion* (Tübingen: Mohr Siebeck, 2004), pp. 230–32.

within God himself; it is important to note that even in the Platonist scheme the constituents of the participatory relationship need not be of the same ontological type. Thus the notion that we somehow merge with the being of God is not a necessary deduction from participation. But some such idea may be read into discussions of theosis where an ontological change to God-likeness is induced by, for example, the sacraments and the work of the Holy Spirit.

Is it proper to say that theosis is the ultimate goal of the creation project? On the positive side, the term has served to mark out widely accepted aspects of Christian hope. As often as not the fathers used 'deification' to stress the *ethical* likeness of redeemed humanity to God. It is hard to imagine a Christian who would want to disavow statements like, 'Be merciful as your Father is merciful' (Luke 6:36). Believers of all stripes embrace the hope of an intimate union with God through Christ and the Spirit in the eschaton. If the strict Platonic associations of 'participation' or 'sharing' are downplayed, even these terms would seem acceptable ways of describing the close fellowship of God and humanity envisioned by Revelation 21–22. Furthermore, the early Eastern tradition was constantly aware of the danger of conflating the uncreated God and created beings. They were careful to deploy the language of deification with abundant qualifications: witness, for example, Pseudo-Dionysius' statement that 'deification is the attaining of likeness to God and union with him *so far as is possible*' (emphasis added).[46] In the same way, they were content to use the language infrequently, or avoid it altogether, in times where it was liable to be misunderstood.[47] Theologians in the West have affirmed what might be deemed the core values of the doctrine, and several have been content to use the language of deification.[48] Calvin himself could write in regards to 2 Peter 1:4, 'We should notice that it is the purpose of the Gospel to make us sooner or later like God; indeed it is, so to speak, a kind of deification.'[49] Acceptance of both the substance and terminology of theosis has spread well beyond the borders of the Orthodox tradition.

There is, then, much common ground in the discussion. But it is reasonable to ask whether the precise term 'deification' is of the most preferable,

---

46. *EH* 1.3; Russell, *Deification*, p. 1.

47. See e.g. the minimal use of the term by Gregory of Nyssa (Russell, *Deification*, p. 226), and its virtual disappearance in the fifth century (Russell, *Deification*, p. 235).

48. See the examples adduced by Myk Habets in 'Reforming Theosis', in *Theosis: Deification in Christian Theology* (2 vols; ed. Stephen Finlan and Vladimir Kharlamov; Eugene, OR: Pickwick, 2006), 1:146–67; for modern Baptist examples, see Mark S. Medley, 'Participation in God', in *Theosis* (ed. Finlan and Kharlamov), 2:205–46.

49. John Calvin, *New Testament Commentary* 12:330, quoted in Habets, 'Reforming Theosis', p. 148.

at least in the Western context. We have seen that in the patristic era, there was a compelling need to situate Christian belief in the Hellenistic religious marketplace. It made sense to press verses like John 10:35 into service as rhetorical foils to pagan notions of the human and the divine: it is a way of saying, 'Here is what it really means to be "divine".' But once the term deification came into use, theologians had to spend much of their time explaining what they *didn't* mean by the term. Since the context of the discussion has changed, why create problems for oneself unnecessarily? The repeated biblical affirmations of our union with Christ, or our need to imitate God's character, would seem sufficient to address the core issues without employing the potentially misleading terminology of 'deification'.

9

The Beautiful World

> God is revealed to man not only as the Wisdom of the world, but also as its Beauty. This means, first of all, that Beauty experienced by man is not only a subjective human feeling, which can, perhaps, claim to exist only as a fashion of the moment. Beauty is an objective principle in the world, revealing to us the Divine Glory.[1]

If Bulgakov is correct that beauty reveals the Divine Glory, then meditating on beauty is a fitting way to conclude our musings on the theology of creation and new creation. The cosmos, we might say, exists to be beautiful. But beauty presents considerable challenges to the theologian. Extolling and analysing God's wisdom comes naturally enough to the philosophic mind: the mechanics of the world can be broken down; its inner ideas can be probed. Beauty resides at the core of things and resists analysis. It is not one thing among others, but the effect of the harmoniously arranged whole. As Balthasar says:

> The word with which we embark . . . is a word with which the philosophical person does not begin, but rather concludes. It is a word that has never possessed a permanent place or an authentic voice in the concert of the exact sciences, and, when it is chosen as a subject for discussion, appears to betray in him who chooses it an idle amateur among such very busy experts.[2]

We can make a start by tracing out the role of beauty in the theological tradition. As Barth has pointed out, 'beauty' as such keeps a fairly low profile in the Bible.[3] There is nothing like a manual of aesthetics in Scripture, nor is beauty explicitly extolled as it is in some later Christian devotion. But it is not altogether devoid of the notion of beauty. The Song of Songs speaks

---

1. Sergei Bulgakov, 'Religion and Art', in *The Church of God: An Anglo-Russian Symposium*, Fellowship of St Alban and St Sergius (ed. E. Mascall; London: SPCK, 1934), p. 176.

2. Cf. Hans Urs von Balthasar, *The Glory of the Lord: A Theological Aesthetics* (7 vols; San Francisco: Ignatius Press, 2009), 1:17.

3. Karl Barth, *Church Dogmatics* (4 vols; Edinburgh: T&T Clark, 1956–75), II/1, pp. 652–53.

at length about the charms of Solomon's beloved, and the text had a rich history as an allegory of Christ and the church; but such a reading is not self-evident. More pertinent are those passages devoted to the construction of the tabernacle and temple, where adornment, proportion, and craftsmanship are central concerns.[4] This mirrors God's own craftsmanship in creation, the glories of which are celebrated in places like Psalm 8 and Psalm 104. The refrain from Genesis 1, 'And God saw that it was good', is surely suggestive of a beautiful order that goes well beyond mere utility. Bulgakov interprets the words to mean, 'He sees it in all its beauty, clothed in glory.'[5]

This association of beauty and *glory* provides a wealth of opportunities for theological reflection. Barth felt compelled to include beauty as an aspect of God's glory, because without beauty we might imagine God's glory was merely a manifestation of power. And so in distinction from much Protestant tradition he concludes:

> The concept which lies ready to our hand here, and which may serve legitimately to describe the element in the idea of glory that we still lack, is that of beauty. If we can and must say that God is beautiful, to say this is to say how He enlightens and convinces and persuades us. It is to describe not merely the naked fact of His revelation or its power, but the shape and form in which it is a fact and is power. It is to say that God has this superior force, this power of attraction, which speaks for itself, which wins and conquers, in the fact that He is beautiful, divinely beautiful, beautiful in His own way, in a way that is His alone, beautiful in the unattainable primal beauty, yet really beautiful.[6]

Barth grounds his assertion both by reference to the tradition—he goes on to cite Augustine and Pseudo-Dionysius as precursors (though he distances himself somewhat from the latter)—and by an examination of the use of 'glory' in Scripture. The joyous response of the saints to God's glory in the Psalter gives particularly vivid testimony to the inherent beauty of God that inspires such praise.[7] While Balthasar may be correct that Barth's emphasis on God's beauty is rare in Protestantism, Barth does have an ally in Edwards: 'for in this glory, which is so vastly and inexpressibly distinguished from the glory of artificial things, and all other glory, does mainly consist the true notion of divinity: God is God, and distinguished from all other beings, and exalted above 'em, chiefly by his divine beauty, which is infinitely diverse from all other beauty.'[8]

4. See e.g. Exod. 36–39.

5. Bulgakov, 'Religion and Art', p. 175.

6. Barth, *CD* II/1, p. 650.

7. Barth, *CD* II/1, pp. 653–56.

8. Jonathan Edwards, 'Religious Affections' 2.5, *The Works of Jonathan Edwards* (26 vols; New Haven: Yale University Press, 1997–2009), 2:298; cf. Kin Yip Louie, *The*

With this association in mind, we are able to look afresh at God's relationship to the creation in Scripture through the lens of beauty. We have seen that the primal 'goodness' of creation in Genesis may equally be seen as its beauty; its natural end, then, would likewise be beauty. The prophetic watchword is: 'For the earth will be filled with the knowledge of the glory of the LORD, as the waters cover the sea' (Hab. 2:14; cf. Isa. 11:9). What is this but a cosmic 'beautification project'? The vision of the New Jerusalem in Revelation 22 harkens back to the divine light of Genesis 1—the light that for many theologians represented the quintessence of God's beauty—and that light illumines a renewed Eden:

> Then he [the angel] showed me the river of the water of life, bright as crystal, flowing from the throne of God and of the Lamb through the middle of the street of the city; also, on either side of the river, the tree of life with its twelve kinds of fruit, yielding its fruit each month; and the leaves of the tree were for the healing of the nations. There shall no more be anything accursed, but the throne of God and of the Lamb shall be in it, and his servants shall worship him; they shall see his face, and his name shall be on their foreheads. And night shall be no more; they need no light of lamp or sun, for the Lord God will be their light, and they shall reign for ever and ever (vv. 1–5).

The encounter with Greek philosophy did not snuff out this appreciation for the beauty of the world. Basil fits squarely in the line of thinkers indebted to Plato, but his *Hexaemeron* is shot through with an appreciation of the glory of creation.[9] He speaks of the 'inexpressible beauty of the stars', which God has strewn about the heavens like flowers (6.1), and describes the creation of various creatures as an 'adornment' of the world, using the verb *diakosmhthnai* and the noun *kosmos* (7.1). The latter point rests on the dual sense of *kosmos* in Greek as 'beautification' and 'universe', and indicates that for Basil this was no mere lexicographical coincidence. Beauty is what makes the world a genuine *kosmos*. While it may pale relative to the ineffable glory of God himself, it is equally true that the beauty of the world becomes a kind of stepping stone to the divine glory:

Beauty of the Triune God: The Theological Aesthetics of Jonathan Edwards (Eugene, OR: Pickwick, 2013), p. 94.

9. See e.g. his comments on the ocean in Basil, *Hex.* 4.6: 'Scripture does not merely wish to say that a pleasing aspect of the sea presented itself to God. It is not with eyes that the Creator views the beauty of His works. He contemplates them in His ineffable wisdom. A fair sight is the sea all bright in a settled calm; fair too, when, ruffled by a light breeze of wind, its surface shows tints of purple and azure—when, instead of lashing with violence the neighbouring shores, it seems to kiss them with peaceful caresses. However, it is not in this that Scripture makes God find the goodness and charm of the sea. Here it is the purpose of the work which makes the goodness.'

> If such is the beauty of visible things, what shall we think of invisible things? If the grandeur of heaven exceeds the measure of human intelligence, what mind shall be able to trace the nature of the everlasting? If the sun, subject to corruption, is so beautiful, so grand, so rapid in its movement, so invariable in its course; if its grandeur is in such perfect harmony with and due proportion to the universe: if, by the beauty of its nature, it shines like a brilliant eye in the middle of creation; if finally, one cannot tire of contemplating it, what will be the beauty of the Sun of Righteousness? If the blind man suffers from not seeing the material sun, what a deprivation is it for the sinner not to enjoy the true light! (6.1).

Basil's reaction of awe at the world's beauty is matched at virtually every strand of the tradition. We may cite again Tertullian in his *Against Hermogenes* (29): 'God, indeed, consummated all His works in a due order; at first He paled them out, as it were, in their unformed elements, and then He arranged them in their finished beauty.' Writing of the Wisdom of God in Proverbs 8 he notes (*Herm.* 18):

> Now, who would not rather approve of this as the fountain and origin of all things—of this as, in very deed, the Matter of all Matter, not liable to any end, not diverse in condition, not restless in motion, not ungraceful in form, but natural, and proper, and duly proportioned, and beautiful, such truly as even God might well have required, who requires His own and not another's?

Poems about nature abounded in the Middle Ages,[10] while St Francis of Assisi's 'Canticle of the Sun' (adapted into English hymnody as 'All Creatures of Our God and King') is one of the best-known paeans to creation:

> Be praised, my Lord, through all your creatures, especially through my lord Brother Sun, who brings the day; and you give light through him. And he is beautiful and radiant in all his splendor! Of you, Most High, he bears the likeness.
>
> Be praised, my Lord, through Sister Moon and the stars; in the heavens you have made them, precious and beautiful.
>
> Be praised, my Lord, through Brothers Wind and Air, and clouds and storms, and all the weather, through which you give your creatures sustenance.[11]

10. See Sarah Foot, 'Plenty, Portents, and Plagues', in *God's Bounty? The Churches and the Natural World* (ed. Peter Clarke and Tony Claydon; Woodbridge: Boydell, 2010), pp. 18–21. Foot argues that some of the 'hermit' poems were more probably written by educated urbanites than actual hermits, but this does not diminish the affection for nature they evidence.

11. Cf. Bonaventure's praise of Nature's 'most beautiful song', pulcherrimum carmen, *Breviloquium* Prolog. 2: t.V, 204b, in Leo Scheffczyk, *Creation and Providence* (trans. Richard Strachan; New York: Herder & Herder, 1970), pp. 141–42.

What Is Beauty?

While we have associated beauty in some way with glory, we are still in need of a more precise definition of the term. We have some concern here with general aesthetics—what elements or combination of elements warrant the designation 'beauty'?—but we are seeking even more to articulate a theology of beauty—what does God have to do with a thing being beautiful? As in so many other areas, theologians leaned heavily on classical antecedents for their aesthetics. Basil can take it as a given that 'beauty in bodies results from symmetry of parts, and the harmonious appearance of colours' (*Hex.* 2.7). Such harmony is writ large in the cosmos as a whole: 'Moses almost shows us the finger of the supreme artisan taking possession of the substance of the universe, forming the different parts in one perfect accord, and making a harmonious symphony result from the whole' (1.7). Augustine approaches beauty in the same way: 'In all the arts it is symmetry that gives pleasure, preserving unity and making the whole beautiful. Symmetry demands unity and equality, the similarity of like parts, or the graded arrangement of parts which are dissimilar.'[12] Number plays a particularly important role in his aesthetic.[13] Aquinas adds the critical element of *splendour*: 'For beauty includes three conditions, "integrity" or "perfection", since those things which are impaired are by the very fact ugly; due "proportion" or "harmony"; and lastly, "brightness" or "clarity" [NB: 'brightness' and 'clarity' render the single Latin word *claritas*], whence things are called beautiful which have a bright color.'[14]

---

12. Augustine, *Ver. Rel.* 55, in *Augustine's Early Writings* (trans. John H. S. Burleigh; Philadelphia: Westminster, 1953), p. 252; see Étienne Gilson, *The Christian Philosophy of Saint Augustine* (trans. L. E. M. Lynch; New York: Random House, 1960), p. 213. On Augustine and beauty, see esp. Carol Harrison, *Beauty and Revelation in the Thought of Saint Augustine* (Oxford: OUP, 1992).

13. See C. Harrison, 'Measure, Number, and Weight in Saint Augustine's Aesthetics', *Augustinianum* 28 (1988): pp. 591–602. In this, as in so many other things, he shows his debt to Plato, cf. *Timaeus*; Plato in turn seems to have been influenced by the Pythagoreans. Compare the comments of Erich Przywara, who speaks of art oscillating between the poles of a 'bare mathematics' such as we see in Cubism and abstract art, and a 'veiled mathematics, which—as a secret "measure, number, and weight"—is the ultimate mystery of the "stylization of the real" in any given work of art . . . That is to say, what constitutes the "stylized reality" in the work of art is its essentiality, which (being opposed to what is too much or too little) consists in an oscillating proportion and clarity, understood as the splendor of this internal proportion—in other words, as the quality of Pythagoreanism's "musical number"'. Erich Przywara, 'Beautiful, Sacred, Christian', in *Analogia Entis: Metaphysics—Original Structure and Universal Rhythm* (trans. John R. Betz and David Bentley Hart; Grand Rapids: Eerdmans, 2014), p. 540.

14. Aquinas, *ST* 1.39.8.

This provides a serviceable definition for what the word 'beauty' is pointing towards. But it does not get to the essence of *how* something in the creation becomes beautiful. The logical starting point to answer that question would seem to lie in the beauty of God which is somehow given to, or shared with, or participated in, or reflected by, creatures. Theologians who pay attention to aesthetics generally agree that God's beauty is foundational for the beauty of creation.

Since Christ is described as the 'image of the invisible God' (Col. 1:15) and the 'effulgence of His glory', it is not surprising that beauty of the Son takes on particular importance in the theological tradition. Augustine repeatedly refers to Christ as the *forma* or beauty of God.[15] This proves an extremely useful trope in his hands. On the one hand, the fact that *forma* corresponded directly to Plato's *Idea* helped him express his Platonically tinged doctrine of Christ as the *logos*. Thus he can write that 'by participation in the Son whatever things are alike are alike either to one another or to God, for the Son is the first species by which, so to speak, all things are specified, and the form by which all things are formed.'[16] At the same time, the aesthetic connotations of *forma* allowed him to integrate a theology of beauty into this idealistic schema. Christ is not merely the abstract blueprint of the cosmos; he is the perfect expression of God's beauty, who therefore can beautify all things. Augustine deploys this to especially good effect in his teaching on salvation, spinning out the whole of salvation history from *forma*. He puts it in concise form in his commentary on the Psalms: 'First let your deformity displease you and then you will deserve beauty from Him . . . For He who formed you will reform you.'[17]

Aquinas follows in Augustine's train, with his customary philosophical precision. How is it that Christ is the beauty of God? Given the threefold definition of beauty seen above, Aquinas details how Christ embodies each one of the characteristics: he displays integrity or perfection 'inasmuch as He as Son has in Himself truly and perfectly the nature of the Father'; he

15. Michael Hanby, *Augustine and Modernity* (London: Routledge, 2003), pp. 27ff.; cf. C. Harrison, *Beauty*, pp. 192–238.

16. Augustine, *Div. quaest. LXXXIII* 23, in Augustine, *Eighty-Three Different Questions* (trans. David Mosher; Washington, DC: Catholic University of America Press, 2010), p. 50.

17. Augustine, *Expositions of the Psalms* 103.1.4, in C. Harrison, *Beauty*, p. 232. As we will see below, Augustine was even able to integrate the deformity of Christ's crucifixion in his theological aesthetics. Paul hints at something like this in Philippians, where Christ is seen to have the 'form'—*morphē*—of God (and then to take up the *morphē* of a servant; Phil. 2:6–7), and believers are said to be 'conformed (*summorphizomenos*) to Christ's death' (3:10) and equally 'transformed' (3:21; the verb is *metaschēmatisei*, but cf. *schēma* in 2:8) and 'conformed (*summorphon*) to the body of his glory' (3:21) (my translations).

displays proportion or harmony 'inasmuch as He is the express Image of the Father. Hence we see that an image is said to be beautiful, if it perfectly represents even an ugly thing'; and he displays *claritas* 'as the Word, which is the light and splendor of the intellect'.[18]

The Christology of Augustine and Aquinas surveyed above hints at the relationship between the foundational beauty of God and the beauty visible in the creation, and the way in which Plato offered one route to a more theologically refined exploration of the source and meaning of beauty. Basil has already suggested that the beauty of the sun lies in its reflection of the divine ideal of light. Gregory Nazienzen echoes him. He compares the human lights of the Paschal procession to greater lights above:

> This is a symbol of the great light, both the heavenly light that makes fire signal from above, shining on the whole world in its own beauty, and equally the light above heavens, in the angels—the first nature illumined after the First and springing from it—and equally in the Trinity, by which every light has been produced, divided off from the undivided light and honored.[19]

Augustine develops this idea further. He acknowledges that created things, though they are subject to changeableness, are 'beautiful in their own way'. But the splendour of this world always slips through our fingers: 'Time in all the beauty of its changefulness holds on its appointed course, and the thing desired escapes him who loved it. It torments him by passing beyond his power to sense it, and disturbs his mind with errors.'[20] It will do no good to simply imagine more of the same corporeal reality, since it is constitutionally subject to passing away and thus can never satisfy the soul. True beauty resides in the ideal world with the unchanging God. Christ, as we have seen, is the mediator of this beauty to the world, both in the beauty of primal formation flowing from Christ as the Word, and the beauty of reformation consequent upon his incarnation.

Bulgakov's understanding of beauty follows along similar lines. It is connected to his rather complex understanding of divine wisdom or Sophia, but

---

18. Aquinas, *ST* 1.39.8.

19. Gregory Nazianzen, *Or. Bas.* 45.2.

20. *Ver. Rel.* 40; compare his response to his grief at the death of a friend in *Conf.* 4.10: '"Turn us again, O Lord God of Hosts, cause thy face to shine; and we shall be saved." For wherever the soul of man turns itself, unless toward thee, it is enmeshed in sorrows, even though it is surrounded by beautiful things outside thee and outside itself. For lovely things would simply not be unless they were from thee. They come to be and they pass away, and by coming they begin to be, and they grow toward perfection. Then, when perfect, they begin to wax old and perish, and, if all do not wax old, still all perish. Therefore, when they rise and grow toward being, the more rapidly they grow to maturity, so also the more rapidly they hasten back toward nonbeing. This is the way of things.'

even those who hesitate to embrace his entire philosophy may be helped by his observations.[21] His system is very much in the stream of Orthodox idealistic understandings of the world, though put forward with a unique vocabulary. For Bulgakov, the triune God is never without his idea for the world, which is an expression of his glorious being; this reality he terms the divine wisdom: 'God's revelation of Himself in the Holy Trinity, God's Wisdom . . . is the primordial reality in which the Divine *all*, contained in the word (*Logos*) is realized in Beauty, and is clothed in Glory.'[22] This 'divine Sophia' is matched by 'the creaturely Sophia', which is the actualized framework for the visible creation.[23] While Bulgakov may balk at the comparison, the creaturely Sophia bears some resemblance to Plato's 'world soul' and Cudworth's eternal plastic nature. Bulgakov's language will sound strange to many a Western ear, and his views have elicited controversy within Orthodoxy as well; one may well question whether his positing of the two Sophias is the most judicious. But we may charitably regard him as attempting to articulate afresh the close connection between God, his wisdom, and the world which suffuses Proverbs 8 and much mainstream Christian thought on creation.

For thinkers like Basil, Augustine, and Bulgakov, we are not meant to merely look *at* nature, as if it carried its meaning in itself apart from God; but neither are we meant to look *past* nature, as if it were an illusion. Rather we are to look *through* it, as a window into the world of God's eternal life where true and enduring beauty resides. While there are certainly other ways one might construe the purpose of beauty in the world, their views are still a far cry from the stereotypical Platonic denigration of the world which too often substitutes for considered analysis of their theology.

We see much the same thing in Jonathan Edwards, whose sustained reflections on beauty are rare in Protestant theology. As we have seen previously, Edwards believed in the closest possible ties between the visible and invisible worlds, and he did not hesitate to use the language of *analogy* to describe the connection:

> If there be such an admirable analogy observed by the Creator in his works throughout the whole system of the natural world, so that one thing seems to be made in imitation of another, and especially the less perfect to be made in imitation of the more perfect, so that the less perfect is as it were a figure or image of the more perfect—so beasts are made in imitation of men, plants are [a] kind of types of animals, minerals are in many things in imitation of plants why is it not rational to suppose that the corporeal and visible world should be

21. For an extended discussion, see Sergei Bulgakov, *The Lamb of God*; a synopsis may be found in 'Religion and Art', p. 175.

22. Bulgakov, 'Religion and Art', p. 175.

23. Sergei Bulgakov, *Lamb of God*, chs 1 and 2.

> designedly made and constituted in analogy to the more spiritual, noble and real world? 'Tis certainly agreeable to what is apparently the method of God's working ('Images' 59, pp. 69–70).

It is particularly, to borrow a phrase associated with Balthasar, the analogy of beauty:

> He who by his immediate influence gives being every moment and by his Spirit actuates the world, because he inclines to communicate himself and his excellencies, doth doubtless communicate his excellency to bodies, as far as there is any consent or analogy. And though beauty of face and sweet airs in man are not always the effect of the corresponding excellencies of mind, yet the beauties of nature are really emanations, or shadows, of the excellencies of the Son of God.
>
> So that when we are delighted with flowery meadows and gentle breezes of wind, we may consider that we only see the emanations of the sweet benevolence of Jesus Christ; when we behold the fragrant rose and lily, we see his love and purity (*Miscellany* 108, 13:279).[24]

Barth is wary here. Much of the explanation for his caution lies in the meandering path of German theology, which to him had wandered dangerously close to collapsing God into a creationally determined 'beauty'. For many Romantics, the encounter with beautiful objects was ipso facto an encounter with God. To paraphrase Keats: Beauty is God, and God Beauty, that is all ye know on earth and all ye need to know. This is intolerable for Barth. To equate God and beauty in this way is effectively to deny that God is Creator. If our judgements about what is beautiful become determinative for the being of God

> [d]o we not bring God in a sinister because in a sense intimate way into the sphere of man's oversight and control, into proximity to the goal of all human striving? Do we not bring the contemplation of God into suspicious proximity to that contemplation of the world which in the last resort is the self-contemplation of an urge for life which does not recognize its limits?[25]

---

24. See discussion in Louie, *Beauty*, p. 81. Cf. Edwards, 'Images' 212, *Works* 11:129–30: 'The immense magnificence of the visible world, its inconceivable vastness, the incomprehensible height of the heavens, etc. is but a type of the infinite magnificence, height and glory of God's work in the spiritual world: the most incomprehensible expression of his power, wisdom, holiness and love, in what is wrought and brought to pass in that world; and in the exceeding greatness of the moral and natural good, the light, knowledge, holiness and happiness which shall be communicated to it. And therefore to that magnificence of the world, height of heaven, those things are often compared in such expressions. "Thy mercy is great above the heavens, thy truth reacheth [unto the clouds]"; "Thou hast set thy glory above the heavens," etc.' In 'Images' 58, *Works*, 11:69, Edwards speaks of the 'various beauties of the Spirit of God' signified by the various colours of the light of the sun.

25. Barth, *CD* II/1, p. 651.

But this does not mean that for Barth created beauty is set adrift on its own aimless way, with only a happenstansical verbal connection to divine beauty. Once we recognize that God is the Creator, and especially that he has joined himself to the creation in the Son, we may justly reflect God's glory back to him: 'Therefore we can now say (supplementarily) that God's glory is not only pleased to accept at a distance its glorification through the creatures, but that it makes this glorification its own in all its creatureliness. There is, then, a genuine creaturely *glorificatio*.'[26] While Barth does not speak explicitly in this part of *CD* II/1 about God beautifying the creature (and indeed the discussion seems to focus on humanity rather than created things in general) there is a warrant for this in his prior association of glory and beauty.

Balthasar appreciates Barth's concerns about conflating divine and creaturely beauty, but he is more optimistic about tracing the points of connection between them—so much so that his major project is precisely a 'theological aesthetics'. There are undoubtedly risks in the venture, but 'may it not be that we have a real and inescapable obligation to probe the possibility of there being a genuine relationship between theological beauty and the beauty of the world and—in spite of all the dangers inherent in such an undertaking—to probe the feasibility of a genuine encounter between divine revelation and antiquity?'[27] Balthasar roots his project in the centrality of *form*, specifically 'the form of divine revelation in salvation history, leading to Christ and deriving from him.'[28] For Balthasar, Christ's beauty as the form of God does not simply refer to the luminosity visible in a vision like that of Ezekiel 1. Christ's form embraces his whole life experience in the incarnation.[29]

The Cross and Beauty

But if the beautiful God creates a beautiful world, what of ugliness? This is analogous to questions surrounding the divine design of the cosmos, though it presses the question of what 'design' is by enquiring not only into functionality but aesthetics. For this reason, Augustine's move to see things as beautiful *in the grand scheme of things* is only partially successful. It is

26. Barth, *CD* II/1, pp. 668–69.

27. Von Balthasar, *Glory*, 1:80.

28. Von Balthasar, *Glory*, 1:29. See von Balthasar, *Glory*, 1:463ff.; and Brendan Leahy, 'Theological Aesthetics', in *The Beauty of Christ* (ed. Bede McGregor and Thomas Norris; Edinburgh: T&T Clark, 1994), pp. 29–30.

29. Cf. von Balthasar, *Glory*, 1:465: 'the facilitating manner in which Christ's Gospel—that is, Christ's form—can and should be presented and proclaimed by the Church to each age'.

true that an untimely death or a natural disaster might be deemed useful *sub specie aeternitatis* as part of the grand pattern of cosmic history. But it is more difficult to label it as 'beautiful'.

A more promising apologetic lies in the way of the cross, and God's ability to transcend conventional paradigms of the beautiful. Here we see the wisdom in the cautions of Barth and Balthasar on a merely aesthetic theology. A theology based solely on measures of proportion and propriety must stand silent before the cross, and therefore silent altogether, since this manifestly ugly act stands at the heart of Christian discourse. Yet John can see in the crucifixion of Christ the moment of his supreme glorification, and thus his supreme beautification: 'I, when I am lifted up from the earth, will draw all men to myself' (John 12:32). Divine beauty thus paradoxically reveals itself within a situation of death and injustice. Human standards of beauty are relativized. The Suffering Servant has no *form* that would attract us to him, and ends his career in humiliation; yet as John makes clear, this Servant is in fact the Lord of Glory.[30] Augustine recognized this, and tied it into his discourse on the form of Christ: '"He had no form or comeliness that we should look at Him." The deformity of Christ forms you. For if He had not wished to be deformed you would not have received back the form that you lost. Therefore, he hung deformed upon the cross, but His deformity was our beauty.'[31]

As Barth notes, Jesus presents himself to us precisely in the form of humiliation:

> It is not self-evident that even—and precisely—under this aspect He has form and comeliness, that the beauty of God shines especially under this aspect, that the crucified is revealed and known as the risen Christ. We cannot know this of ourselves. It can only be given us. If the beauty of Christ is sought in a glorious Christ who is not crucified, the search will always be in vain. But who does not do this? And who finds it at this point? Who of himself does not find the opposite here? Who sees and believes that the One who has been abased is the One who is exalted, that this very man is very God? The glory and beauty of God shines out in this unity and differentiation. In this it persuades, convinces, and conquers.[32]

30. John achieves this through a subtle interweaving of texts from Isa. 6 and Isa. 53 in chapter 12 of his gospel. See Richard Bauckham, *Jesus and the God of Israel: God Crucified and Other Studies on the New Testament's Christology of Divine Identity* (Grand Rapids: Eerdmans, 2009), pp. 46–50.

31. Augustine, *Serm.* 27.6, in C. Harrison, *Beauty*, p. 234. In *Expositions of the Psalms* 127.8 Augustine makes it clear that Christ's beauty is particularly evident in the ugliness of the crucifixion, *for those with eyes to see*: 'Only because he looked ugly to them [his persecutors] could they do these things, for they lacked the eyes to see Christ's beauty.'

32. Barth, *CD* II/1, p. 665.

It is not the case that injustice and death have themselves become intrinsically beautified; but they have become the vessel for God's beauty to shine forth in the suffering of Christ. Even the sin that led to the crucifixion thus becomes the occasion for this display of divine purpose; in a strange manner they feed and enhance the beauty of the cross. It is surely not a coincidence that so much Christian art has focused on the crucifixion. These works are not mere eucharistic adornment; they are visible expressions of the theological truth expressed above by John, Augustine, and Barth.

Reflecting Beauty

Of course theological exposition is hardly the only way that the church has expressed the beauty of creation. As we saw in the previous chapter, the creative reflection of beauty, and the affirmation of life in God's good world, has been with the people of God from its formation. The anti-iconic stance of Torah should not obscure the fact that the tabernacle and temple were thoroughly creative endeavours. The detailed accounts of measurements and construction techniques for these worship centres may not make for the most scintillating reading, but part of the intent of the texts is to stress the order and proportionality of the structures. Bezalel was famously gifted with the very Spirit of God to adorn the tabernacle: 'See, I have called by name Bez'alel the son of Uri, son of Hur, of the tribe of Judah: and I have filled him with the Spirit of God, with ability and intelligence, with knowledge and all craftsmanship, to devise artistic designs, to work in gold, silver, and bronze, and cutting stones for setting, and in carving wood, for work in every craft' (Exod. 31:1–5). Most importantly, as we have already seen, it is likely that the temple was meant to serve as a mirror of the cosmos.

The worship itself was likewise meant to be beautiful. This is most evident in careful provisions for the music of the temple (e.g. 2 Chr. 29:25–26), and the enduring appeal of the Psalter. While the isolation of hymns in the New Testament may be more difficult than the scholarly tradition suggests, there is certainly a poetic grace to passages like Philippians 2:6–11 or Colossians 1:15–20, and it is evident that music played a central role in early Christian worship (cf. Eph. 5:19). Space will not permit us to expound on the subsequent glories of liturgical text and music, so we will let one fascinating piece from the Middle Ages speak for the whole:

> We beseech thee Omnipotent God,
> that you might bless these first fruit of the trees,
> so that we who were punished in the first father with the just sentence of death for [eating] the deadly fruit of the forbidden tree,

> may eat, in a salutary manner, the plants which the earth will produce as a result of this annual day of solemnity,
> since through the revealing of your only Son, our Redeemer and Lord Jesus Christ and by the blessing of the Holy Spirit,
> all has been blessed and sanctified, and the treachery of the ancient Enemy, plot[ter] of the original sin, has been driven out and cast away.[33]

The liturgy is telling on any number of points. The idea that the church swapped its creation-affirming biblical inheritance for a mess of Greek philosophical potage is belied by the practical use to which this liturgy was presumably put: blessing the earth and the fruit of the tenants' everyday labours. But it also avails itself of the opportunity for theological instruction afforded by fruit trees. In the hands of the liturgist, the fruit before them evokes not only the lamentable past of primal humanity, and the present provision of God for food, but also the atoning provision for humanity in Christ which opens up the prospect of eternal life. The 'secular' fruit is sacramentalized in a way that goes beyond mere symbology: somewhat like the miracles of Christ's public ministry, the now-blessed food itself becomes a foretaste of unending bliss.

Far better-known artefacts give testimony to the vibrancy of the visual arts in the life of the church as it celebrates God's good world. We have touched upon the great medieval cathedrals as emblems of a creative fusion between Christian faith and Aristotelian philosophy; but we would not want to miss the sheer beauty of these and other monuments. Hagia Sophia in Istanbul is an architectural marvel that dwarfs the visitor in an immense enclosed space capped by domes meant to echo the heavenly firmament. The massive York Minster has a similar, if squarer, effect; the theme of creation and new creation is captured in the Great East Window, which features stunning panels from the books of Genesis and Revelation. Time would fail us were we to detail the magnificent sculptures and paintings that have adorned these spaces, or the sacred music that has filled them. Whether one counts this all as 'theology' naturally depends on how one defines the term. But Barth was happy to give Mozart a place in theology, for all his faults, and defends his decision thus:

> He had heard, and causes those who have ears to hear, even today, what we shall not see until the end of time—the whole context of providence. As though

33. *Benedictio Pomorum* (*Liber Vitae* of New Minster, Winchester, Portiforium of St Wulfstan), trans. Gwenfair Walters; Latin text may be found in Tamsin Rowe, '"Bless, O Lord, This Fruit of the New Trees": Liturgy and Nature in England in the Central Middle Ages', in *God's Bounty: The Churches and the Natural World* (ed. Peter Clarke and Tony Claydon; Woodbridge: Ecclesiastical History Society, 2010), p. 64.

> in the light of this end, he heard the harmony of creation to which the shadow also belongs but in which the shadow is not darkness, deficiency is not defeat, sadness cannot become despair, trouble cannot degenerate into tragedy and infinite melancholy is not ultimately forced to claim undisputed sway. Thus the cheerfulness in this harmony is not without its limits. But the light shines all the more brightly because it breaks forth from the shadow.[34]

Protestantism, of course, introduces something of a lacuna in the church's expression of beauty—when it comes to ornament, one might more readily speak of a 'Protestant ascetic' than a Protestant aesthetic. It is no wonder that a tradition birthed in strident opposition to the medieval church should want to slough off the material reminders of its ecclesial forebears. The doctrine of *sola scriptura* encouraged the anti-iconic stance, particularly when viewed through the lens of a New Testament which seemed to dismiss the visible signs of the Old Testament as mere shadows surpassed by the reality of Christ and his kingdom. But this does not mean that beauty was shunted aside altogether. Music continued to flourish. Hymnody maintained a central place in worship, enriched by authors like Isaac Watts and Charles Wesley. Even church architecture developed a lean aesthetic culminating in the meeting-houses of colonial New England.

Interestingly, one of the clearest apologetics for this minimalist 'Protestant' tendency comes from the Catholic theologian Erich Przywara. He argues that 'Christian sacrality' presents fundamental problems, epitomized by Jesus' displacement of the temple as the centre of holiness. As Jesus makes clear to the Samaritan woman, worship is no longer focused at a particular geographical location, but is rather done 'in the Spirit'.[35] He concludes:

> Seen from this radical Christian perspective, all Christian sacred art produced within time, however 'divine' it may be, is—from its root, through its development, and to its end—fundamentally destined for dissolution: in the sign of Christ who, as the original Christian temple, is 'destroyed' in order to be 'raised'—not into a 'divine temple,' but into the 'God who is Spirit,' as the only temple of the definitive nuptial reality between 'God is Spirit' and 'humanity as bride'.[36]

This does not eliminate Christian art altogether, but it does mean that such art must bear within itself the humility and the agony of the crucifixion. In Przywara's view, the traditional modes of Christian sacred art have 'exhausted themselves'. Perhaps the only way to recapture art for the gospel is

34. Barth, *CD* III/3, p. 298.
35. Przywara, 'Beautiful, Sacred, Christian', p. 553.
36. Przywara, 'Beautiful, Sacred, Christian', p. 554.

to return (and here Przywara seems to echo the Reformation in its most radical Anabaptist strains) to the 'apostolic style of profane homes and tables', the 'truly simple village church' or 'a style in which towering sacred edifices are reduced to the "without form or comeliness" of ordinary, communally shared private rooms'. Such simplicity exhibits the 'authentic "style of the kingdom of God'" which does not come with signs so as to be seen (Luke 17:20).[37]

Saving Beauty

The Prince in Dostoevsky's novel *The Idiot* famously declared, 'Beauty will save the world.' The meaning of the phrase is somewhat obscure: the Prince has a deep aesthetic sensibility, particularly with respect to the ravishing Nastassya Filippovna, but it is equally likely that he is referring to the saving beauty of Christ. But while we may debate whether beauty in any sense saves the world, we may say with confidence that the world is saved for beauty. God declared his world good in the beginning, and whatever emerges in the way of redemption is designed to reclaim and enhance that goodness, that the creation might stand as an enduring theatre for his eternal glory.

37. Przywara, 'Beautiful, Sacred, Christian', p. 555.

10

Conclusion

> But there are also many other things which Jesus did; were every one of them to be written, I suppose that the world itself could not contain the books that would be written (John 21:25).

The final verse of John's gospel is a rather curious conclusion to the book—it seems almost a sigh of resignation that the evangelist's job is not really completed.[1] The key to understanding the verse (and the key to understanding the present volume) is to see that John is subtly summing up all that has gone before in his gospel. 'In the beginning was the Word', and in the end John confesses that all the words in the world will fail to fully capture the deeds the Messiah has wrought in creation and new creation.

The Word made all things in the beginning. God faced nothing but his own Image as he set about the task of creation: 'all things were made through him, and without him was not anything made that was made' (John 1:3). Whatever things exist in the world exist because the Father has called them into being through the Son and Spirit.

This alone might seem to warrant the sweeping nature of John's conclusion . . . but something is still missing. John does not say, 'there are also many other things which the Word did . . .' He says, 'there are also many other things which *Jesus* did . . .' As astounding as the work of creation in the beginning had been, God had something more remarkable in store with the venture of the Son into the world he had made. The Word became flesh; the Light shone in the darkness; the Eternal One entered time; the Creator joined in solidarity with the creation. There he set about beginning the work of restoring the fallen world. The echoes of the creation narrative sound clear in John's prologue and in places like John 9, where Jesus declares that he is 'the light of the world'. They are muted, but still faintly audible, in the gospel's *seven* signs and its interest in numbering

1. There are those who dispute whether this is the 'original' ending of the gospel, but see the strong arguments defending its authenticity in Richard Bauckham, 'The 153 Fish and the Unity of John's Gospel', in *The Testimony of the Beloved Disciple* (Grand Rapids: Eerdmans, 207), pp. 271–84.

days.[2] We have noted already the recreative nature of the signs themselves, culminating in the raising of Lazarus from the dead.

But this recreation week reaches its paradoxical climax in the decreative work of the cross: Jesus declares, 'It is finished', on the eve of the Sabbath (19:30–31). It is his suffering that completes his work in the world; it is his humiliation that most clearly reveals his divine glory. Here in the nadir of the cross, his solidarity with the broken world reaches its greatest depth. As Barth says:

> But the self-humiliation of God in His Son is genuine and actual, and therefore there is no reservation with respect to His solidarity with us. He did become—and this is the presupposition of all that follows—the brother of man, threatened with man, harassed and assaulted with him, with him in the stream that hurries downwards to the abyss, hastening with him to death, to the cessation of being and nothingness. With him He cries—knowing far better than any other how much reason there is to cry: 'My God, my God why hast thou forsaken me?' . . . *Deus pro nobis* means simply that God has not abandoned man in the unlimited need of his situation, but that He willed to bear this need as His own, that He took it upon Himself, and that He cries with man in this need.[3]

In one sense Jesus' work was finished on the cross—but through the Spirit it continues. The book of divine creativity is still being written. Throughout John's gospel, Jesus invites others to share with him in fulfilling the creation project. Just as Jesus has been 'sent from the Father', so he sends others to continue the mission he has begun: the blind man is 'sent' to the pool of Siloam because he will shortly be sent to testify to Jesus' mighty works before the Pharisees. Jesus promises to send his Spirit to the disciples not only to comfort them, but to equip them to carry out his mission. If the cross represents the infinite contraction of the old world into the *nihil*, the resurrection and sending of the Spirit are nothing less than the Big Bang of the new creation: 'Truly, truly, I say to you, he who believes in me will also do the works that I do; and greater works than these will he do, because I go to the Father' (John 14:12). Redeemed humanity can resume its role in God's creation project, as men and women continue the work of Jesus through the power of the Spirit.

2. See e.g. 2:1, 'On the third day there was a marriage at Cana in Galilee' (the third day may also evoke resurrection); 2:11, 'this, the first of his signs'; cf. Murray Rae, 'The Testimony of Works in the Christology of John's Gospel', in *The Gospel of John and Christian Theology* (ed. Richard Bauckham and Carl Mosser; Grand Rapids: Eerdmans, 2008), pp. 302–10.

3. *CD* II/1, p. 215.

By the end of chapter 21, John can write no more, because the story of creation and new creation is written by the infinite wisdom of the creating and redeeming God. God's resourcefulness transcends even the Eagle's ability to capture it. But far from engendering wistfulness, it should inspire us to throw ourselves ever deeper into the divine mystery. We remember the words of Gregory of Nyssa:

> You see how boundless is the path for those rising up to God, yet how it is that what the soul has comprehended is the beginning of something beyond her? [He who looks at] the divine boundless beauty . . . continues to wonder at God's continuous revelation; he never exhausts his desire to see more because what he awaits is always more magnificent and more divine than anything he has seen.[4]

4. Gregory of Nyssa, in *Cant.* 11, in Morwenna Ludlow, *Universal Salvation: Eschatology in the Thought of Gregory of Nyssa and Karl Rahner* (Oxford: OUP, 2000), p. 63.

Bibliography

Acar, Rahim. *Talking About God and Talking About Creation: Avicenna's and Thomas Aquinas' Positions* (Leiden: Brill, 2005).

Adams, Robert M. 'Leibnitz's Theories of Contingency.' In *Gottfried Wilhelm Leibniz: Critical Assessments* (ed. R. S. Woolhouse; London: Routledge, 1994): 243–83.

Athanasius. *Contra Gentes: introduction, translation, and commentary* (trans. E. P. Meijering; Leiden: Brill, 1984).

Ayres, Lewis. 'On Not Three People: The Fundamental Themes of Gregory of Nyssa's Trinitarian Theology as Seen in *To Ablabius: On Not Three Gods*.' Pages 15–44 in *Re-thinking Gregory of Nyssa* (ed. Sarah Coakley; Malden, MA: Blackwell, 2003).

Balthasar, Hans Urs von. *The Glory of the Lord: A Theological Aesthetics* (vol. 1; San Francisco: Ignatius Press, 2009).

———. *Cosmic Liturgy: The Universe According to Maximus the Confessor* (trans. Brian E. Daley; San Francisco: Ignatius Press, 2003).

Barbour, R. S. 'Creation, Wisdom, and Christ.' Pages 22–42 in *Creation, Christ, and Culture: Studies in Honour of T. F. Torrance* (ed. Thomas F. Torrance and Richard W. A. McKinney; Edinburgh: T&T Clark, 1976).

Barkman, Adam. *C. S. Lewis & Philosophy As a Way of Life: A Comprehensive Historical Examination of His Philosophical Thought* (Allentown, PA: Zossima, 2009).

Barrett, C. K. *The Gospel According to St. John: An Introduction with Commentary and Notes on the Greek Text* (Philadelphia: Westminster Press, 1978).

Barth, Karl. *Church Dogmatics* (4 vols; ed. G. W. Bromiley and T. F. Torrance; Edinburgh: T&T Clark).

Bartlett, Robert. *The Natural and the Supernatural in the Middle Ages* (Cambridge: Cambridge University Press, 2008).

Bauckham, Richard. *Jesus and the God of Israel: God Crucified and Other Studies on the New Testament's Christology of Divine Identity* (Grand Rapids: Eerdmans, 2009).

———. *The Theology of the Book of Revelation* (Cambridge: Cambridge University Press, 1993).

———. *The Climax of Prophecy: Studies on the Book of Revelation* (London: T&T Clark, 2007).

———. 'Eschatology in The Coming of God.' Pages 1–34 in *God Will Be All in All: The Eschatology of Jürgen Moltmann* (ed. Richard Bauckham; Edinburgh: T&T Clark, 1999).

Bautch, Kelley C. *A Study of the Geography of 1 Enoch 17–19* (Leiden: Brill, 2003).

Bayer, Oswald. *Martin Luther's Theology: A Contemporary Interpretation* (Grand Rapids: Eerdmans, 2008).

Beale, G. K. *The Temple and the Church's Mission: A Biblical Theology of the Dwelling Place of God* (Downers Grove: IVP, 2004).

———. *The Book of Revelation: A Commentary on the Greek Text* (Grand Rapids: Eerdmans, 1999).

Berdyaev, Nikolai. *The Beginning and the End* (trans. R. M. French; New York: Harper, 1952).

Berry, R. J. 'Does Disputing Darwinism Discourage Creation Care?' Pages 217–38 in *As Long as the Earth Endures* (ed. Jonathan Moo and Robin Routledge; Downers Grove: IVP, 2013).

Blowers, Paul M. *Drama of the Divine Economy: Creator and Creation in Early Christian Theology and Piety* (Oxford: Oxford University Press, 2012).

Borgen, Peder. *Philo of Alexandria: An Exegete for His Time* (Leiden: Brill, 1997).

Braine, David. *The Reality of Time and the Existence of God: The Project of Proving God's Existence* (Oxford: Clarendon, 1988).

Broad, C. D. *Leibnitz: An Introduction* (ed. C. Lewy; Cambridge: Cambridge University Press, 1975).

Brownlee, William. *Ezekiel 1–19.* (Waco, TX: Word, 1986).

Bulgakov, Sergius. *The Lamb of God* (trans. Boris Jakim; Grand Rapids: Eerdmans, 2008).

———. 'The Corpse of Beauty.' In *A Bulgakov Anthology* (trans. Natalie Duddington and James Pain; London: Westminster, 1976), pp. 67–72.

———. Religion and Art.' Mascall, E.: *The Church of God: An Anglo-Russian Symposium by Members of the Fellowship of St Alban and St Sergius.* (London, 1934): 175–91.

Burney, C. F. 'Christ as the APXH of Creation.' *The Journal of Theological Studies* 27 (1926): 160–77.

Burrell, David B. *Freedom and Creation in Three Traditions* (Notre Dame: University of Notre Dame Press, 1994).

———. *Faith and Freedom: An Interfaith Perspective* (Malden: Blackwell, 2004).

Buxton, Richard. *From Myth to Reason?: Studies in the Development of Greek Thought* (Oxford: Oxford University Press, 2001).

Bynum, Caroline Walker. *The Resurrection of the Body in Western Christianity: 200–1336* (New York: Columbia University Press, 1995).

Byron, John. *Cain and Abel in Text and Tradition: Jewish and Christian Interpretations of the First Sibling Rivalry* (Leiden: Brill, 2011).

Carson, D. A. *The Gospel According to John* (Grand Rapids: Eerdmans, 1991).

Ciampa, Roy E., and Brian S. Rosner. *The First Letter to the Corinthians* (Grand Rapids: Eerdmans, 2010).

Colish, Marcia L. *Review of Dermot Moran's 'The Philosophy of John Scottus Eriugen'*. Isis, 82 (1991), pp. 722–24.

Coleridge, Samuel T. 'Notes on Leighton': *The Complete Works of Samuel Taylor Coleridge* (7 vols; ed. W. G. T. Shedd; NY: Harper, 1854).

Couenhoven, Jesse. *Stricken by Sin, Cured by Christ: Agency, Necessity, and Culpability in Augustinian Theology* (New York: Oxford University Press, 2013).

Cosmos. *Christian Topography* (trans. J. W. McCrindle; London: The Hakluyt Society, 1897).

Cragg, Gerald R., ed. *The Cambridge Platonists* (New York: Oxford University Press, 1968).

Craig, William Lane. 'Divine Eternity and Einstein's Special Theory of Relativity.' Pages 145–55 in *God, Eternity, and Time* (eds. Christian Tapp and Edmund Runggaldier; Farnham: Ashgate, 2011).

Crisp, Oliver. *Jonathan Edwards on God and Creation* (New York: Oxford University Press, 2012).

Cross, Richard. *Duns Scotus on God* (Aldershot: Ashgate, 2005).

Cudworth, Ralph, and Thomas Birch. *The True Intellectual System of the Universe* (2 vols; Andover: Gould and Newman, 1837).

Davies, W. D., and Dale C. Allison. *A Critical and Exegetical Commentary on the Gospel According to Saint Matthew* (3 vols; London: T&T, 2004).

Dawkins, Richard. *The Blind Watchmaker* (New York: Norton, 1986).

Dillon, John M. *The Middle Platonists, 80 B.C. to A.D. 220* (Ithaca: Cornell University Press, 1977).

Duns Scotus, John, *Contingency and Freedom: Lectura I 39* (trans. A. Vos. Jaczn, et al.; Dordrecht: Kluwer Academic Publishers, 1994).

Dupré, Louis K. *Passage to Modernity: An Essay in the Hermeneutics of Nature and Culture* (New Haven: Yale University Press, 1993).

Ellul, Jacques. *The Meaning of the City* (trans. Dennis Pardee; Grand Rapids: Eerdmans, 1970).

———. *Apocalypse: The Book of Revelation* (trans. G. W. Schreiner; New York: Seabury, 1977).

Emery, Gilles. 'Trinity and Creation.' Pages 58–76 in *The Theology of Thomas Aquinas* (ed. Rik van Nieuwenhove and Joseph Wawrykow; Notre Dame: University of Notre Dame Press, 2005).

Eriugena, John Scotus. *Periphyseon: On the Division of Nature* (trans. Myra L. Uhlfelder and Jean Potter; Indianapolis: Bobbs–Merrill, 1976).

Foot, Sarah. 'Plenty, Portents, and Plagues.' In *God's Bounty? The Churches and the Natural World* (ed. Peter Clarke and Tony Claydon; Woodbridge: Boydell, 2010): 15–41.

Fouke, Daniel Clifford. *The Enthusiastical Concerns of Dr. Henry More: Religious Meaning and the Psychology of Delusion* (Leiden: Brill, 1997).

Garr, W. R. '"Image" and "Likeness" in the Inscription from Tell Fakhariyeh.' *Israel Exploration Journal* 50 (2000): 227–34.

Gelber, Hester Goodenough. *It Could Have Been Otherwise: Contingency and Necessity in Dominican Theology at Oxford, 1300–1350* (Leiden: Brill, 2004).

Gilson, Etienne. *The Christian Philosophy of Saint Augustine* (trans. L. E. M. Lynch; NY: Random House, 1960).

Gregory, Alan. *Coleridge and the Conservative Imagination* (Macon, GA: Mercer University Press, 2003).

Grenz, Stanley J. *The Named God and the Question of Being: A Trinitarian Theo-Ontology* (Louisville: Westminster John Knox, 2005).

Gunton, Colin E. *The Triune Creator: A Historical and Systematic Study* (Edinburgh: T&T Clark, 2001).

Gurtner, Daniel M., and Benjamin L. Gladd, eds. *From Creation to New Creation: Biblical Theology and Exegesis: Essays in Honor of G. K. Beale* (Peabody: Hendrickson, 2013).

Guthrie, W. K. C. *A History of Greek Philosophy* (6 vols; Cambridge: Cambridge University Press, 1967–1981).

Hanby, Michael. *Augustine and Modernity* (London: Routledge, 2003).

Harrison, Carol. *Beauty and Revelation in the Thought of Saint Augustine* (Oxford: Oxford University Press, 1992).

Hart, Trevor. 'Imagination for the Kingdom of God?: Hope, Promise, and the Transformative Power of an Imagined Future.' Pages 49–76 in *God Will Be All in All: The Eschatology of Jürgen Moltmann* (ed. Richard Bauckham; Edinburgh: T&T Clark, 1999).

Hays, Richard B. *The Moral Vision of the New Testament: Community, Cross, New Creation: a Contemporary Introduction to New Testament Ethics* (San Francisco: HarperCollins, 1996).

Heil, John Paul. 'Jesus with the Wild Animals in Mark 1:13.' *Catholic Biblical Quarterly* 68 (2006): pp. 63–78.

Helm, Paul. *Eternal God: A Study of God Without Time* (Oxford: Clarendon, 1988).

Hill, John Spencer. *Imagination in Coleridge* (London: Macmillan, 1978).

Holmes, Stephen R. *The Quest for the Trinity: The Doctrine of God in Scripture, History, and Modernity* (Downers Grove: Intervarsity Press, 2012).

Horne, Brian. 'Divine and Human Creativity.' Pages 135–48 in *The Doctrine of Creation: Essays in Dogmatics, History and Philosophy* (ed. Colin E. Gunton; London: T&T Clark, 2004).

Ingham, Mary Beth, and Mechthild Dreyer. *The Philosophical Vision of John Duns Scotus: An Introduction* (Washington, DC: Catholic University of America Press, 2004).

Jasper, David. *Coleridge as Poet and Religious Thinker* (Allison Park, PA: Pickwick, 1985).

Jeauneau, Édouard. *Rethinking the School of Chartres* (trans. Claude Paul Desmarais; Toronto: University of Toronto Press, 2009).

Jenson, Robert W. *Systematic Theology* (2 vols; New York: Oxford University Press, 1997–1999).

Johansen, Thomas K. *Plato's Natural Philosophy: A Study of the Timaeus-Critias* (Cambridge: Cambridge University Press, 2004).

Johnson, Luke Timothy. *The First and Second Letters to Timothy: A New Translation with Introduction and Commentary* (New York: Doubleday, 2001).

Kendall, Calvin. 'Imitation and the Venerable Bede's Historia Ecclesiastica.' In *Saints, Scholars, and Heroes: Studies in Medieval Culture in Honor of Charles W. Jones* (ed. Charles Williams Jones, Margot H. King, and Wesley M. Stevens; Collegeville, MN: Hill Monastic Manuscript Library, Saint John's Abbey and University, 1979): 161–90.

King, Stephen A. *Reggae, Rastafari, and the Rhetoric of Social Control* (Jackson, Miss: University Press of Mississippi, 2007).

Kirk, Alex. '1 Timothy.' In *Theology of Work Bible Commentary* (Peabody, MA: Hendrickson, 2016).

Kline, Meredith. 'Space and Time in the Genesis Cosmogony.' *Perspectives on Science and Christian Faith* 48 (1996): 2–15.

———. *Images of the Spirit* (Eugene, OR: Wipf & Stock, 1999).

Lamb, Matthew L. 'Eternity Creates and Redeems Time: A Key to Augustine's Confessions Within a Theology of History.' Pages 117–40 in *Divine Creation in Ancient, Medieval, and Early Modern Thought: Essays Presented to the Rev'd Dr Robert D. Crouse* (ed. Michael Treschow, et al.; Leiden: Brill, 2007).

Laansma, Jon. 'The Cosmology of Hebrews.' Pages 125–43 in *Cosmology and New Testament Theology* (ed. Jonathan T. Pennington and Sean M. McDonough; London: T&T Clark, 2008).

Leahy, Brendan, 'Theological Aesthetics.' Pages 23–55 in *The Beauty of Christ* (ed. Bede McGregor and Thomas Norris; Edinburgh: T&T Clark, 1994).

Leftow, Brian. *Time and Eternity* (Ithaca: Cornell University Press, 1991).

Levenson, Jon Douglas. *Creation and the Persistence of Evil: The Jewish Drama of Divine Omnipotence* (Princeton: Princeton University Press, 1988).

Lewis, C. S. *Voyage of the Dawn Treader* (New York: MacMillan, 1967, 8th edition).

———. *The Pilgrim's Regress; An Allegorical Apology for Christianity, Reason, and Romanticism* (Grand Rapids: Eerdmans, 1959).

———. *The Last Battle* (New York: Macmillan, 1956).

———. *The Great Divorce* (New York: Macmillan Company, 1946).

———. *The Chronicles of Narnia* (New York: Macmillan, 1950).

———. *Mere Christianity* (London: HarperCollins, 2001).

Lierman, John. *The New Testament Moses: Christian Perceptions of Moses and Israel in the Setting of Jewish Religion* (Tübingen: Mohr Siebeck, 2004).

Louie, Kin Yip. *The Beauty of the Triune God: The Theological Aesthetics of Jonathan Edwards* (Eugene, OR: Pickwick, 2013).

Louth, Andrew. 'The Place of Theosis in Orthodox Theology.' Pages 32–44 in *Partakers of the Divine Nature: The History and Development of Deification in the Christian Traditions* (ed. Michael J. Christensen and Jeffery A. Wittung; Grand Rapids: Baker, 2008).

Louth, Andrew. *The Origins of the Christian Mystical Tradition from Plato to Denys* (Oxford: Clarendon, 1981).

Lovejoy, Arthur O. *The Great Chain of Being: A Study of the History of an Idea* (Cambridge: Harvard University Press, 1936).

Ludlow, Morwenna. *Universal Salvation: Eschatology in the Thought of Gregory of Nyssa and Karl Rahner* (Oxford: Oxford University Press, 2000).

Macaskill, Grant. *Union with Christ in the New Testament* (Oxford: OUP, 2013).

Mâle, Emile. *The Gothic Image; Religious Art in France of the Thirteenth Century* (New York: Harper, 1958).

Mann, William E. 'The Best of All Possible Worlds.' Pages 250–77 in *Being and Goodness: The Concept of the Good in Metaphysics and Philosophical Theology* (ed. Scott McDonald; Ithaca: Cornell University Press, 1990).

Maximus. *On the Cosmic Mystery of Jesus Christ: Selected Writings from St. Maximus the Confessor* (trans. Paul M. Blowers and Robert Louis Wilken; Crestwood: St. Vladimir's Seminary Press, 2003).

May, Gerhard. *Creatio ex Nihilo* (trans. A. S. Worrall; London: T&T Clark, 2004).

McClymond, Michael J. 'Salvation as Divinization: Edwards, Palamas, and Neoplatonism.' In *Jonathan Edwards: Philosophical Theologian* (ed. Paul Helm and Oliver Crisp; Aldershot: Ashgate, 2003): 139–60.

McDonough, Sean M. *Christ As Creator: Origins of a New Testament Doctrine* (Oxford: Oxford University Press, 2011).

———. *YHWH at Patmos: Rev. 1:4 in Its Hellenistic and Early Jewish Setting* (Tübingen: Mohr Siebeck, 1999).

———. 'Paradise by the Desolation Trail.' In *As Long as the Earth Endures* (ed. Jonathan Moo and Robin Routledge; Downers Grove: IVP, 2013).

McDowell, Catherine. *The 'Image of God' in the Garden of Eden: the Creation of Humankind in Genesis 2:5–3:24 in Light of the* mis pi pit pi *and* wpt-r *Rituals of Ancient Mesopotamia and Egypt* (Winona Lake, IN: Eisenbrauns, 2015).

McInerny, Ralph. *A History of Western Philosophy* (2 vols; Notre Dame: University of Notre Dame Press, 1963–1970).

McPhee, John. *Annals of the Former World* (New York: Farrar, Straus & Giroux, 1998).

Meredith, Anthony. *Gregory of Nyssa* (London: Routledge, 1999).

Midgley, Mary. *Evolution As a Religion: Strange Hopes and Stranger Fears* (London: Routledge, rev. edn., 2006).

Millard, Alan R., and Pierre Bordreuil. 'A Statue from Syria with Assyrian and Aramaic Inscriptions.' *Biblical Archeologist* 45 (1982): 135–41.

Mobley, Gregory. *The Return of the Chaos Monsters—and Other Backstories of the Bible* (Grand Rapids: Eerdmans, 2012).

Moltmann, Jürgen. *God in Creation: A New Theology of Creation and the Spirit of God* (Minneapolis: Fortress Press, 1993).

Moo, Jonathan. 'New Testament Hope and a Christian Environmental Ethos.' Pages 146–68 in *As Long as the Earth Endures* (ed. Jonathan Moo and Robin Routledge; Downers Grove: IVP, 2013).

Moran, Dermot. *The Philosophy of John Scottus Eriugena: A Study of Idealism in the Middle Ages* (Cambridge: Cambridge University Press, 1989).

———. 'Nature, Man, and God in the Philosophy of John Scottus Eriugena.' Pages 91–106 in *The Irish Mind: Exploring Intellectual Traditions* (ed. R. Kearney; Dublin: Wolfhound, 1985).

More, Henry, and Alexander B. Grosart. *The Complete Poems of Dr. Henry More (1614–1687) for the First Time Collected and Edited: With Memorial Introduction, Notes and Illustrations, Glossarial Index and Portrait, Etc.* (Edinburgh: Printed for private circulation by T. and A. Constable, 1878).

Nauta, Lodi. 'The Preexistence of the Soul in Medieval Thought.' *Recherches de Théologie ancienne et medieval* 63 (1996): 93–135.

Newsome, David. *Two Classes of Men: Platonism and English Romantic Thought* (London: John Murray, 1972).

O'Meara, John J. *Eriugena* (Oxford: Clarendon, 1988).

Orlov, Andrei. *Heavenly Priesthood in the Apocalypse of Abraham* (Cambridge: Cambridge University Press, 2013).

Osborn, Eric Francis. *Irenaeus of Lyons* (Cambridge: Cambridge University Press, 2001).

Otten, Willemien. 'The Parallelism of Nature and Scripture: Reflections on Eriugena's Incarnational Exegesis.' In *Iohannes Scottus Eriugena* (ed. Gerd van Riel, Carlos G. Steel, and J. J. McEvoy; Leuven: Leuven University Press, 1996): 81–102.

Pannenberg, Wolfhart. *Jesus, God and Man* (Philadelphia: Westminster Press, 1968).

Patrides, C. A. *The Cambridge Platonists* (Cambridge: Cambridge University Press, 1980).

Pauw, Amy Plantinga. *The Supreme Harmony of All: The Trinitarian Theology of Jonathan Edwards* (Grand Rapids: Eerdmans, 2002).

Pennington, Jonathan T. *Heaven and Earth in the Gospel of Matthew* (Grand Rapids: Baker, 2009).

Pitman, J. H. *The Old English Physiologus* (New Haven: Yale University Press, 1921).

Pinckaers, Servais. *The Sources of Christian Ethics* (trans. Mary Thomas Noble; Edinburgh: T&T Clark, 1995).

Plantinga, Alvin. *Where the Conflict Really Lies: Science, Religion, and Naturalism* (New York: Oxford University Press, 2011).

Polkinghorne, John. 'The Hidden Work of the Spirit in Creation.' Pages 3–10 in *The Spirit in Creation and New Creation* (ed. Michael Welker; Grand Rapids: Eerdmans, 2012).

———., ed. *The Work of Love: Creation As Kenosis* (Grand Rapids: Eerdmans, 2001).

Possekel, Ute. *Evidence of Greek Philosophical Concepts in the Writings of Ephrem the Syrian* (Louvain: Peeters, 1999).

Powicke, Frederick J. *The Cambridge Platonists: A Study* (Westport, CT: Greenwood, 1970).

Przywara, Erich. 'Beautiful, Sacred, Christian.' Pages 537–55 in *Analogia Entis: Metaphysics—Original Structure and Universal Rhythm* (trans. John R. Betz and David Bentley Hart; Grand Rapids: Eerdmans, 2014).

Robertson, Jon M. *Christ As a Mediator: A Study of the Theologies of Eusebius of Caesarea, Marcellus of Ancyra and Athanasius of Alexandria* (Oxford: Oxford University Press, 2007).

Rose, Matthew. *Ethics in Barth: God, Metaphysics and Morals* (Farnham: Ashgate, 2010).

Rosenberg, S. P. 'Forming the Saeculum: The Desacralization of Nature and the Ability to Understand It in Augustine's Literal Commentary on Genesis.' Pages 1–14 in *Studies in Church History* (ed. P. Clarke and T. Claydon; London: Thomas Nelson & Sons, 2010).

Runia, David T. *Philo of Alexandria and the Timaeus of Plato* (Leiden: Brill, 1986).

Russell, Norman. *Deification in the Greek Patristic Tradition* (Oxford: Oxford University Press, 2004).

Scheffczyk, Leo. *Creation and Providence* (New York: Herder & Herder, 1970).

Scott, Alan. *Origen and the Life of the Stars: A History of an Idea* (Oxford: Clarendon, 1991).

Scott, James M. *On Earth As in Heaven: The Restoration of Sacred Time and Sacred Space in the Book of Jubilees* (Leiden: Brill, 2005).

Shanley, Brian J. 'Beyond Libertarianism and Compatibilism: Thomas Aquinas on Created Freedom.' In *Freedom and the Human Person* (ed. Richard L. Velkley; Washington, DC: Catholic University of America Press, 2007): 70–89.

Skinner, T. H. *Coleridge and the Moral Tendency of His Writings* (New York: Leavitt, Trow, & Co, 1844).

Smith, Christopher R. 'Chiliasm and Recapitulation in the Theology of Ireneus.' *Vigilae Christianae* 48 (1994): 313–31.

Sorabji, Richard. *Time, Creation and the Continuum: Theories in Antiquity and the Early Middle Ages* (London: Duckworth, 1983).

Steel, Carlos. 'The Return of the Body into the Soul: Philosophical Musings on the Resurrection.' In *History and Eschatology in John Scottus Eriugena and His Time* (ed. Michael Dunne and J. J. McEvoy; Leuven: Leuven University Press, 2002): 581–610.

Stout, Harry S., ed. *The Works of Jonathan Edwards* (26 vols; New Haven: Yale University Press, 1957–2009).

Tabernee, William. *Fake Prophecy and Polluted Sacraments: Ecclesiastical and Imperial Reactions to Montanism* (Leiden: Brill, 2007).

Tanner, Kathryn. 'Creation and Providence.' Pages 111–26 in *The Cambridge Companion to Karl Barth* (ed. John B. Webster; Cambridge: Cambridge University Press, 2000).

Tapp, Christian, and Edmund Runggaldier, eds. *God, Eternity, and Time* (Farnham: Ashgate, 2011).

Thiselton, Anthony C. *The First Epistle to the Corinthians: A Commentary on the Greek Text* (Grand Rapids: Eerdmans, 2000).

Thunberg, Lars. *Microcosm and Mediator: The Theological Anthropology of Maximus The Confessor* (Eng. rev., A. M. Allchin; Copenhagen: Munksgaard, 1965).

Tolkien, J. R. R. 'On Fairy Stories'. In *The Tolkien Reader* (New York: Ballantine, 1986).

Tollefsen, Torstein. *The Cosmology of St. Maximus The Confessor* (Oxford: Oxford University Press, 2012).

Torrance, Alan. 'Creatio Ex Nihilo and the Spatio-Temporal Dimensions, with special reference to Jürgen Moltmann and D. C. Williams.' Pages 83–103 in *The Doctrine of Creation* (ed. Colin Gunton; T&T Clark, 1991).

Torrance, Thomas F. *Space, Time and Resurrection* (Edinburgh: T&T Clark, 1998).

Tertullian. *Adversus Marcionem* (trans. Ernest Evans; Oxford: Oxford University Press, 1972).

Vishnevskaya, Elena. 'Divinization and Spiritual Progress in Maximus the Confessor'. In *Theosis: Deification in Christian Theology* (2 vols; ed. Stephen Finlan and Vladimir Kharlamov; Eugene, OR: Pickwick, 2006).

———. 'Divinization as Perichoretic Embrace in Maximus the Confessor.' In *Partakers of the Divine Nature: The History and Development of Deification in the Christian Traditions* (ed. Michael Christensen and Jeffrey Wittung; Grand Rapids: Baker, 2008): 132–45.

Ward, Michael. *Planet Narnia: The Seven Heavens in the Imagination of C. S. Lewis* (Oxford: Oxford University Press, 2008).

Watts, Rikki E. *Isaiah's New Exodus in Mark* (Grand Rapids: Baker, 2000).

Webster, John B. *Barth's Ethics of Reconciliation* (Cambridge: Cambridge University Press, 1995).

Wenham, Gordon. *Genesis 1–15* (Word Biblical Commentary, vol. 1; Nashville: Thomas Nelson, 1987).

Westphal, Merold. *Transcendence and Self-Transcendence: On God and the Soul* (Bloomington: Indiana University Press, 2004).

Whichcote, Benjamin, Antony Tuckney, and Tod E. Jones, eds. *The Cambridge Platonists: A Brief Introduction* (Lanham, MD: University Press of America, 2005).

White, Joel. 'Paul's Cosmology: The Witness of Romans, 1 and 2 Corinthians, and Galatians.' Pages 90–106 in *Cosmology and New Testament Theology* (ed. Jonathan T. Pennington and Sean M. McDonough; London: T&T Clark, 2008).

Whitrow, Gerald J. *The Natural Philosophy of Time* (Oxford: Clarendon, 1980).

Williamson, Ronald. *Philo and the Epistle to the Hebrews* (Leiden: Brill, 1970).

Winter, Bruce W. *After Paul Left Corinth: The Influence of Secular Ethics and Social Change* (Grand Rapids: Eerdmans, 2001).

Wolter, Alan B., and William A. Frank. *Duns Scotus on the Will and Morality* (Washington, DC: Catholic University of America Press, 2012).

Wyatt, Peter. *Jesus Christ and Creation in the Theology of John Calvin* (Allison Park, PA: Pickwick, 1996).

Zakai, Avihu. *Jonathan Edwards's Philosophy of History: The Re-enchantment of the World in the Age of Enlightenment* (Princeton: Princeton University Press, 2003).

———. *Jonathan Edwards' Philosophy of Nature: The Re-enchantment of the World in the Age of Scientific Reasoning* (London: T&T Clark, 2010).